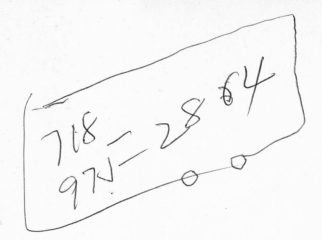

718
97N — 28 64

The Israeli-Egyptian War of Attrition, 1969–1970

A Case-Study of Limited Local War

A Case-Study
of Limited
Local War

The
Israeli-Egyptian
War
of Attrition,
1969-1970

Yaacov Bar-Siman-Tov

Columbia University Press   New York   1980

Library of Congress Cataloging in Publication Data

Bar-Siman-Tov, Yaacov, 1946–
  The Israeli-Egyptian war of attrition, 1969–1970.

  Includes bibliographical references and index.
  1. Israel-Arab Border Conflicts, 1949–   —Egypt.
2. Israel—Foreign relations—Egypt.   3. Egypt—Foreign
relations—Israel.   I. Title.
DS119.8.E3B37   956'.046   80-11124
ISBN 0-231-04982-X

Columbia University Press
New York   Guildford, Surrey

To Ronit

Contents

Preface

THE WAR OF ATTRITION of March 1969 to August 1970 between Israel and Egypt which has been regarded as a passing event in the course of the Arab-Israeli wars is the one most disregarded by researchers. But the War of Attrition was a major confrontation and acquired a very unique character distinguishing it from the other wars for two main reasons: its special type of war attrition and superpowers' direct military intervention, and its special theoretical characteristics from the point of view of strategic, conflict, crisis, and bargaining studies. For these reasons it deserves a more theoretical study than this war has previously received.[1]

This study is based on the idea that the War of Attrition was a special case of "limited local war." Therefore, the main concern of this research is an attempt to fill the theoretical gap in the recent literature about the War of Attrition by offering a theoretical framework for the study of limited local war like the War of Attrition. Our research will, however, utilize the framework for the study of limited local war to test the War of Attrition between Israel and Egypt for characteristic limited local war features, the better to understand its nature.

The literature about the so-called "limited war" or "local war" represents an attempt by analysts and scholars to capture the special implications of that type of conflict from the point of view of the superpowers' behavior, but not from the point of view of the local and small actors. What we hope to develop in this research are some ideas about the characteristics of limited

local war geographically remote from the superpowers' home-
lands and involving mainly small nations as in the Arab-Israeli
conflict.

This study utilizes a variety of source materials: interviews,
documents, Middle Eastern newspapers and transcripts of
radio broadcasts. I held interviews with Israeli officials and military people who belonged to the inner group of Israeli decision
makers during the War of Attrition. For obvious legal and security considerations and due to the positions held by some inter-
viewees (most of them still active in public life and politics), I
am prevented from naming some of my sources of information.
Therefore, conversations with high Israeli officials or military
people are quoted with anonymous acknowledgments. Being an
Israeli I could not interview any Egyptian officials and the study
lacks this kind of information.

The archives of the Shiloah Institute for Middle Eastern
Studies of Tel-Aviv University were a major source. These ar-
chives hold very useful Israeli and Arabic documents, Middle
Eastern newspapers, and transcripts of radio broadcasts.

Among the people who have provided assistance and support for this effort, two individuals in particular are owed a deep
debt of gratitude. In its earliest and difficult phases of the research and throughout the research period, Mr. Daniel Dishon, a
senior researcher of the Shiloah Institute and the editor of the
Middle East Record provided a wealth of wise advice about the
topic and research directions, methodological and substantive.
Without his direction, understanding, and encouragement, this
study would not have been completed.

Professor Alexander L. George of Stanford University gave
me a comprehensive critical analysis of the theoretical chapter
and provided invaluable suggestions for the empirical chapters.
Professor George contributed to this book far beyond the call of
duty by sponsoring my year at Stanford. Indeed, his encouragement and intellectual stimulation made it possible.

I am also indebted to Dr. Amnon Sela from the Hebrew University and Mr. Ami Ayalon from the Shiloah Institute for their
valuable suggestions.

This study is indebted to some institutional friends. It was supported by a grant from the Fo. d Foundation received through the Israel Foundation Trustees. The Shiloah Institute kindly permitted me to use its archives and its facilities and gave me the opportunity to carry out this study. I am also grateful to the Hebrew University and to the Leonard Davies Institute for International Relations, especially to its director, Professor Nissan Oren, for having financed my year at Stanford University during the last stage of the research. The mistakes and inadequacies of the final product that remain are solely mine.

Mrs. Dafna Allon, Lydia Gareh, and Barbara Sullivan worked very hard in translating and typing. Finally, I would like to acknowledge the indispensable contribution of my wife, Ronit, for without her love, patience, understanding, and sacrifices, this research would never have been completed.

The Israeli-Egyptian War of Attrition, 1969–1970
A Case-Study of Limited Local War

A Rubbing out or Grinding down, as by friction

Introduction

*A gradual
Gradual wearing down
or weakening - a war
of attrition -*

THE WAR OF ATTRITION between Israel and Egypt from March 1969 to August 1970 was the outcome of problems created by the Six-Day War. That war had had decisive results on three levels and therein lay the seeds of the War of Attrition. The most momentous result of the Six-Day War, and at the same time the most problem-laden, was the new territorial situation that was seen from the start by all the parties concerned—Israel, the Arab States, and the superpowers—as a situation that would have to be altered. The second outcome of the Six-Day War was the decisive gap in the relative military strength of Israel and Egypt, given the overwhelming Israeli victory in the war. The third outcome was a central function of the other two: the increased involvement of the superpowers, mainly the USSR, in the Arab-Israeli conflict. These three decisive consequences of the Six-Day War added up to a crucial change in the structure of political-strategic relations between Israel and Egypt. The relative strategic stability that had characterized the Arab-Israeli conflict as a whole and the Egyptian-Israeli conflict in particular since the Israeli withdrawal from the Sinai at the end of the Suez crisis in March 1957 was severely shaken by the Six-Day War. The conditions for insuring strategic stability in the Arab-Israeli conflict in general and the Egyptian-Israeli conflict in particular depended on finding a way out of the dilemma created by the outcome of the war, i.e., changing the territorial situation to the satisfaction of both sides and at the same time providing an assurance of a certain balance in the relative strength of the sides.

At the close of the Six-Day War both sides to the dispute, Israel and Egypt, sought to find a political solution to the crisis created as the war's aftermath, but the kind and shape of the political solution was conceived of in different fashion by each side. The basic difference in the stands adopted by each of the two sides centered around the essence of the connection between a solution to the problem created after the Six-Day War and a solution to the Arab-Israeli conflict as a whole. While Egypt sought a solution only to the later minor crisis, Israel sought to settle the Arab-Israeli conflict in its entirety. Given this essential breach between the basic positions of the two sides and their unwillingness to introduce any concessions into these positions, the various diplomatic initiatives undertaken at the time were incapable of promoting any political solution whatsoever.

The difference in the relative strengths of the two sides also made the diplomatic efforts more difficult. Israel's strategic superiority made it difficult for her to envisage basic concessions since she hoped to secure a political arrangement that would reflect, even if only partially, that superiority. Egypt's strategic inferiority, on the other hand, made it difficult for her to accept a political settlement. The Egyptians thought that as long as the decisive gap continued to exist between the relative strengths of the two sides, the political settlement would necessarily reflect Israel's victory in the Six-Day War. In these circumstances, it would seem a new war was automatically called for. The two sides in the conflict continued to cling to a political solution as their guiding idea, except achieving it was seen by Egypt in terms of military initiatives which would give added impetus to her diplomatic moves made with a view to achieving the political solution.

The War of Attrition thus marked the recognition that there was no possibility of promoting a political solution in the absence of military initiatives. This recognition characterized the Egyptian concept at the start of the war and as the war went on, it came to influence the Israeli concept as well.

The War of Attrition between Israel and Egypt of March 1969 to August 1970 differed in many respects from the other armed confrontations in the history of the Arab-Israeli conflict.

Apart from the October 1973 War, the War of Attrition was the only one where the side that started the war, Egypt, was not out to defend but to change the existing military, political, and territorial status quo. In the other wars the initiator tried to prevent the status quo from being overthrown. In the 1948–1949 War it was the Arabs who wanted to defend the status quo, while in the Suez campaign of 1956 and in the Six-Day War it was Israel that started the war in order to prevent a change in the status quo.[1]

The War of Attrition was also the first in which the Arab-Israeli conflict was interlocked directly with the superpower conflict. Direct military intervention by a superpower occurred at the point where the two conflicts met and overlapped. When the gap between the relative strengths of Israel and Egypt reached a point judged critical by Egypt and the Soviet Union, the latter intervened directly with military means in order to neutralize Israel's strategic superiority. The point reached was judged critical because beyond it lay the danger of one side's achieving a military decision of the war.

The War of Attrition acquired the unique character distinguishing it from other wars in the course of the Arab-Israeli conflict largely because of special theoretical characteristics, which this study focuses on as defining a special type of limited war, in accordance with the definitions of limited war propounded in the extensive literature on the subject.

The Duration of the War

The duration of the war has been fixed as from the date when it began in March 1969 to its close in August 1970, according to a number of criteria: the war aims of the parties and the relation between these aims and the basic politico-strategic aims embraced by both sides since the Six-Day War; the military means utilized; the kinds of military activity and the nature of the interaction between military and diplomatic activity; identification of escalatory moves in the fighting; examination of the network of relationships between the superpowers and the belligerents; and an examination of the relations between the superpowers.

According to these criteria, the War of Attrition can be divided into four main stages:

First stage: March 8 to July 19, 1969. The Egyptians impose their strategy.

Second stage: July 20 to end of December 1969. Breakdown of Egyptian strategy.

Third stage: January 7 to April 17, 1970. The Israelis impose their strategy.

Fourth stage: April 18 to August 7, 1970. Direct Soviet military intervention, strategic draw, and end of the war.

My research examines each stage of the war from the following points of view: the belligerents' aims; their strategies; kinds of military activity; principal military means utilized; the initiative in belligerent activity; and the nature of the interaction between belligerent activity on the canal and diplomatic activity on the part of the superpowers relating to the Middle East. The transition from one stage of the war to the next came as a result of escalation by one of the belligerents. Examination of the escalatory moves reveals the changes that took place in the belligerents' concept of the war as well as the development of the war itself.

1 Framework for the Study of Limited Local War

THE THEORETICAL CONCEPT of "limited war" was originally meant to assist analysis of political and strategic relations—not between small actors involved in local wars, but between two superpowers in the nuclear age. Fear of a "total war" in the nuclear age in the manner of World Wars I and II, with the potential threat of extermination for all taking part in it, led to development of the theory and doctrine of limited war. The aim was to clarify the possibility of preventing total war by allowing for wars that would be less than total—wars that would be limited and controlled in accordance with a specific sequence of recognized restrictions. Limited war strategy was developed in order to discern the presence of intermediate situations in politico-strategic relations between the two superpowers. This strategy was intended to neutralize the dangers of total war while making certain options available in crisis situations, mainly by indicating actions that might be taken in local conflicts involving superpower interests.[1] While limited war theory aimed at reducing the danger of superpower confrontation, this does not exclude the possibility that limited wars have become the main substitute for total war in the nuclear age. Limited wars have certainly proved of practical relevance to international politics, for since World War II more than fifty limited wars have occurred without resulting in a world war. The majority of these wars did not directly involve superpowers; most were fought between small actors.[2] But there is no discrimination between those wars in which superpowers are involved on opposite sides, even if only by proxy, and those in which neither of the two superpowers is directly or indirectly involved. It is desirable, however, to recognize that a war that is limited from the point of view of the superpowers may not be limited from the point of view of the small actors.[3] For the superpowers, the Korean and Vietnam wars were limited (despite direct military intervention on the part of the United States), but for the small actors (South and North Korea, South and North Vietnam) the war came near enough to being a total war.

This study aims to develop a theoretical framework of the characteristics of limited war that is geographically remote from the superpowers and involves mainly small actors. It is desirable to identify a variety of factors that affect the limitation and expansion of local wars between small actors: the types of constraints and limitations and their relationships, patterns of bargaining between small actors, and the problems of terminating such wars.

Problem of Defining Limited Local War

Various definitions of limited war are to be found in the literature; they emphasize various limitations that the participants are prepared to impose on themselves. For the war to be limited, the limitations have to apply to at least one of the following aspects (more often to a combination of them): the aims of the war, the military means employed, the geographical demarcation of the battle zone, the targets attacked (mainly military ones), participants and the like.

The listing of the aspects of warfare that are liable to limitation in various combinations makes it clear that limited war is not a uniform phenomenon. A war can be limited variously in some senses but not in others. Thus, for example, it can be limited to a defined geographical region but not to the means of warfare or the targets. It can be a war in which one or the other belligerent makes full use of the military and economic potential available even though those capabilities may not be sufficient for achieving the country's ultimate political goals (because there is no parity in power between the adversaries). Moreover, the war can be limited in the view of one side while it is seen by the other side as unlimited. The combinations of the various restrictions can be few or many.

Generally, these limitations referred only to the interactions between superpowers in war, as Bernard Brodie notes:

As a rule we do not apply the term "limited war" to conflicts which are limited naturally by the fact that one or both sides lack the capability to make them total. . . . We generally use it to refer to wars in which the United States on the one side and the Soviet Union or Communist China are involved, perhaps directly but usually through proxies, on one or both sides.[4]

Brodie's definition is too restrictive to be applicable in the present study. The definition of war as limited does not always have to include or necessarily imply the possession of a capability to wage unlimited war or nuclear war at choice, although this element of capability *per se* weighs heavily in arriving at the definition.[5] It is more useful to define limited war as applying to any war in which the actors, whether they are superpowers or not, have decided to observe some significant restrictions in their use of force. The term "limited local war" can be applied to any war where the small actors have themselves decided or have been persuaded by others to observe such restrictions. This term is now often reserved for local conventional war in which neither of the superpowers is directly involved.[6]

Sources for Limiting Local War: "Constraints" and "Limitations"

This study proposes to distinguish between major sources of restrictions in local war: "constraints" and "limitations." The term constraints refers to all restrictions imposed on the local actors' behavior, sometimes against their will and sometimes because they lack the capability or do not believe it useful to wage unlimited war. The term limitations refers to restrictions that the local actors prefer to observe in order to keep the war limited and that are adopted as a result of a unilateral judgment of self-interest or through mutual agreement of some kind.[7]

External Political Constraints
The term "limited local war" is most applicable to situations where external political constraints imposed in some way by the superpowers narrow the possibilities open to local powers for expanding the war, with particular reference to soundly defeating the opponent.[8]

By using one or another means of pressure on their respective clients and on their client's opponent, the two superpowers can bring their influence to bear on the belligerents to keep the war limited with respect to its political objectives and/or the military means employed. The superpowers can exert these pressures, for example, by means of an embargo on arms supplies and/or economic aid or by withholding political-diplomatic support in international forums. Pressures can also take the form of threats by a superpower to induce the client's opponent to observe limitations of objectives or military means or to face the risk of intervention by the superpower. Such threats can be backed by naval demonstrations or maneuvers near the war zone or by limited forms of intervention.

Domestic Political Constraints
Limits occur not only when external political constraints are imposed, but also when domestic political considerations constrain the objectives pursued and/or the military means employed. Domestic constraints may arise as a result of disagreement within the decision-making elite or between this elite and other political actors such as competing elites, interest groups, or public opinion regarding the nation's political objectives in that local war, the value to be accorded to these objectives, and the level of costs and risks considered acceptable in the pursuit of these objectives.[9] Sometimes the necessity to mobilize support for the government's policy or the government's wish to be continued in office could also serve to keep the war limited.[10] But it should be recognized that in other situations similar considerations could push the government to expand the war.

Constraints Arising from Limited Military Capabilities or
Resources for Fighting a War

A war can also be kept limited because the local states suffer
from a shortage of military capabilities or resources for fighting a
war, and/or economic capabilities. Similarly, a local state may
limit its military operations and objectives so as to conserve military resources that are needed to deter or deal with other ene-
mies. A combatant may also hold back the use of some of its
military resources simply because it does not believe their em-
ployment would be sufficiently cost-effective in influencing the
outcome.[11]

Self-Interest Limitations

Local war may be limited by just one side. Self-interest limitations, motivated by a desire to keep the war limited, may be
coupled with the following considerations:

(a) a fear of the possibility of reprisals by the opponent who
    has military capability for such actions;

(b) a fear of the possibility of reprisals or reactions by the
    opponent's patron (superpower) or by other actors who
    are allied to the opponent in situations where the oppo-
    nent himself has no appreciable military capabilities for
    significant reprisals;

(c) a desire to maintain political, military, and economic
    support from one's patron superpower;

(d) a fear that escalation will lead the superpowers to im-
    pose a military-political termination of the conflict that
    may be contrary to one's political interest;

(e) a desire to signal to the opponent an interest in keeping
    the war limited and to encourage him to behave like-
    wise.[12]

The readiness to keep the war limited by self-interest gives
an important significance to behavior that distinguishes it from
situations of readiness to keep the war limited because of lack of
capability, considerations of military utility, or the threat of intervention by the superpowers. Self-interest limitation is a ratio-
nal political strategy insofar as it attempts either to avoid future

situations that might otherwise bring external political constraints into play or to create useful "rules of the game" to regulate the conflict with the adversary.

Consensual Limitations

Local war may be limited also by an interactive consensual process. Thus, limitations may emerge as a result of a jointly perceived interest to formulate a set of limitations via interaction and some type of communication with the adversary—in other words, a cooperative two-sided interaction for this purpose even while the two sides are engaged in military conflict. Schelling has developed a "tacit bargaining" model in order to explain the rationale and modus operandi for the emergence of consensual limitations in limited war.[13] Tacit bargaining, according to Schelling, takes place in a situation where—despite their conflicting interests—the two sides try to settle their dispute, not in the first instance by means of an immediate compromise over the interests involved, but by indicating at least a provisional willingness to accept an outcome to be reached within the framework of a mutually acceptable pattern of limitations. In other words, achieving a set of limitations to prevent undesired escalation of the war has priority in their calculations for the time being over the determination of the exact shape or content of an acceptable outcome. Tacit bargaining is a way in which the opposing sides can communicate with each other when the main vehicle for doing so is via the military actions they do not engage in; the objective is to achieve mutual coordination of behavior and expectations.

Bargaining of this type may result in a tacit agreement between the two sides to limit their actions in specific respects. The existence of limitations is dictated by their mutual fear of escalation and of extension of the conflict beyond what is aimed and desired by the sides. The tacit agreement between the sides to limit their actions creates a series of unwritten "rules"— perhaps "expectations" is a better description—governing their behavior. The success and duration of the tacit agreement depends, of course, on whether both sides share the same understanding of it and remain willing to refrain from actions likely to be judged as infractions of the unwritten rules.

These rules may be respected, as Schelling suggests, "because if they are once broken, there is no assurance that any new ones can be found and jointly recognized in time to check the widening of the conflict."[14]

Non-consensual Limitations
Schelling's "tacit bargaining" model is applicable, as Halperin notes, only to those situations in which a limit is in fact established as a result of both sides engaging in an effort to establish a simple limitation or a more complex set of limitations.[15] In other words, tacit bargaining implies limits that are perceived as symmetrical enough by both sides as to be acceptable. Logically speaking, each side presumably believes that the utility of the limitations to prevent undesired escalation is preferable to whatever dis-utility those limitations may impose on efforts to secure the most favorable outcome.

But limitations in local war may also emerge, as Alexander George indicates, without bargaining. In some cases, limitations may be adopted by both sides without any agreement and without conditions being formulated or indicated.[16] The limitations are liable to be asymmetrical in scope or in type. Both sides may keep some, but not the same, limitations. One side refrains from doing something that the other side is doing. The motives that give rise to this state of affairs do not have to be symmetrical, and it is likely that there will be a variety of calculations that favor accepting the different types of limitations. The limits may actually be based on misunderstanding, misperception, miscalculation, or at least a different understanding of what is taking place. Others may be based on domestic or external political constraints, or on negotiating and bargaining with the superpowers or actors other than the opponent.

The Interrelationship of Constraints and Limitations

We have identified the major sources for limiting local war, but it may be very difficult to answer the question whether a decision not to expand the war reflects constraint behavior of one type rather than another. The motives for not expanding the war may be complicated and may appear in any local war. It may be a matter of importance to ask: what is the role of each source for limiting local war? This is a very complicated question because the role of each source varies in importance from one decision to the next and from one war to another. In some situations both sides may be very conscious of the need to agree on consensual limits. In other situations external political constraints or domestic political constraints may motivate the actors' behavior. This study suggests that external political constraints rather than other sources may sometimes be the most effective for limiting local wars. The reasons are the following:

1. All other sources grow out of self-constraint, limitation, or interdependence relationships. External political constraints may enforce limitations regardless of the local actors' preferences.
2. Sources of self-imposed constraint or limitation (domestic political constraints, or capability and military constraints) are based on self-interest. Sources that do not stem from a dependent relationship with outside powers are easier to change than others because they need only self-approval.
3. Consensual limitations seem to be a more stable source for limiting a war because they are based on an interdependent relationship. If both sides share a common understanding regarding the importance of the limitations, then according to Schelling, such an understanding may be an important factor for keeping the war limited. But what happens in those situations when both actors do not share such a common understanding? Or where there is no parity in power between the two actors? Or when there is no equalization of advantages from the limitations?

Alexander George rightly remarks:

A common clear-cut understanding by the two sides regarding the criticality of individual limitations is not essential for maintaining a pattern of limitations. Stability of a set of limitations may also rest on uncertainty (and on skillful manipulation of uncertainty) regarding their inter-relationship and the consequences of violating one of them. Moreover, a common, clear-cut understanding on the interconnection between some of the prevailing limitations may be accompanied by uncertainty regarding the interrelationship between others.[17]

We may conclude that self-interest or consensual and non-consensual limitations or constraints frequently do not suffice to restrain one or both sides.

The external political constraints may be the best source for limitations, especially in situations where there is no parity of power between the local actors and/or where there is no equalization of advantages from the limitations, but rather some special patron-client relationship between local actors and superpowers. In those situations the opponent may choose not to adopt certain courses of action because of the need to consider the external political constraints very seriously. The motives for accepting limited local war are based not only on interdependence of local actors' actions but on interdependence between local actors and superpowers' reaction as well. Consequently, each actor must take into account not only the actual and potential actions of the other actor, but also the actual and potential reactions of the superpowers. The uncertainty for one or both of the opposing sides concerning the superpowers' reactions may be essential for maintaining the limitations. The patterns of limitations may be changed according to the degrees of this uncertainty. When two superpowers, each backing one of the local actors, participate in the limitations process, then many of the preceding observations also apply to the superpowers' motives for limiting the conflict.

Major Types of Limitations in Limited Local War

Five general types of limitations in local war are usually identified: objectives, military means, geography, targets, and participants.

Limitation of Objectives

A limited local war must be defined mainly by limited political objectives. Preference for limited war strategy is based on the belief that in the given circumstances, especially with the existence of external political constraints, it is not possible to secure absolutely conclusive results, but only partial ones that do not always correspond to the national interest. While it is not possible to achieve all the national aims, a war of this kind nevertheless offers the great advantage that it does not involve a threat to the very survival of the nation.[18] This contention is correct in principle on the condition that the side initiating the limited war has reason to believe that the other side is in fact willing to accept the restrictions of limited war. Where the other side refuses to accept these restrictions, there is a danger of events threatening the national survival, a danger underestimated by the side initiating the limited war.

The aim of limited local war from the military point of view is to inflict losses on the enemy or make him face dangers out of proportion to what is at stake in the conflict. The lower the stakes, the less violent need be the war.[19] In limited war, the military means are directed by the political aims and interact with them constantly. In spite of the fact that limitation of military means does not necessarily suit the war as it develops, it is necessary to maintain the dominance of the political aims over the military means. Compromise at the expense of this principle is liable to damage the definition of the aims of the war as limited ones. Permanent subordination of the military means to the political aims is also dictated by the constant fear lest the military aims become an end in themselves and thereby nullify the limited character of the war.[20]

Limitations on Military Means

Limitations affect not only quantitative utilization of military means but also weapon systems utilized.[21] Since the limitations concern both quantity and types of military means, there is a range of varied possibilities in the use of military means. In limited war it is sometimes necessary to refrain from securing absolute air superiority.[22] Absolute air superiority is liable to increase the danger of extending the war, either because the side enjoying this superiority will be tempted to exploit it in the hope of bringing the war to a speedy end, or because the weaker side will be bound to seek other military means that are also judged as an infringement of the limitations of means utilized. Each and any such resort to increased military means—the deployment of advanced anti-aircraft systems (sophisticated missiles) or a request for direct military assistance from an external supporting factor (foreign power)—is liable to extend the war.

Limitations on Targets

Limitations on targets usually include refraining from hitting non-military targets (economic and civilian targets) but go beyond this to include certain types of military targets. The limitations regarding targets can be measured both quantitatively and qualitatively—for example, according to the relations between the number of weapons utilized and the type or types of targets. A distinction can be drawn between "anti-force" and "anti-value" strikes, that is to say between striking at military targets (the enemy's means of waging war) and at economic and civilian targets (the means of sustaining civilian life). Striking at non-military targets is liable to be seen as a serious violation of the limitations on the war and may provoke reprisals on the part of the adversary.[23] In local wars where the superpowers are involved directly, it is especially important to avoid attacking military targets manned by the superpowers' personnel.

Geographical Limitations

Geographical limitations generally involve restriction of the fighting to specific regions, excluding certain areas so-called "sanctuaries" where no attempt will be made to inflict damage. Geographical limitations are laid down by delineating clear front lines denoted by topographical boundaries (rivers, mountains, etc.), according to legalistic frontiers—the political frontiers that existed prior to the outbreak of the war—or according to freshly drawn lines.[24]

Once the boundaries are thus delimited by tacit agreement, any move across these lines is liable to be interpreted as an infraction of the limitations or as an escalation of the war. These boundaries serve as "signal lines" by which the adversaries effect tacit communication and reassure each other regarding the limitation of the war. Honoring these boundaries as the limit to violent action is of very considerable importance in keeping the war limited. Geographical expansion by one side, threats of military action, or action initiated in other regions comprise what is called "compound escalation." Such actions are taken in order to deter the opponent from aggression in one place by creating the threat of counteraction in another place. The opponent's fear of an advance or reinforcement of the enemy in a given area can restrain him from provocative action in another place. Or an attempt is made to secure military, political, and strategic advantages by means of attacks in depth in other regions outside the frame of the geographical limitations initially accepted.[25] The geographical limitation is liable to be the most important on the further count that it is the easiest to operate. Nevertheless, localizing the war is not an absolute limitation. In the light of the changing circumstances of the war as it develops, there may well be reprisal attacks by air, sea, and land that strike deeper than the zones of the limited war. These reprisals themselves must be undertaken with the recognition that they are liable to lead to an extension of the war beyond the boundaries initially agreed on; there must be a conscious decision that it is necessary to take the risks involved.[26]

Other Limitations

Other relevant aspects that are subject to limitation are those of participants (type and number), outside assistance (receipt of military and economic aid from protagonists not taking an active part in the conflict), or an increase in the number of active protagonists (intervention by a foreign power or intervention by protagonists that are not superpowers). These limitations reflect wishes rather than realities since there is, in fact, no way of imposing limitations on protagonists. In most limited wars these additional limitations have not been among those mutually accepted.[27]

Ideally, as Kaufmann indicates, ". . . one might wish to see a war confined as to area, weapons, time, and tempo, but it seems doubtful that so many limitations could be imposed or maintained simultaneously."[28] Kaufmann's conclusion is that the most we can hope and work for are restrictions of area and weapons. For Kaufmann, weapons and area are the critical limitations.

Schelling indicates: "The most powerful limitations, the most appealing ones, the ones must likely to be observable in wartime, are those that have a conspicuousness and simplicity, that are qualitative and not a matter of degree, that provide recognizable boundaries." [29] But the question is how one can define the criticality of limitations, or in other words, which type of limitation is likely to be more critical than others for keeping the war limited. George defines the following limitation as critical, ". . . if its alteration or violation would make unstable the pattern of limitations of which it is a part, i.e., would lead to a change in other limitations. Conversely, a limitation is not critical if its violation or alteration would not lead to alteration of other limitations." [30] Degrees of criticality, according to George, ". . . may be postulated in terms of the extent of spiralling in the level of violence that would be set into motion by violation of different limitations." [31]

It is widely believed that one's limited political objectives and the value placed upon them are what basically determine the magnitude and the level of violence. Political objectives basically determine the military means, but the value placed upon political objectives may determine the decision to limit or expand the war, even though the objective itself remains the same. [32] It is also believed that qualitative limitations such as type of target or type of weapon are more critical than quantitative limitations. This belief is controversial. Sometimes quantitative limitations may be more critical. The interrelationship between the limitations is such that the dynamics of the war itself may indicate which limitation is more critical. The criticality of limitations may vary from war to war or from one situation to another according to the circumstances.

Patterns of Bargaining in Limited Local War

This study distinguishes six types of bargaining relationships in those situations characterized by war between two local actors and by patron-client relationships between the two local actors and the two superpowers:

(a) bargaining relationship between local actors a and b;
(b) bargaining relationship between local actor a and its superpower patron A;
(c) bargaining relationship between local actor b and its superpower patron B;
(d) bargaining relationship between local actor a and superpower B;
(e) bargaining relationship between local actor b and superpower A;
(f) bargaining relationship between the superpowers A and B (see figure).

In a usual and simple bargaining relationship each actor has to bargain and coordinate expectations only with the other one. In this type of local war, however, each actor has three different types of bargaining relationships—with the other local actor and with the two superpowers. This complicated bargaining relationship has some interesting features:

1. The capacity to gain or avoid losing some portion of the object is limited for the local actor, not only by the bargaining power of the other local actor, but also by the bargaining power of the two superpowers.[33]
2. This complicated interdependence means that a local actor cannot exercise full control over the course of in-

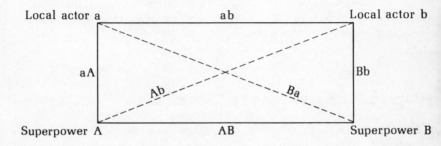

teractions. Nevertheless he may have superiority in military strength. Military inferiority of one party may be compensated for by its greater ability to convince its patron to deter its adversary because there is a great danger not only to the interests of that local actor, but also to the interests of the superpower.

3. Schelling identifies several types of bargaining relationships that are relevant to our study: bargaining about the conduct of the war (the bargaining about the way the war is to be fought, bargaining about the cease-fire, truce, armistice, or whatever brings the war to a close, and bargaining about the actor's authority to negotiate).[34]

4. Bargaining relationships between local actors and their superpowers may help to keep the war limited in those situations where the local actors fail to reach any agreement. Those bargaining relationships are based on the superpowers' commitments to the local actors, and on the dependence of the local actors for the massive support of the superpowers. By utilizing a system of pressures on their respective clients and on their client's opponent, the two superpowers can bring their influence to bear on the belligerent to maintain the limitations.

5. The bargaining relationship between the two superpowers in a local war where their interests are directly involved is based on two opposing aims. On the one hand, the two desire their clients or proxies to win *or at least to avoid a total/major defeat*. On the other hand, they are aware of the danger of the war's expanding. In order to win or at least avoid defeat, the superpower may support the client militarily (supplying arms, providing military advisers, operating given weapons), economically (stepping up economic assistance), and politically-diplomatically. The latter may include pressures and threats directed against the client's adversary or against the other superpower in order to get it to use its influence to restrain its own client. The superpower's support may encourage the client to expand the war but may also serve as a constraint on the client's adversary. In this

sphere of activity the two superpowers may negotiate some "rules of the game" concerning their involvement in the war, their respective commitments to either side in the conflict, and their definition of thresholds in a war whose outbreak will mean direct intervention by the superpowers. The fear that expansion of the war is liable to involve both superpowers directly in the conflict, given their respective commitments, has indeed prevented the two superpowers from intervening militarily with their own forces in most of the limited wars. The very fact that the local war may expand spurs the two superpowers' efforts to bring the war to an end, or at least to insure that it remains limited. In situations where it is clear that one superpower has more at stake in the local war than the other, especially because the results are negative for its client or because the client's adversary broke some limitations, it may decide by tacit agreement with the other superpower to intervene in the war in order to prevent its client's defeat.

6. Due to the superpowers' fears of the war's expansion, local actors may be able to maneuver between them in order to secure favorable treatment in certain respects, and also in order to resist and overcome the superpowers' pressures and constraints. If they can recognize and identify the conflict of interests between the superpowers, the level of commitment of each power vis-à-vis its own client, and the superpowers' fears of direct confrontation or change in the strategic and political balance between them, the local actors can enjoy some freedom of action and the superpowers will have difficulty in limiting the war or bringing it to an end. In situations like this the bargaining power of the local actors will increase.[35]

Escalation and Limited Local War

The concept of limited war and the concept of escalation are interrelated. As Richard Smoke describes it, "Escalation is the process by which the previous limits of a war are crossed. . . . Conversely the limits of a war are the barriers or thresholds or stages of the escalation process."[36] Violation of the limits entails the danger that the escalation process will get out of control and drastically increase the levels of violence.

It was widely believed that the most likely way for escalation to occur in limited war would be accidental—the result of miscalculation or of incomplete verbal or tacit communication between the adversaries.[37] But escalation may be viewed as a deliberate strategy that actors in a local war may use to achieve specific and immediate advantages. The quest for military or political advantages necessarily entails the risks of greater and uncontrollable escalation.[38] Before expanding the war, each actor must consider the possibility of the other's response. According to Halperin, the enemy's reaction may be to take parallel action, but he may also react in a different way.[39] It is also necessary for one side to be aware of the hazards. Once particular observed limits are broken, it may become impossible to prevent total destruction of other limits.[40] The basic problem, however, is how to use escalation as a deliberate, controlled strategy, i.e., how to use escalation for improving tactical or strategic developments without total destruction of the limits.

Schelling suggests the use of saliencies or thresholds in order to keep escalation under control. By escalating only to the level of another salience, one actor may signal his intentions to keep the war under control. The opponent, while he retaliates, may consider these intentions and act in proportion. In this escalation process, according to Schelling, only some particular limits become discredited and new limits appear in the new stage of the war. A controlled escalation represents a tacit proposal by one actor for new limits.[41]

Schelling suggests the use of an escalation ladder. The breakpoints or the thresholds in the escalation ladder represent the limits of controlled escalation. Crossing a threshold is always a significant escalation, but every threshold represents a different level of violence. If both sides are aware of the idea of thresholds, then during a war, instead of reacting out of proportion to each other's initiatives they can make calculated and appropriate

moves that will not cross the critical threshold. "It is undoubtedly in the interest of limiting war that some obvious firebreaks
and thresholds occur. There are subclasses or patterns or conventional boundaries to help find a stopping place. It is hard to stop
without an obvious stopping place . . . some thresholds have
made a claim to being the 'ultimate limit,' the last stopping place
before all-out war."[42]

In a limited local war, escalation may continue until both
sides decide that it is not in their interest to expand the war, or
until one or both superpowers decide to stop it. In situations
where local actors cannot define or recognize the critical threshold for controlled escalation, the superpowers may help by signaling explicitly or tacitly to one or both actors to stop the war
because they are about to cross a threshold or have already done
so. Controlled escalation may not be a result of a bargaining situation between local actors, however, but of one between local
actors and superpowers. Or else, as suggested by Richard Smoke,
"Much of the non-bargaining significance of limits and escalation lies in various deep-seated features of the context or
situation within which limits are formed or escalation occurs. . . ."[43]

Escalation is likely to occur in situations when one or both
sides are no longer interested in observing certain limitations.
This may happen because of asymmetries in capabilities, asymmetries in availability of options to belligerents and their ability
to use them, or asymmetries of interests and motivations.[44] A
number of specific factors are liable to push either of the sides
into expanding the war:

1. The initial pressure for escalation of military activity is
   likely to come from the perception that such an increase
   in the level of violence will improve the likelihood of
   securing military ends (strategic or tactical).[45]
2. One side may accord more importance (interest or motivation) to the disputed issue and judge that it cannot
   achieve its objectives within restrictions previously accepted.[46]
3. While striving to secure strategic and political advan-

tages, one side may judge, with or without justification, that the extant balance of power is favorable to it.[47]

4. It may appear to one side that as a result of an added external development (arms deliveries, intervention of a third party in the war), the adversary is likely to expand the war and it will be better to forestall him.

5. If one side judges that the other side is trying to impose limitations not to its liking, it may counter this supposed "dictate" by an increased degree of belligerence.[48]

6. In certain situations internal pressures exist that make for a speedy end to the war. There may be internal opposition to suffering a high rate of casualties to gain limited aims.[49]

7. When one side feels that it is losing the war or judges that the other side is likely to win, it is liable to feel itself less bound by the rules of limitation that were initially agreed. Furthermore, when the losing side feels trapped in a situation that will result in unlimited war, it may expand the war as the sole alternative to defeat. This can be done by permitting unlimited use of military means, by introducing more sophisticated military means, or, in the most serious situation, by bringing an additional protagonist into the war—a superpower, for instance.[50]

8. Extreme conditions proposed for terminating the war are likely to lead to the expansion of a limited war.[51]

9. The personal motives and psychology of decision makers provide another source of escalation. Sometimes decision makers may feel either that they need a victory in order to stay in power or that their place in history will be determined by such a victory.[52]

Tempo and Dynamics of Limited Local War

The tempo and the dynamics of limited local war can be determined by examining the dimensions of intensification and deintensification of the violence of the war, in terms of escalation of military actions. A distinction can be drawn between two patterns of escalation: a gradual rise in military activity—"expansion of the war," or a sharp jump in the frequency of interaction between the warring sides marked by a sharp rise in the level of military action and the violence of the war—"explosion of the war." This latter escalation, which can lead to a situation of unlimited war, is generally caused by the intervention of additional factors not previously present in the war—the introduction of sophisticated weapons, utilization of new strategic doctrines, direct intervention by a third party, or an essential change in policy makers' objectives (or changes in the value placed upon them).[53]

By examining the tempo and level of military activity, we can determine the developments that lead to these two patterns of escalation. The tempo can be discerned by correlating the type of military activity (the type of arms utilized), the level of violence (rate of losses, extent of material damage), the level of military activity (small, medium, or large-scale incidents), the targets (military or civilian), the number of military actions such as air strikes (per day, per week, per month, etc.). It is also possible to consider the relationships among these variables and their effects on the acceleration or deceleration of war intensification—for example, the connection between the targets and the type of military activity or bombing of enemy territory in depth and the reduction of the enemy's military activity, or on the contrary, the connection between installation of antiaircraft missiles and reduction of the number of daily air strikes, or the type of military activity and the level of violence (utilization of weapons systems such as planes and reduction of rate of losses). A situation can arise where utilizing certain weapons systems is likely to decelerate military actions in the first phase but increase military activity in the next phase.

The dimension of time can assist in determining the degree of intensification of the conflict by comparing the intervals between attacks or actions by one side and the reactions of the other side, i.e., the length of the intervals between the exchange of blows and the length of the intervals between military actions and diplomatic initiatives. The degree of deintensification or deescalation of the conflict can be determined by considering the interaction between diplomatic activities and military actions. Increase in the tempo of diplomatic activities can assist the deintensification of the war. On the other hand, intensification of military actions can also impel one side or both sides to seek diplomatic initiatives in face of the rising danger of extension and expansion of the war, lest serious expansion of the war mean increased damage inflicted on both sides.[54]

The tempo and dynamics of limited local war can also be determined by examining one actor's changing his political objectives and the influence of this on the other actor, or the changing values placed on political objectives and their influence on escalation or deescalation of the war.

Limited Local War Management

The term "limited local war management" in this study is taken to mean an exercise of control by the small actors and the superpowers' decision makers in order to minimize the danger of a limited local war getting out of control. In other words, the term "crisis management" is used in this study to mean avoidance of risk of unlimited war. Decision makers in a limited local war are interested in more than just avoiding major escalation or superpowers' constraints. They are also interested in advancing their political objectives or protecting them, and in maximizing gains and minimizing losses. Both sides are interested in winning or gaining ends but without the risk of a major escalation that will encourage superpowers to threaten intervention. The goals of the parties are in conflict with outside constraints. This bargaining situation is characterized by a mixed motive that represents an interaction between the mutual interests of both sides to advance political gains and their desires to prevent outside constraints. Each actor, as Snyder and Diesing mention, ". . . wishes to manage the crisis so as to maximize its values in the outcome, which means it wants to coerce prudently or accommodate cheaply, or some combination of both."[55] Self-management of limited war is limited only to those situations in which the local actors manage the war by consensual limitation. In situations where local actors fail to manage the war by themselves, the superpowers' role in management of the war becomes more predominant. The superpowers' management may be used by one or both actors as a constraint on the opponent in order to coerce him to avoid expansion of the war.

George suggests criteria or requirements for controlled measures, use of force, and effective crisis management between superpowers. These criteria may apply to limited local war: top-level presidential control of military options, pauses in military operations, clear and appropriate military options demonstrations, coordination between military action and political-diplomatic action, confidence in the effectiveness and discriminating character of military options, military options that avoid motivating the opponent to escalate, or avoidance of impression or resort to large-scale warfare.[56] The utility of these requirements in limited local war is especially valid in self-management situations.

Patterns of War Termination

Basically limited local war, unlike total war, aims at decision not by destruction or surrender of the enemy's forces, but by insuring the furthering of limited political objectives. The presentation of flexible and moderate objectives by the sides is likely to be most conducive to the termination of a local war.[57] Since the major purpose of the limited war is a limited political objective, the tendency is to limit war so it can result in a limited victory, a limited defeat, or a stalemate.[58]

The termination of a local war will come from a variety of pressures: external (superpowers' constraints), domestic (pressures against suffering a high rate of casualties), or capability and military constraints (lack of military and economic capabilities to continue the war, or need to avoid the economic costs of continuing it). We may identify three patterns of war termination: self-termination, agreed termination, and imposed termination. Self-termination occurs in situations in which one side decides to terminate the war. Agreed termination occurs in situations where both sides agree to finish the war. Imposed termination occurs where the superpowers impose termination conditions. Self-termination will be the result of several factors: one side's belief that it has achieved its limited objectives, fear of total defeat, fear of a superpower's direct intervention, or fear of an imposed solution. Agreed termination will be a result of the same factors and also of a mutual fear of the war's expansion. An imposed solution will be entailed by failure of the local actors' attempts to terminate the war on their own.

Superpowers' motivation for imposed termination are: fear of direct confrontation, fear of total defeat or total victory of the client, and self or mutual understanding that stalemate termination is the best condition for subsequent negotiation between the local actors. During the course of the war both sides may bargain over conditions for ending the war and over the nature of the settlement. Schelling notes, "There would be bargaining about the cease-fire, truce, armistice, surrender, disarmament, or whatever it is that brings the war to a close—about the way to halt the war and the military requirements for stopping it." [59] Bargaining over conditions for ending the war or over the nature of the settlement may develop between the local actors and the superpowers, and between the superpowers themselves. War termination conditions that reflect success on the battlefield will promote bargaining situations between superpowers and local actors. In some situations where there is no clear understanding between the superpowers about war termination conditions, the local actors can maneuver for better ones that will reflect their success on the battlefield. The political constraints are less effective in situations where the bargaining relationship between the superpowers may neutralize the ability of one superpower to employ effective constraints against his client's adversary.

Conclusions

This study attempts to unify in a coherent theory some of the factors that affect the limitation and expansion of local wars between small actors in which the superpowers take sides and render indirect assistance but where neither of them is directly involved with its own forces. The reasons for limiting a local war are not always the result of direct interaction between the local actors. Limitations are not always required, as the "tacit bargaining" model suggests. The external political constraints or the types of interactions between superpowers and small actors in a local war seem to be the major factors limiting it. The element of uncertainty about superpowers' reactions or direct superpowers' pressures or threats may enforce limitations on small actors' behavior in local wars. It is important to examine local wars or case studies in order to apply the results to interrelationships between sources of constraints and limitations in local war. The aim of this study is to examine the 1969–1970 War of Attrition between Egypt and Israel as such a case study.

2 The Theory and Definition of "War of Attrition"

A CLEAR, GENERAL DISTINCTION must be made between two types of wars of attrition: (a) the war of attrition as politico-military strategy, declared and adopted as such by one side in the war and seen by it as most-favored strategy; (b) a war of attrition that is not a politico-military strategy adopted from the outset, but that has developed from another type of war as a consequence of tactical and strategic circumstances—in other words, a war that was not originally meant to be a war of attrition, but turned into one as the result of a connected chain of events.

A war of attrition as a politico-military strategy, declared and adopted, is extremely rare in the long history of war, and accordingly it has not been the subject of theoretical treatment in the literature on war and strategy on such a wide scale as have other types of war.[1] War of attrition as politico-military strategy is generally conceived as undesirable by the side initiating it, as a strategy of *faute de mieux* (for lack of a better alternative) and it is adopted as preferable only in the absence of objective capability to develop any other strategy. War of attrition as politico-military strategy is what concerns us in this study and we shall discuss its various characteristics.

In the history of war, most of the situations known or defined as wars of attrition were not basically such wars. Attrition was generally forced on the belligerents as a result of the unforeseen evolution of the war into a prolonged and static conflict, characterized by a high level of erosion of forces on both sides and/or paucity of tactical or strategic offensives.[2] In his *Study of War*, Quincy Wright describes the conditions that can lead to wars of attrition, or that make wars of attrition more likely to occur. "Modern military techniques," he writes, "have increased the possibility of a deadlock and a war of attrition between powers both of which are equally skilled in the use of these methods. . . . On the whole, increasing mechanization and capitalization of military techniques have favored the war of attrition."[3]

In two world wars and in the Vietnam War (1963–1973) situations developed where the belligerents waged wars of attrition when all attempts to develop other strategies had failed. The war of the French and British allies against Germany on the western front in the years 1915–1917, and the fighting between the USSR and Germany on the eastern front—at Stalingrad from September 1942 to January 1943 and at Leningrad from October 1941 to January 1944—began as German offensives and turned into wars of attrition. Those wars on the western front in World War I and on the eastern front in World War II were characterized by prolonged warfare at static positions, use of similar military techniques on both sides, a high degree of reciprocal erosion of the forces engaged, and a paucity of tactical and strategic offensives. Under these conditions the war of attrition was not preferred and the belligerents wanted to change it and develop a broad offensive. On the western front the Allied forces launched this offensive in 1917, while on the eastern front the Russian offensive was launched at Stalingrad early in 1943 and at Leningrad early in 1944.[4] During the Vietnam War, too, developments took place that were seen as presenting the features of war of attrition. The U.S. massive bombing of North Vietnam in 1965, 1968, and 1972 constituted "air attrition" as part of the effort to bring the war to an end.[5]

War of Attrition as Politico-Military Strategy

The strategy of war of attrition is generally adopted by a belligerent with limited military capability and inability to develop any other politico-military strategy. It is a strategy adopted by the side that is weaker from the military point of view in an attempt to alter the given politico-military situation by imposing a war of attrition on its adversary, since it sees this as the only military option it can adopt.[6]

It is characteristic of the war of attrition that the side initiating it is without the capability to develop not only an inclusive military option but even limited strategies of various kinds such as mobile warfare. To adopt a strategy of attrition is to recognize that the adversary possesses clear superiority on the political plane (superpower's political support of its political policies) and on the military plane, and that the success of attrition depends on success in achieving limited political objectives by depriving its opponent the use of its superiority.

The side initiating a war like this judges that by manipulating political and/or strategic limitations, it will prevent the adversary from using his military superiority to force the initiator to fight on lines contrary to his own nature. On the political plane, the side choosing a strategy of attrition assumes that the adversary's politico-strategic concept is one of maintaining the existing political and military situation. Hence it judges that the adversary, fearing a breakdown of this existing politico-military situation, is not interested in the outbreak of a violent conflict and is therefore likely to refrain from making use of his full military capability and his superiority in various military strategies (mobile warfare, preventive war, preemptive strike, etc.) and from exceeding the military bounds thus imposed on him.

This assumption can work successfully in situations involving considerable superpower interests that are liable to be endangered by the outbreak of a violent conflict. The pressure of vital superpower interests in the region concerned is likely to be decisive for the success of the strategy of attrition from the purely political point of view. The mere possibility of a clash between the superpowers in the event of a violent conflict getting out of their control is enough to create a tense and menacing atmosphere. If the side initiating the strategy of attrition can produce this atmosphere, it can bring about speedier diplomatic activity to help alter the given diplomatic-military situation unacceptable to itself.

From the purely military point of view, the strategy of attrition tries to hit at the weak point in the adversary's military strategy by exploiting the military advantages accruing to the side that starts the war. The side initiating a war of attrition, which by definition does not enjoy the advantages of speed and mobility, will try to adopt a strategy that suits its own military talents and that runs counter to the military nature and talents of its adversary. A limited strategy (local and static) that exploits any advantages (quantitative and qualitative) of the initiator in manpower and certain weapons systems (mainly artillery), as well as its advantages of better staying power (economic, political, and social), is effective in a situation of tactical proximity of the belligerent forces—an essential condition for operating a strategy of attrition. The aim of the strategy of attrition, from the military standpoint, is to delay and prevent a decision on the strategic level at a stage when a wide gap still exists between the strengths of the relative forces, and to speed up a decision on the tactical level.

Calling attrition a strategy does not imply that it is necessarily a final strategy. It is a temporary strategy that reflects the existing politico-strategic circumstances. It is a *pis aller*, a "last resort." Attrition is no more than a necessary strategic phase and is directed toward securing no more than limited political and military results. On the political plane, the aim is to disrupt a given politico-military situation by exercising political and military pressures in order to produce accelerated diplomatic moves and bring about the desired political solution. On the military plane, the aim is to wear down the enemy over a lengthy period by physical and moral attrition until he consents to the political and military concessions the initiator is interested in securing. By eroding the enemy's strength, the initiator also hopes to bring about a change in the balance of forces between the sides to secure military superiority for himself or at least draw level with the adversary. When the stage of equality of forces or of superiority for the initiator is reached, the latter must adopt a different strategy in order to secure his ultimate aims, now that attrition has secured him only limited aims.[7]

The Limitations of War of Attrition as Politico-Military Strategy

The great weakness of the strategy of attrition deliberately adopted at the outset of hostilities is that it is based on one fundamental assumption—that the adversary will in fact refrain from utilizing his military superiority on account of political and/or military limitations. If the adversary does not accept and observe the rules of the military setup, the entire politico-strategic infrastructure of attrition collapses. Further, attrition strategy relies on a unilateral concept of the war, which is seen as a special type of limited war. All the limitations that the side starting the war tries to impose are unilateral. They will be accepted and applied to the conduct of the war only if the adversary agrees at the outset and consents to them in their entirety. Since these limitations are imposed without the declared permission and consent of the adversary, but in the belief that he will tacitly accept them on account of his own political and military limitations, there is no real guarantee that they will in fact be observed.

The strategy of attrition is dependent on the capacity of the side initiating it to "persuade" the adversary to keep within the military setup that the initiator is attempting to dictate. To neutralize the adversary's freedom of action, a system of political and/or military pressures and threats is necessary, such as the threat to extend the war, to turn it into a war of outright destruction, to invoke the intervention of a foreign power, etc.

The prospects of attrition as military and political strategy are better in situations where considerable superpower interests are involved. The pressure of vital superpower interests in the region concerned, including a high level of commitment to the superpowers' respective clients (the initiator and his adversary), is liable to make it easier for the side choosing the strategy of attrition to achieve its aims. Keeping the war within the bounds desired by the side starting it will also be facilitated by that side's success in manipulating the opposed interests of the superpowers in balance with their common interest in preventing an extension of the war.

The nature of the commitments of the patron superpower to its client who started the war constitutes an important basic condition for the strategy of attrition. The more extensive the superpower commitment, the greater the likelihood that the client's adversary will be prepared to accept real limitations on the conduct of the war. Extensive superpower commitment is also likely to reduce the risks if the client's adversary should nevertheless decide to make use of his military superiority.

Another important condition for the success of attrition as a strategy is the initiator's recognition that this strategy is indeed limited in its politico-military effects. Its achievements are limited, just as the level of risk is thought to be limited. Attempts to achieve more are liable to bring about an extension of the war, set off by either party. The more the side starting the war feels likely to succeed, and the more it extends the war, the more liable this side is to cause an escalation of the war from one of attrition to another type of war. The adversary is liable to become more and more apprehensive and deduce that the war is developing beyond its initial limitations. The more successful the side starting the war is in making its limited aims clear, the greater the likelihood that it will be able to secure its adversary's acceptance of the limitations even against his will.

Motivation is of prime importance in every war—even more so in a war of attrition. The side adopting the strategy of attrition has to be more determined to reach its aims than the adversary is in defending his positions. In other words, the "balance of vital-ness"[8] (the importance attached to the achievement of aims judged to be vitally important, and the readiness to make the maximum efforts—military, economic, and political—needed for this purpose) has to be higher for the side starting the war of attrition than for its adversary. In situations where the adversary's "balance of vital-ness" is higher than or equal to that of the initiator, the adversary will be readier to defend the given military and political position. His readiness to make use of his military superiority is also likely to be greater.

The prospects of success for a strategy of attrition (always on the assumption that the adversary will, in fact, be prepared to wage a war of attrition) depends on the staying power of the belligerents. This is a direct function of the duration of the war and the degree of erosion. Since attrition means a high degree of reciprocal erosion over a relatively long period of time, obviously the side that suffers a greater degree of physical and moral fatigue is likely to lose the war. In order to withstand the rate of erosion in the war of attrition, the side initiating this strategy must possess larger economic resources and reserves of manpower than its enemy. It must also have stamina—high civilian and military morale and readiness to bear heavy casualties. The rate of erosion of economic and human resources and of civilian and military morale is likely to determine which side wins the war. The longer the war of attrition, the higher is likely to be the rate of erosion. A long war of attrition with a high rate of erosion can sometimes be so costly to the victor that attrition ceases to be an effective policy instrument.

The duration of the war is necessarily a function of the rate of erosion. The higher the rate of erosion, the shorter the war must be. Moreover, the longer the war goes on and the higher the rate of erosion inflicted on the adversary, the more likely the adversary will be to decide to change the nature and the course of the war in the hope of bringing it to a speedy and successful end.[9] The war of attrition therefore has to be confined to a very limited period of time, after which it is liable to lose its character. The high rate of erosion is liable to impel the belligerents to try to end the war quickly by means of some other strategy.

War of Attrition as Limited War

The war of attrition as a politico-military strategy is a specific type of limited war. The limited military capability of the initiator of attrition is of importance in considering the war limited, at least from the standpoint of the initiator. Not every limited war necessarily implies the component of physical capability to wage an unlimited war, but in a war of attrition the question of capability is a dominant consideration. In other types of limited war, reluctance to utilize military capability to the full helps to keep the war limited, but in a war of attrition there is the objective problem of the absence of capability to develop an unlimited war. At bottom the strategy of attrition is limited, at least from the standpoint of the initiator, not only because he has no possibility of developing a less limited general strategy, but also because there is no possibility open to him for utilizing limited strategies of other kinds. The adversary's outstanding advantage—his superior capacity to use other military strategies—compels the side initiating attrition to stay within the bounds of this very limited military strategy. His limited military capability forces the initiator of attrition strategy to accept limitations in a number of spheres: a limit to his war objectives, a limit to the military means utilized, a geographical limit to the war, a limit to the type of targets selected (mainly military ones), and a limit to the duration of the war. Whether these limitations will in fact be applied in the war depends mainly on the adversary's consenting to honor all or some of them.

Limit to the Objectives
War of attrition as politico-military strategy is employed for attaining limited political and military objectives. The basic politico-strategic aim of the initiator of the strategy of attrition is a certain change in the given political and military situation that he hopes to bring about by utilizing limited military and political pressures. The side initiating the attrition does not possess the capability to bring about this change in the given political and military situation by a decision in war—by the destruction or defeat of his enemy. The success of attrition will be determined by the increasing rate of erosion of the enemy's strength and resources, leading him to recognize the need to make political concessions to the initiator of the war or to agree to negotiate. The choice of the limited aims is of course a function of the initiator's limited capability to attain wider aims. Since the adversary enjoys clear military superiority, the initiator's political and military achievements will necessarily be limited. Recognition of this is a primary condition for keeping the conduct of the war limited, at least from the standpoint of the initiator. Moreover, setting politico-military aims that are clearly limited can help induce the adversary to refrain from going beyond the bounds of the war limitations the initiator seeks to impose.

Limit to the Military Means Utilized
The limit set on the war objectives necessarily imposes a limited utilization of military means. Further, since the war of attrition is characterized by the use of certain weapons systems (mainly artillery), care must be taken to utilize those only. Qualitative and quantitative limitation is also necessary, in spite of the fact that this limitation is damaging to the initiator's power to inflict erosion on his adversary. Full utilization of his quantitative or qualitative potential would lead the adversary to start escalation by utilizing those military means in which he does possess clear superiority. To exploit quantitative or qualitative potential to the full would be utilizing unlimited means in the supposedly limited war. Limitations are a matter of quantity and types of specific military means; hence exists a range of possible limitations.

Geographical Limit to the War
War of attrition is by definition a war that limits the battle zone. Initiation of the strategy of attrition is based on the tactical proximity of the belligerents. The battle zone is likely to be geographically reduced (both in breadth and depth), because of the limited capacity of the military means utilized (except the air force) to cover larger geographical areas with fire. In light of the way the war develops, the initiator can go outside the battle zone by means of commando raids, for example, but these actions have to be taken with the knowledge that they are liable to lead to a change in the nature of the war.

Limit to the Targets Selected and to the Duration of War
Given the tactical proximity of the belligerents and the geographical limits to the battle zone, the strategy of attrition will generally concentrate on enemy military targets in this zone only. The erosion of the enemy's human and military resources is the central aim of attrition from the military point of view. The belief is that increasing erosion of the enemy's army will suffice to sap its strength, moral and physical, at the front and in the rear. If the rate of erosion is high, the adversary will be forced to devote more and more economic and human resources to strengthening the front, thereby probably damaging his national

economic effort. The rate of erosion must not get too high, therefore, if the adversary is to be deterred from extending the war.

Communication Between Belligerents and the Breakdown of Limitations

The subject of communication between the sides in a war of attrition is very complex because the initial proceeding to put the
limitations of this war into effect is unilateral. In order to insure
that all or part of these limitations go into effect, the side initiating the war has to try to create channels of communication with
the adversary. The only way to insure that the war will have the
character of attrition and be kept limited is for the initiator to
make his intentions and his war aims clear from the start.

The communication most likely to take place between the
sides in a war of attrition is tacit bargaining. The military actions
of the side initiating the war may in fact constitute the best communication signals in the absence of any possibility of open and
direct communication since these actions are in themselves the
clearest indicators of the initiator's intentions and aims. The less
dense the "fog of war," the greater the initiator's hope of success
in making his intentions clear. Tacit bargaining can also be accompanied by additional signals, such as speeches and declarations by the policy makers on the side initiating attrition. While
these signals can help clarify aims and intentions, their effectiveness will be doubtful if the military actions do not display
the same spirit.

Tacit bargaining is also useful to the adversary before he
decides whether to escalate the war (e.g., by limited use of certain weapons systems such as the air force as a deterrent).
Whether the adversary will refrain from escalation depends on
the success of the tacit bargaining initiated by the side starting
the war of attrition.

Attrition as a strategy thus relies on a unilateral concept of
the war as a type of limited war. All the limitations that the side
initiating the war tries to apply are basically unilateral. The development of the war as limited thus depends on whether the ad-

versary is willing to observe all or some of the limitations it proposes to impose on him. Insofar as the adversary does agree to observe some of the limitations, these will hold for both sides. There is a possibility that the adversary will agree to keep the war limited and a war of attrition, but on conditions and with limitations that he wants to impose.

In this situation, the adversary attempts to seize the initiative in the war and even to develop a counterstrategy of attrition, of wearing down the other fellow. In other situations, the adversary may agree in principle that the war should stay limited, but will want it to stop being a war of attrition. Even if the initiator of attrition strategy fails to persuade his adversary to stay within the military bounds that he, the initiator, wants to set up, the war will probably remain limited, though not within the military setup the initiator intended. In this case, gradual escalation of military activity is liable to occur; there will be what is called "expansion of the conflict." It is of course possible that the adversary will reach the point of deciding to make use of his military superiority and will go beyond the bounds of limited war restrictions. In this case escalation can amount to "explosion," a situation where the conflict turns into total war.

The war may also lose the character of a war of attrition and its restriction to limited war if the side initiating the attrition is no longer interested in keeping within the limitations it imposed on itself (the essence of attrition strategy), or if it simply loses control over the conduct and development of the war. A number of factors are liable to impel the side initiating the war to expand the conflict:

First, if the initiator attaches great importance to the specific issue at stake (that is, the "balance of vital-ness" is very high), and if it judges that in the conditions of attrition it cannot achieve its aims (either because of its low level of military success or because serious political initiatives fail to materialize), then the initiator is likely to reach the opinion that it is preferable to take the risk of expanding the war in order to produce a real shift in events and more effective diplomatic moves.[10]

Second, if arms supplies arrive in greater quantities and of higher quality than before (better planes and/or air defense systems), or if the patron superpower commits itself further than in the past to direct, if limited, military intervention, all or some of these things can lead the initiator of attrition to judge that the balance of forces has changed in his favor and he will then decide to drop attrition strategy, adopted only as a *pis aller* in the first place.

Third, there are situations where internal pressures for a speedy end to the war begin to make themselves felt. On the one hand there is opposition to suffering heavy losses for the sake of limited aims, and on the other hand it is foreseen that the war will not secure adequate military and political results. The regime fears for its survival if it does not produce significant military or political achievements, and this too is likely to contribute to a decision to expand the war.

Finally, if the side initiating attrition judges that it is losing the war or that the war has stopped being limited as far as it is concerned (on account of the enemy's countermoves), it can be impelled to adopt a strategy of "threatened defeat" in order to increase the pressure on its patron superpower and other international bodies to intervene in the war and bring it to an end by serious diplomacy. "Threatened defeat" is a strategy of blackmail directed against the patron superpower. The threat is that without direct, real military assistance or the desired political solution to the war, the side that initiated the attrition will probably initiate military actions that may lead to a serious defeat, necessarily endangering the interests of the patron superpower in this region of the world. The side that initiated attrition believes that its own defeat runs counter to the patron superpower's interests and that the latter will intervene directly in order to improve its own military and political standing.[11]

Summary

1. *Aims of the war on the politico-strategic plane:* Function of a military capability too limited to develop other types of strategies. Achievement of limited political and military aims;

limited political and military concessions by the adversary. A given, limited change in the given politico-military situation.

2. *Aims of the war on the military-operation plane:* Delay, postponement, or prevention of decision on the strategic level, but thrust for speedy decision on the tactical level by means of limited erosion of enemy strength.

3. *Military means:* Exploitation of quantitative and qualitative advantages in certain types of arms (artillery).

4. *Geographical war zone:* Very restricted because of belligerents' tactical proximity.

5. *Targets for strikes:* Exclusively military targets at the front (also because of limited military means for covering a larger range of targets).

6. *Duration of war and rate of erosion:* High rate of erosion of manpower and material resources. Length of the war a function of the rate of erosion.

7. *Communication between the sides:* "Tacit bargaining" (military actions) plus signaling by means other than military actions (threats and declarations).

8. *Conditions for success as political and military strategy:*

(a) Consent of the adversary to accept the limitations specific to a strategy of attrition, and punctilious observance by the initiator of the limitations devised by him.

(b) High degree of involvement of superpower interests plus high degree of commitment to the client on the part of the patron superpower.

(c) Recognition of the limited nature of the political and military achievements to be attained by utilizing this strategy.

(d) Very high "balance of vital-ness."

(e) A low rate of erosion during a given period of time.

9. *Results of the war:* Limited, on both the military and the political planes, so long as all the above mentioned conditions for the success of attrition as political and military strategy continue to be observed.

3 Egypt Imposes Its Strategy

The Military Option

EGYPT APPARENTLY REACHED its decision in favor of the military option toward the end of 1968 as a result of the Egyptian leadership's reappraisal on the one hand of the effectiveness of diplomatic initiatives in securing a political solution of the crisis in the region, and on the other of the Egyptian military capability for a limited military confrontation with Israel. In the autumn of 1968 the Egyptian leadership judged that there was no chance of realizing the immediate aims of Egypt—Israeli withdrawal from the Sinai—by means of a political solution that would be acceptable from the Egyptian standpoint (general Israeli withdrawal without Egypt's signing a peace treaty with Israel).[1]

From the political point of view, the Egyptian leadership judged that the diplomatic initiatives taken since the end of the Six-Day War (including the Jarring Mission) would not bear fruit as long as there was no substantial change in Israel's political stand, that is to say as long as Israel refused to withdraw from the conquered territories unless a political settlement of the conflict providing for secure boundaries was reached by direct negotiation. There had been a whole series of these diplomatic initiatives in the course of 1967 and 1968: the contacts between the two superpowers that began with the first "Summit Conference" at Glassboro between President Johnson and Premier Kosygin, the Egyptian plan at the end of 1967 for the reopening of the Suez Canal, and principally the Jarring Mission, which was intended to secure the implementation of United Nations Security

Council Resolution 242. The fact that all these initiatives failed constituted the clearest indication for the Egyptians that all such efforts were of no value.

Thus the judgment by the Egyptians in the autumn of 1968 was that Israel—and the United States who supported Israel's political stand—must be pressured into changing their attitudes in order to open the way for more effective diplomatic initiatives.[2] The military option was seen by the Egyptian leadership as the only way likely to pressure Israel and the United States into changing their stand. The concept that only by a certain utilization of the military option would it be possible to reach a solution acceptable from the Egyptian viewpoint was not a new idea, but it only took shape finally at the end of the autumn of 1968.

This concept was based on two assumptions. First, as long as Israel retained strategic superiority there was no prospect of Israel's agreeing to a political solution that would be acceptable from the Egyptian point of view (that is, Israeli withdrawal from the Sinai without Egypt's signing a peace treaty with Israel). Israel would want the political solution to reflect its strategic superiority.[3] Second, a political solution that would be acceptable from the Egyptian point of view would have to be a reflection of real military achievements. These would only become possible if equilibrium were attained with Israeli power or by neutralizing Israel's military superiority. This would demand a considerable reinforcement of Egyptian power, but more than this the readiness to choose the military option that fit the conditions of reinforced Egyptian strength, in accordance with the balance of power between Israel and Egypt.[4]

President Abdel Nasser summed up this approach in an interview published in the newspaper *Al-Ahrām* on January 21, 1968:

The first priority, the absolute priority in this battle is the military front, for we must realise that the enemy will not withdraw unless we force him to withdraw through fighting. Indeed there can be no hope of any political solution unless the enemy realizes that we are capable of forcing him to withdraw through fighting.[5]

The Egyptian decision to adopt the military option was therefore taken from the standpoint that war is nothing other than the continuation of politics by other means, as Clausewitz defined it.[6] For Egypt war was nothing other than the only way to secure a political solution acceptable to Egypt, since political means had failed to secure such a solution from the adversary. The artillery "incidents" of September–October 1968 were apparently a sort of trial run, a preliminary to the utilization of a limited military option.[7] The Israeli reprisal action against Naj' Ḥamādī, deep inside Egypt, on November 1, 1968, revealed serious shortcomings in Egypt's military readiness and led the Egyptians to postpone further military activity until March 1969 in order to get the Egyptian army better prepared for a more effective utilization of the military option.[8]

Military Calculations Affecting Decision
The Egyptian decision reached in the autumn of 1968 to adopt the military option was connected in the first place with the Egyptian leadership's reappraisal of Egypt's military capability for a limited confrontation with Israel. The judgment that a substantial change had taken place in the relative strengths of Israel and Egypt (at least on the Suez Canal front) was the central factor in reaching the decision.

In the autumn of 1968, the Egyptian leadership judged that Israel no longer enjoyed the decisive strategic superiority that it had had before, as a result of Egypt's having made up for the equipment lost in the Six-Day War and having improved its relative strength generally and on the Suez front in particular.[9] The Egyptians now judged that they had more and better planes at their disposal than Israel, a large number of well-trained airmen, and an improved air defense system that had been installed in part along the canal.[10] On the other hand Israel's intensive utilization of its planes on the eastern front (the IAF lost six planes on this front up to April 1969) meant loss through high and constant wear.[11]

Besides the change in relative strengths in the air, the Egyptian military chiefs judged that Egypt had absolute superiority over Israel in manpower, armor, and artillery, especially in view of the massive deployment of Egyptian forces along the Suez Canal Front, opposite the thin Israeli security deployment along this line.[12] The effort expended by Israel to create the Bar-Lev Line after the incidents of September–October 1968 had an effect on the Egyptian decision to advance the activation of the military option. The decision itself to adopt the military option had preceded the creation of the line. The Israeli effort to create the Line was seen by Egypt not only as an attempt to insure the continuation of the military status quo along the canal (by maintaining Israeli military superiority along the canal and blocking any possibility of an Egyptian crossing), but also as an attempt to fix the line of the canal as the political border between Israel and Egypt. The Bar-Lev Line therefore signified the perpetuation of the territorial, political, and military status quo that the Egyptians were determined to alter.[13]

The construction of the Bar-Lev Line did indeed speed up the Egyptian decision to start a war, but it was not the cause that brought about the war. The decision to utilize the military option (the first indication of which was the artillery fire of September–October 1968) was achieved before the construction of the line began and was linked to a larger set of considerations than the fact of the creation of the line. It is erroneous to contend that the establishment of the Bar-Lev Line led to the outbreak of the War of Attrition, but it did bring about the actual decision on attrition as the form Egyptian military strategy would take, given the tactical proximity of the Bar-Lev Line to the Egyptian line of deployment. The Egyptian judgment was that the completion of the Bar-Lev Line was liable to change the balance of forces between Israel and Egypt along the canal and increase the cost in lives of Egyptian military actions.[14]

Egyptian and Soviet Attitudes
There is nothing to indicate that the Egyptian decision to start a new war was agreed on beforehand with the Soviet leadership in the course of the political contacts between the two countries during 1968, but it is possible that the Soviets knew of Egypt's intentions. It is not at all certain that the Soviets had any interest in seeing belligerent action in the region, in view of possible effects on their relations with the United States and their appreciation of the fact that Egypt could not launch an offensive war.[15]

The Soviet political leadership judged that all the diplomatic means available should be tried first, that new diplomatic moves should be initiated differing in character from the Jarring Mission, and that this could only be done through close contacts between the superpowers. In talks held with President Abdel Nasser in July 1968 and in talks conducted by the Soviet Foreign Minister Andrei Gromyko in Egypt in December of that year, the Soviets tried to persuade the Egyptians that only the two superpowers could produce a political solution of the crisis and even impose their solution.[16]

From September 1968 on, the USSR submitted a number of new diplomatic suggestions to the United States, France, and Britain regarding a settlement of the crisis. The first "Peace Program" was put forth to the United States toward the end of September 1968. A further Soviet initiative was put forward in November of the same year, calling for the convening of a committee of the four powers. After both these two proposals were rejected, the USSR on December 30, 1968, proposed a new plan for summoning a four power conference to discuss a new peace program for the Middle East.

Egyptian Aims in the War of Attrition

The Egyptian aims in the War of Attrition were to compel Israel to withdraw from Sinai, perhaps not by means of general war (liberation of Sinai by force) but by means of manipulation of a limited military strategy (war of attrition) and political strategy (adopted to secure an acceptable political solution). The Egyptian strategy in the War of Attrition was aimed at something that could be secured in a general war (sc. Israeli withdrawal from the Sinai), but aimed at getting it by means of a limited war, without having to fight a general war of liberation.[17]

Egyptian aims in the War of Attrition are characterized in this study as limited ones, because in the winter of 1969 and in the course of the war, Egypt was in no position to start anything more than a very limited military operation. It is the matter of military capability that defines the aims of Egypt as limited ones, and not her aspirations and intentions; the aims were limited in spite of the fact that without question she aspired to securing less limited aims (such as the liberation of the Sinai by force) if she only had the military means to do so. This aspiration could be realized only by means of a general offensive war. In the light of the gap between the strengths of Israel and Egypt in March 1969, total war was not possible from the Egyptian point of view.[18]

In March 1969, the Egyptian political and military leaders judged that the liberation of the Sinai by force was possible only by means of a general war. To start a general war would only be possible, according to the Egyptians' evaluation, by realizing certain basic preconditions, which were very far from being realized in the winter of 1969. These conditions were: readiness in the Arab world to render Egypt active assistance in starting a general war; equilibrium of Israeli and Egyptian forces and/or neutralization of Israeli superiority by other means; and assurance of suitable international circumstances for the conduct of a general war, given the fear of intervention by the superpowers in order to stop the war immediately (this referred mainly to the United States).

The fundamental precondition for a general war to be started by Egypt was the opening of several fronts against Israel, which would force her to extend her forces and thus help neutralize her superior strength. The other fronts beside the Egyptian front were supposed to be the Syrian and Jordanian (sometimes called the "eastern front," and including Iraq). Unless this condition were fulfilled, it would not be possible to start a general war, for the main Israeli military effort would then be concentrated on the Egyptian front alone. Nor would there be any possibility of insuring the existence of the second condition without the first, since the way to secure a balance of power with Israel and/or to neutralize her superiority was to create an eastern front.[19]

The second fundamental precondition was securing a balance of relative strength between Israel and Egypt and/or neutralizing Israel's military superiority. This superiority referred mainly to the air, since the Israeli Air Force was considered stronger than that of all the Arab countries put together. Israeli superiority in the air was judged the main thing rendering it impossible for Egypt to wage a general war.[20] In spite of the speedy rehabilitation of the Egyptian Air Force (the purchase of a large number of planes of high quality plus the training of numerous airmen), the Egyptians still considered themselves in the winter of 1969 unable to achieve superiority or even equality with Israeli air power. Two alternatives offered themselves for counterbalancing or neutralizing Israeli air power. The first alternative was to open another front, the eastern one, while the second was to install an improved air defense system.[21] In March of 1969, Egypt failed to make sufficient use of either alternative to permit waging a general war.[22]

The third condition for starting a general war was an assurance of proper international conditions, i.e., neutralizing any American moves to support Israel with supplies. In the absence of any possibility of securing the first two preconditions, the third was of less immediate concern.

Some additional preconditions needed from the operational angle were indicated by Muḥammad Heikal. They included the capability of the Egyptian forces to reach a level of armament and preparedness for battle that would with absolute certainty insure them the possibility of dealing the Israeli forces very damaging blows in the first attacks after crossing the canal, constant superiority of the Egyptian forces over the Israelis in the open spaces of the Sinai, and constant support for the Egyptian forces along the supply lines stretching the whole length of the Egyptian advance into the Sinai.[23]

In the absence of the basic preconditions needed for launching a general war, the Egyptian leadership judged that the only military option available to Egypt was a limited war. The fact that Egypt adopted the War of Attrition as politico-military strategy in itself confirms that Egypt lacked the capability to initiate a general war or even to utilize limited strategies of a different nature, such as a war of movement. The War of Attrition that Egypt initiated in the winter of 1969 was the kind described in strategic studies as a "war of compellence," intended to compel the adversary to agree to a certain, specific change in the political and/or military situation.[24] Egypt hoped to secure this result by manipulating the political constraints implicit in the Israeli-Arab conflict and in the superpower conflict. Limited military constraints would be used to stiffen the political constraints. In other words, the War of Attrition was a twofold strategy—both political and military—thought to hold the best prospect of success.[25]

Egyptian Political Strategy
The Egyptians wanted to create a serious threat of strategic destabilization, and by so doing they hoped to give a real impetus to diplomatic initiatives in support of an acceptable political solution—Israeli withdrawal from the Sinai without a political settlement of the Israeli-Arab conflict. (After direct USSR military intervention in the War of Attrition, President Abdel Nasser demanded the implementation of Security Council Resolution 242, according to the Egyptian interpretation, as a condition for ending it—Israeli withdrawal from all the occupied territories and a solution to the Palestine question without a political settlement of the Israeli-Arab conflict.)[26]

The political concept behind Egypt's strategy relied on a manipulation of the high degree of involvement of superpowers' interests in the region as well as on the high level of superpowers' commitment to their clients, Egypt and Israel. The central assumption was that the outbreak of a violent if limited conflict that would escape from the control of the superpowers would be liable to endanger the superpowers' interests in the region. The superpowers would be interested in preserving strategic stability in the region, not only out of concern for their interests there, but also from fear of a clash between them. This fear of a possible clash between the superpowers in the event of violent conflict would be likely, the Egyptians thought, to speed up diplomatic activity on the part of the superpowers and bring about a change in the given territorial and military status quo. This whole concept was clearly stated by Heikal in *Al-Ahrām* of August 23, 1968:

If escalation of the crisis occurs—and this is likelier than many people think—it will turn into a problem between the great powers. Our world is becoming a small one and interests are so closely interlocked that no one is able to act separately on his own . . . especially so in a sensitive region like the Middle East, where the weightiest forces come up against each other. What I am trying to say is that it is not enough if we ourselves feel that the field of battle is the only alternative left us. It is important that many others too should be of the same opinion and that they should be fully convinced that this is the choice forced on us. The importance of political action becomes clear against this background. If political action brings results, we shall have achieved something of importance. But if it does not produce results—and that is the probable prospect—we shall have achieved something still more important. We shall have persuaded influential elements that the battlefield is the only choice left, that there is no other way out. Thus we shall see that the USA and the USSR cannot ignore what happens in the Middle East. If they do not succeed in moves to bring about real peace in the region, they will not be able to stand aside from the fighting that will inevitably ensue, fighting that will settle the fate of the region. Therefore the very fact of reaching the brink of war demands precisely political activity on our part, massive patience and staying power—until we reach our goal.

The threat to upset the strategic stability of the zone was intended to bring about a change in U.S. policy. The belief was that the United States was interested in maintaining strategic stability in order to protect its vital interests in the region on the one hand and on the other prevent confrontation with the USSR. Egyptian strategy was therefore directed to persuading the United States that Egypt was ready to risk war in order to bring about a political solution acceptable to itself,[27] and that only a change in U.S. policy on a settlement of the crisis and/or reduction of massive U.S. support for Israel could prevent a violent, if limited, conflict from developing into a situation threatening American interests in the region.[28] The most important component of this politico-military strategy was the threat of increased Soviet intervention in Egypt. By means of this increased Soviet intervention in the region and more particularly in Egypt, Abdel Nasser also hoped to increase the political and military ties between Egypt and the USSR to the point where another Egyptian defeat would be their defeat. He hoped in this way to make certain that the USSR would not permit Egypt to be defeated again, that is, he hoped that Soviet involvement in Egypt would deter Israel from activating the total military option against Egypt,

once Egypt had activated the limited military option against
Israel. This strategy was adopted by Nasser shortly after the end
of the Six-Day War, as attested by Heikal in his memoirs:

Inevitably the Russians regarded Egypt's defeat as to some extent their
defeat also, and Nasser encouraged this attitude because he thought it
would lead to greater Russian involvement in the Middle East, which
was the only way in which American superiority in that area could be
offset. . . . He was trying to make the Russians see Egypt's defeat as
their defeat and to increase their aid to Egypt, even to the extent of taking over, temporarily at least, Egypt's air defenses.[29]

The Egyptian leadership judged that the USSR would also
be concerned about keeping control over the level of violence in
the region, for the same reasons that led the United States to try
to secure strategic stability in the region. Egypt's activating the
limited military option was also intended to get the USSR to
desist from trying to settle the crisis in the region in order to
buttress her relationship with the United States on the global as
well as the regional plane.[30]

In the sphere of Israeli-Egyptian relations, Egypt's political
strategy was based on manipulating the political and strategic
limitations that restrained Israel from adopting a total military
option. The Egyptian leadership judged that given Israel's
achievements in the Six-Day War and the changes in its security
doctrine, mainly in view of Soviet involvement in Egypt, Israel
would find it difficult to break out of the confines of limited war.
This judgment was based on the assumptions that Israel had no
need to attack again, but wanted to make the status quo secure,
since its victory in the Six-Day War had won it the best defense
lines she could wish, and that Israel was not interested in seeing
a violent conflict break out in the region, for fear of upsetting the
existing territorial and military arrangement, and it would therefore refrain from initiating total military activity and would seek
to preserve limited boundaries of a violent conflict.[31]

If Israel were to escalate the violence in a situation of limited
conflict, it would be risking total war, the military and political
costs of which would be too great and too dangerous. From the
military standpoint, any Israeli attack that involved her military

forces' crossing the canal would see those forces submerged by a dense Arab population without any possible way of coping with it. Nor could Israel attack Egypt frontally, given the massive and practically impenetrable deployment along the canal. Any attempt to break through this front would cost Israel very heavy losses indeed.[32] From the political standpoint, it would also be difficult for Israel to adopt the total war option if Egypt initiated a limited local war, given the probable reaction of international public opinion and given Soviet involvement in Egypt. If the Israelis were not deterred by Soviet involvement in Egypt and decided to exert their full strength, the Egyptians thought that the USSR would then in all likelihood intervene directly to prevent Egypt's being defeated.

Egyptian Military Strategy
Egypt's military aims were to reach certain limited military objectives in order to validate Egypt's political strategy in practical terms. The aims were to conquer footholds on the eastern shore of the canal and to wear down Israel's strength, thereby securing a lever for political pressure on Israel for further withdrawal, a pressure to be exerted by means of renewed diplomatic initiatives.[33] Until the end of July 1969, Egypt aimed at establishing a bridgehead on the eastern bank of the canal. After the attack by the Israeli Air Force on July 20, 1969, Egypt's main thrust was transferred to attrition of Israeli strength.

In the winter of 1969, the Egyptian leadership judged that Egypt could realize its limited military objectives by adopting a limited military option. The main question was which limited military option was the most suitable for Egypt. Fundamentally, the leadership judged that Israel had a clear advantage on the military plane and that therefore Egypt could not hope to succeed unless it could deprive Israel of its military advantage. The Egyptian leadership knew that Egypt could not adopt a total military option, but they also judged that it could not adopt even limited strategies such as a war of movement or a *blitzkrieg* because of Israel's clear military advantage in utilizing these strategies.[34]

Once the idea of a *blitzkrieg* was rejected as the military strategy for crossing the canal, it was necessary to choose a different strategy to fit Egypt's military circumstances and capabilities. What was needed was a military option that would exploit the political and military constraints that prevented Israel from adopting the total military option and/or any other strategy in which she enjoyed superiority, a military option that would give Egypt the benefit of the advantages accruing within a limited war situation, in view of the evaluation of the respective strengths of the two countries. In the last analysis, the military option best suited to Egypt was seen to be a prolonged, limited, local, and static war of attrition.

Prolonged war was the main characteristic of Egyptian military strategy in the War of Attrition. Prolonged war was seen as contrary to the Israeli security conception that was based on waging short, swift wars. Prolonged war was contrary to Israel's security doctrine mainly because of its limited resources of men and material. Prolonged war demands protracted mobilization of human and material resources, which is precisely what Israel cannot afford. It was thought the diversion of human resources and other productive forces from Israel's economy to prolonged service in the reserves should bring about the collapse of the Israeli economy: "Reliable authorities state that the enemy cannot stand the consequences of protracted war because the prolongation of general mobilization—given her limited resources in manpower—is liable to threaten her with complete internal breakdown."[35] Furthermore, since Israel is not used to prolonged war, it would necessarily be deprived of the strategic superiority based on waging a blitzkrieg: "If we succeed in preventing her (from waging a blitzkrieg), then Israel will lose her most important military advantage and will be forced to fight in ways she is less well prepared for."[36]

A prolonged war of attrition is also bound up with a slow erosion of human and material resources, which Israel cannot long stand. The difference in manpower resources between Israel and Egypt, and the great importance Israel attaches to her losses, were seen by the Egyptians as the most important variable in a prolonged war of attrition. The Egyptian advantage in manpower was seen as sufficient to cancel Israel's technological military superiority in the course of time.[37] What is more, differences in manpower resources are of major import in winning a war of this kind. In order to win such a war, Israel would have to inflict absolute defeat on Egypt—something judged impossible, given the existing military and political pressures. On the other hand, an increase in Israeli losses above certain proportion would already constitute a victory for Egypt in such a war. To demonstrate this principle in concrete terms, Heikal gave the following example:

If the enemy succeeds in inflicting on us 50,000 *casualties* in this campaign, we can go on fighting nevertheless, because we have manpower reserves. And if we succeed in inflicting 10,000 *casualties*, he will indisputably find himself compelled to stop fighting, because he has no manpower resources at his disposal. The moment we succeed in increasing the enemy's losses in lives above his capacity to replace them, we can count ourselves the victors (emphasis added).[38]

Thus Egypt's military aims were to wear Israel down, cause it heavy losses, and face it with political and military dangers out of all proportion to the objectives at issue in the conflict. The Egyptians judged that the importance attached by Egypt to the return of the conquered territories was greater than Israel's readiness to defend the status quo. The different evaluation of the importance of the issue by each side was seen as an important element favoring Egyptian aims.

Since prolonged war is characterized by a high rate of erosion, the capacity to hold out and win such a war is largely a psychological matter, a question of the moral readiness to withstand the attrition of a war in which there are no real victories or gains and in which there are, on the contrary, very real losses in manpower and material resources. The difference in manpower resources and in the balance of vital issues was seen by the Egyptians as enabling them to hold out better than Israel, both physically and morally. They believed that after massive erosion (as we have seen, Heikal's estimate was 10,000 Israeli casualties), Israeli morale would be undermined and doubts would develop and questions be raised by the Israeli public as to whether Israel should maintain its presence in the occupied territories and as to whether that presence was the source of all the trouble—the cause of constant and prolonged warfare without any end to the conflict as the Israeli public had hoped for after the Six-Day War. The increased questions and doubts would be likely to produce increased criticism of the Israeli government's policy and possibly even a split between the people and their leaders. The aim of the protracted military action was therefore to shake the foundations of Israeli society and to bring about its collapse. Once Israeli morale was undermined, it would be possible to get political concessions with relative ease.[39]

Prolonged war of attrition was thus a strategy directed toward reversing the balance of power between the warring sides in favor of Egypt (by means of erosion of Israel's strength), or at the very least to create a balance of power between the two sides. Once this balance of power was brought about between the two sides, Egypt could envisage adopting some other kind of strategy in order to realize her aims in full. The effectiveness of the new strategy chosen would be enhanced by the already lowered state of the enemy's morale.[40]

In the first phase (up to July 1969), a protracted war was thought of as one that would last six to eight weeks.[41] After that date, when the Egyptians dropped the idea of crossing the canal and adopted attrition as their strategy, the time dimension was also altered. Prolonged war was now thought of not in terms of weeks but of years—from three to five years.[42]

A second important element in the Egyptian strategy of attrition was the static character of the war. Static warfare was seen by the Egyptians as offering them a number of advantages. First, it exploited the weak point of Israel's security strategy. The creation of the Bar-Lev Line in the winter of 1969 was a signal to the Egyptians of a change in Israel's security doctrine. They saw it as evidence that Israel had abandoned the system of mobile defense in favor of static defense. This canceled out Israel's strategic qualities—the capacity for swift movement of armored forces and infantry in combined action with the air force, and speedy changeover to the offensive. They considered static military deployment unsuited to the character of the Israeli army which needed a long period of preparation in the light of Israel's lack of experience of this kind of deployment.[43] Moreover, the difference between Egypt and Israel in types and quantities of military deployment along the canal secured the Egyptians striking tactical and strategic advantages. Given the static deployment and the thinness of the Israeli forces along the canal, the Egyptians judged that they enjoyed tactical and strategic advantages in static warfare: superior manpower resources (capacity to stand a high rate of losses), superiority in certain weapons systems (artillery), and superiority in the type of deployment of these weapons systems (massive concentration along the canal).[44]

Given the tactical proximity of the Israeli defense line to the Egyptian line, the Egyptians judged that by a static war of attrition they could wipe out the major part of the forward positions of the Bar-Lev Line as well as the Israeli mobile forces near the canal, and that they could then proceed to seize a number of footholds on the eastern shore.[45]

The central question is whether the Egyptians believed they could find some way to compel Israel to enter into a prolonged war of attrition that would go against its nature. This question worried the Egyptian leadership for a long time, as can be learned from Heikal's articles in *Al-Ahrām*.[46] In a general way, the Egyptians' considered view was that by correctly manipulating Israel's political and strategic limitations, they could prevent Israel from exceeding the bounds of limited war, i.e., deter it from initiating a total military option. In the first phase of the war, up to July 1969, the Egyptians judged that they could also compel Israel to keep the war the way the Egyptians wanted it—a prolonged, limited, local, and static war of attrition. They thought that as long as the war was restricted to artillery action and to limited raids by commando units, Israel would refrain from starting any offensives that would exceed the bounds of a static war. They thought Israel would refrain from putting in its air force for fear of escalating the war to more serious proportions and for fear of erosion and loss of planes as the result of the improved antiaircraft defense system now at Egypt's disposal.[47] They thought Israel would limit its reaction to artillery fire on the Egyptian army and Egyptian economic and civilian objectives along the canal, as well as to limited commando raids in depth in Egypt against economic and civilian targets, like the raid on Naj' Ḥamādī.[48]

Until July 1969 Israel did not put in the air force and limited its reaction to artillery counterfire and a limited number of commando raids on economic targets in the Egyptian rear. This strengthened the Egyptian belief that Israel would go on fighting the war the way Egypt wanted it. Moreover, the Egyptians' belief that they had succeeded in destroying the major part of the Bar-Lev Line reinforced their feeling that the limited military option they had chosen matched their basic assumptions and that it was possible to carry on in accordance with their original plan, i.e., crossing the canal and taking a number of footholds on the eastern shore as a lever for accelerated diplomatic activity.[49]

Some doubts were expressed all the same in the Egyptian press, even in the early phase of the war, over Egypt's ability to impose a long, static war of attrition on Israel. The general view was rather that a war of attrition was not only opposed to Israel's military character but was liable to inflict such a high rate of erosion of manpower and material resources that Israel would not be able to hold out for long and would therefore be liable to break out of the constraints of the war of attrition established by Egypt. It was thought, however, that she would still remain within the framework of limited war, i.e., abandon static defense and pass over to limited military offensive in order to rob the Egyptians of the initiative and change the nature of the war.[50]

The Concept of Attrition in the First Phase of the War

In the first phase of the war (up to July 20, 1969), the Egyptian military strategy was based on a tactical conception of attrition. Attrition was seen as a military tactic to prepare the ground for crossing the canal. Attrition was supposed to be the first of four phases that were planned, and was to continue for perhaps six to eight weeks,[51] during which time Egypt would make use of its massive artillery deployment to bombard the artillery deployment of the Israeli defense along the canal. The aim of the artillery bombardment was to upset the Israeli security balance by destroying the Bar-Lev Line and inflicting heavy losses on the Israeli troops on the canal line.

After the destruction of the greater part of the Bar-Lev Line would come the second phase. Egypt would send in commando units with the aim of completing the destruction that had been begun by the Egyptian artillery and to hit Israeli supply lines. After completing these tasks, the Egyptian forces would return to Egyptian territory.

In the third phase, larger Egyptian units would carry out actions deeper on the other side of the canal. The tasks of these units would be similar to those of the commandos but on a larger scale. These actions would make it possible to train as many units as possible in techniques of crossing the canal and give them the experience of direct clashes with Israeli forces. After completing their operational tasks, these units too would return to Egyptian soil.

In the fourth and last phase, the operation of crossing the canal would be carried out on a large scale with the objective of conquering the eastern shore of the canal or part of it. This would be the political lever with which to break the stalemate in diplomatic activity and promote the desired political solution.[52]

Israeli Aims in the War of Attrition

The main politico-strategic aim of Israel in the War of Attrition was basically defensive—to preserve the territorial, political, and military status quo created after the Six-Day War. This aim characterized Israeli leadership before the War of Attrition too, but striking importance was especially attached to it all through that war when the continued existence of the status quo was seen as really endangered. To preserve the status quo, various intermediate aims took shape:

First, to stand firm along the existing line, simply to prove that Israel had the power to hold on over a long period and reinforce its security presence along the line.[53]

Second, to prevent the Arab States, especially Egypt, from crossing the lines and attempting to conquer the Sinai or the eastern bank of the canal, or even to seize footholds there.[54]

Third, to prevent war, especially total war. A new war was

not wanted by Israel since its main significance would be to upset the status quo. A new war would be liable to lead to a prolonged crisis that would be bound up with political pressures for a change in the status quo without Israel's realizing its po-litico-strategic aims, namely the conclusion of positive peace treaties with the Arab States and the creation of fair conditions and arrangements of a nature to prevent additional war.[55]

Fourth, to refrain from infringing on the cease-fire, thereby "warming up" the frontier area, as this would be liable to lead to serious escalation and total war.[56]

Fifth, in the event of the other side's initiating incidents and "warming up" the frontier areas, to refrain from escalation that would intensify and extend the war beyond a certain point.[57]

Israeli Perception of Egyptian War Initiatives

In the course of 1968, and more particularly after the artillery in-cident in the autumn of 1968, the Israeli leadership was per-suaded that Egypt was liable to initiate a new war, not only be-tween Egypt and Israel, but also between Israel and a coalition of Arab States with Egypt at their head. It was assumed that the main threat of renewed war came from Egypt and that the other Arab States would not start a war against Israel unless Egypt took the lead.[58]

The Israeli leadership judged that three causes were likely to bring Egypt and the Arab States to the point of starting another war. If the Arab States (and Egypt in particular) saw the situation created after the Six-Day War as intolerable, and if diplomatic ef-forts failed to secure Israeli withdrawal, they would have no choice but to adopt the military option in order to force Israel to withdraw. The Egyptian decision to make use of force would be dependent on an evaluation that something would in practice be achieved by going to war.[59] Second, Arab judgments regarding the balance of power between Israel and the Arab States, based on the speedy rehabilitation of the Arab armies and mainly the Egyptian army, were mistaken. Toward the end of the first year after the Six-Day War, the Israeli view was that the Arab States had recuperated their full military strength.[60] A third cause con-sisted of internal political pressures in the Arab States to start the war again. The existence of the Arab regimes was to a large degree dependent on their responding to these pressures.[61]

The Israeli leadership judged that if Egypt and the Arab States decided to renew the war, they would not do so in the 1967 pattern.[62] In spite of the speedy process of reconstruction of her army, Egypt was not thought to be militarily capable of changing the territorial and military status quo since she was not capable of initiating a general war against Israel, but only a limited and local war or local incidents (also dubbed "interim flare-ups")—a situation marked by a certain degree of belligerent activity, but not real war.[63]

This opinion was strengthened as a result of incidents in late 1968 and early 1969. Israeli policy makers judged that Egypt was about to initiate military activities in the near future on the lines of previous artillery incidents.[64] A clear indication of this was a large concentration of Egyptian forces on the western bank of the canal. The Israeli work on setting up the Bar-Lev Line was connected with this judgment that the Egyptians were about to renew military activity along the length of the canal.[65]

When the Israeli policy makers weighed the likelihood of a new war, they did not fail to attach importance to what stand the USSR would take regarding an Egyptian decision to start a new war and they concluded that in spite of the rehabilitation of the Egyptian army, Egypt could not adopt the military option without Russian agreement. Thus, in February 1968, Moshe Dayan stated:

Even when they [the Egyptians] complete their military reorganization, they will not be strong enough to be able to allow themselves to go to war relying on their own force alone. The key to their going to war or their not going to war lies in the answer to the question whether they can rely on an *outside power,* which will be giving them the "green light" to go ahead and even provide them with assistance. In other words, the Arabs' decision whether to renew the war now a year after [the end of the Six-Day War] depends on the readiness of the USSR to give them its backing.[66]

The very fact of the Soviet military presence in Egypt was seen as a source of psychological encouragement to go to war, since the Egyptians believed that the USSR would back their military effort and would not let the Arabs suffer another defeat.[67] Presumably when the Israeli policy makers considered the question of the Soviets' giving the "green light" or "backing" Egypt, they were thinking of the possibility of a general Egyptian war. Nevertheless, the Israeli leadership appears to have thought that the relations between Egypt and the USSR—the very presence of Soviet military advisers in Egypt—would also oblige the Egyptians to consult the USSR to some extent before adopting even such a limited military option as a static war of attrition.[68]

The Bar-Lev Line—A Changed Israeli Security Conception?
The massive artillery incidents initiated by the Egyptians in September and October 1968 were the primary reason for the construction of the Bar-Lev Line. The question for Israel was how best to insure the lives of the men posted along the line of the canal in case the Egyptians' bombardments should be repeated.[69] When the Israeli General Staff reached the view that a substantial change was needed in ways of defending the canal and in the extent to which the positions there should be fortified, the question of how best to insure the canal line and the defense of the Sinai was thoroughly examined. At bottom the debate was between those who believed in a system of mobile defense, defense not based on fortifications along the water line but on mobile forces, and those who believed in a defense based in the first place on an advanced fortified line along the water. The problem of holding the line of the canal turned on two main issues: how to secure the line in conditions of static warfare such as a war of attrition, and whether the effort should be made to prevent a general Egyptian crossing by means of a line of fortifications along the eastern bank.[70] These questions were debated at length by the Israeli military high command both during the War of Attrition and after it—a debate which reached its apogee in the Yom Kippur War.

At first the debate turned mainly on the question whether a line of fortifications along the canal would in fact prevent an Egyptian crossing. In the next stage, the debate centered on the question of how to guard the canal line in a situation of static war, with incidents multiplying along the canal and developing into a war of attrition. The earlier problem of the danger of an Egyptian crossing remained, however, the order of the day.[71]

Those who were for building the Bar-Lev Line were Major General Yeshiyahu Gavish, head of Southern Command; Major General Avraham Adan, Commander of the Armored Forces; and Lieutenant General Haim Bar-Lev, Chief of the General Staff. Against it were Major Generals Ariel Sharon (then Head of Training in the IDF—the Israeli Defense Forces) and Israel Tal (then developing means of warfare at the Ministry of Defense). Those in favor of the line were not thinking only in terms of static defense; they saw the line as just one component in the overall defense network, of which only the forward line would be static and the rest mobile. Their idea was to build a forward line of fortifications the length of the canal and to post infantry there, while armored and other mobile forces would be put in in the spaces between the fortified positions. Artillery units would be deployed at a certain distance further back to support the forces along the canal and to fire on targets on the other side of the canal.[72] According to this school of thought, the line of fortifications along the canal was not meant to stand up to a large-scale Egyptian crossing, but to prevent crossings by small forces attempting to seize a foothold. The strongholds would be strung out along the canal at points where there was a high degree of likelihood of Egyptians' attempting such crossings.[73] The mobile forces were thought capable of filling this task only in part, given the belief that every Egyptian penetration would lead to large-scale fighting in which Zahal would be bound to suffer heavy losses. A permanent presence along the length of the canal would have additional advantages such as the possibility of setting up lookout points to keep watch on army deployments on the Egyptian side, to facilitate judgment of Egyptian intentions, and to report developments at once in the event of Egyptian attempts to deploy their forces for a large-scale crossing. In other words, a forward line of fortifications was meant to provide an early warning system. It was also thought that in the event of a massive Egyptian crossing, the fortified posts would be able to disrupt the Egyptians' moves to some extent and perhaps delay their penetration into the open spaces of the Sinai.

As against this view held by Gavish, Adan, and Bar-Lev, Tal and Sharon were of the opinion that a line of fortifications could not play an effective role in preventing a crossing of the canal, but was only good for concealment and cover in time of war. When the moment came for the Egyptians to cross the canal, a heavy Egyptian artillery barrage would neutralize the capacity of the soldiers there to hinder the crossing. The fortifications were therefore absolutely superfluous. The canal and the Sinai did not necessarily have to be defended along the water line. A line to block any advance should be built in the rear at a good distance from the canal (from Belusa in the north to Tasa in the south). Mobile forces—mainly armored—should operate in the space between the canal and the barrier line in the rear in order to wipe out invading Egyptian forces. The infantry should not be posted along the line of the canal but only in the barrier line to the rear.[74]

The debate over the Bar-Lev Line marked not only a division of opinion on mobile as against static defense, but also a change in Israeli political strategy in the period after the Six-Day War. Once the Israeli government decided that its political strategy would be based on preserving the territorial, political, and military status quo, a decision that was at heart political, it became necessary to reappraise Israeli defense doctrine. The central problem of strategy was in essence how Israel would conduct the next war. Should it initiate a preemptive strike against any warlike initiative on the other side, or should it take the shock of the first enemy attack and not try to forestall it? In other words, should Israel continue to act in accordance with the criteria of offensive strategy that had been its guidelines up to the Six-Day War, or should it adopt principles of defensive strategy which it had never before accepted? Once the political strategy was decided in favor of preserving the existing state of affairs, the defensive strategy followed almost as a matter of course. In the new politico-strategic conditions, the political constraints linked with initiating a preemptive strike, backed by the belief that the new strategic lines were Israel's best possible defense lines, helped finalize the decision.[75]

If political strategy was based on preserving the existing

state of affairs, this clearly dictated preferring static defense to mobile, also for political reasons. Creating a security presence on the canal line was a central expression of Israel's political presence there. The construction of the Bar-Lev Line was the direct result of the preference given to political over military considerations. Although the political echelons recognized that mobile defense was preferable to static defense from the purely military point of view, the static system of defense was decided on for purely political reasons.[76]

From the purely military viewpoint, the Israeli decision to rely on a static defense system helped the Egyptians to crystallize their strategy of attrition. The tactical proximity of the Bar-Lev Line to the Egyptian line enabled the Egyptians to wage a war of attrition the way they wanted to at various stages during the course of the war. Finding itself without adequate military means for waging a war of attrition on the terrain chosen by Egypt, in a state of strategic inferiority, Israel had no choice but to escalate the war in order to rob the Egyptians of the initiative. Escalation, effected by activating the air force in the second half of July 1969, was definitely the outcome of the failure of static defense in the War of Attrition. The construction of the Bar-Lev Line itself endowed the Egyptians with the capability to stage a limited military confrontation and there was no way of depriving them of it except by escalating the war.

Israeli Perception of Egyptian Aims and Strategy in the First Phase

In the first months of the war, March and April 1969, there was no change in the Israeli views on Egyptian aims in the War of Attrition. Evaluations, arrived at late in 1968 and early in 1969, held good in the first months of the war when Israeli judgment was guided by appraisal of the balance of power between Israel and Egypt. In the light of this appraisal, the possibility was discounted that Egypt was likely to initiate a general war in order to change the territorial status quo by force.[77] It was thought that the Egyptians would make no such attempt until they judged that they really could "achieve a result of some kind by means of war."[78] The Israeli leadership was of the opinion at this stage that limited Egyptian offensive activity could not change the existing territorial and military situation and that in any case it was not within the Egyptians' military capability to attempt even a limited offensive. The Minister of Defense, Moshe Dayan, declared that an Egyptian crossing of the canal in order to invade the Sinai by force was not a real possibility.[79] The fact that Egyptian military activity in the months of March and April 1969 was limited to massive artillery bombardments strengthened the Israeli opinion that this activity was intended to be limited and local. The Egyptian military activity was variously described as "local incidents," "local flare-ups," "local waves of aggression," etc.[80]

From the political angle, the Egyptians' activity was seen as expressing their refusal to resign themselves to the territorial and military status quo as permanent and as intended to persuade world public opinion that war was liable to break out again, thus transmitting signals in support of the view that the Middle East was a "powder keg" liable to explode at any moment.[81] Egyptian political aims were already seen at this stage as furtherance of a political settlement that would meet Egyptian wishes. This evaluation was reinforced by the superpowers' efforts to cope with the Middle East crisis.[82] In addition to all this, the Israeli leadership believed that by means of belligerent activity Egypt hoped to restore her prestige in the Arab world that had been badly damaged by her defeat in the Six-Day War and by the absence of any organized military action along the canal since the end of that war.[83] As in the past, belligerent Egyptian actions were also perceived as a safety valve for internal criticism directed against the regime.[84]

The Israeli leadership judged that from the operative military point of view Egypt's aims were to damage the Israeli presence along the canal and to harass IDF movements on the eastern bank and in the Sinai.[85] Egyptian military activity, which from the second half of April 1969 included raids by commando units in addition to massive artillery fire, brought some change in the Israeli evaluation of Egyptian aims. The Egyptian actions were seen not only as a limited "warming up" of the front, but as directed toward achieving wider results. There was a reevaluation of the possibility of general war and/or a large-scale Egyptian military operation to cross the canal.[86] But at this stage too general war and/or an Egyptian crossing were not seen as possibilities for the near future.[87] The Israeli leadership nevertheless judged that the military action along the canal was no longer a matter of local incidents or sporadic flare-ups but was a real war waged along the front lines, a continuing war, a war of attrition, but not a downward course to general or total war.[88] For the first time since the Six-Day War, Israel judged that a war situation existed from the Egyptian point of view. This meant an absolute Egyptian breach of the cease-fire status, but not of the cease-fire line, defined as the line of the canal. Non-breach of the cease-fire line therefore meant not crossing the canal.[89]

Israel judged that Egypt was putting all its military strength in the war along the canal, while refraining from sending its air force across the cease-fire line on account of the inability of the air force to confront the Israeli Air Force.

Toward the end of the first phase of the war (May and June), Israel appraised the War of Attrition as an Egyptian politico-military strategy in the conduct of the war or as an attempt to evolve such a strategy. It was seen that a war of attrition was the strategy most preferable for Egypt, given its reluctance to risk general war and its view that in this kind of war Egypt enjoyed strategic advantages which were *ipso facto* Israeli disadvantages.[90]

Israeli Military Reactions in the First Phase

Israeli operative reactions were the result of weighing the following elements: what were conceived to be Egypt's aims in the war, the operative nature of Egyptian military action, Israeli politico-strategic aims and intermediate aims, and the stand taken by the superpowers (interpower deliberations). The single most important indicator for determining Israeli reactions was the nature of Egyptian military activity along the canal. Given the opinion held at the outset that Egyptian aims in the war were limited in character and that Egyptian military activity along the canal was limited and local, Israel framed its own limited aims in the first phase of the war—protecting and fortifying the Israeli presence along the canal and reimposing the cease-fire on Egypt.[91]

The Israeli strategy was at bottom a defensive one, pointing to Israel's capacity to hold out in a prolonged static war. This was indicated by expressions such as: "Israel is not in a weak position along the canal," "We are stationed on the canal with large and sufficient forces," "The Israeli deployment along the canal cannot be fractured," "It is not within the Arabs' power to push us even a pace or two back from the canal," and "The Egyptians are not capable of crossing the canal and evicting the IDF from the eastern bank." [92] The strategy took the operative form of increased effort put into fortifying the positions along the canal line in order to secure maximum reduction of vulnerability and minimum penetration by Egyptian commando units.

Defensive strategy also dictated the nature of operative military activity. The starting point was that Israel must refrain from escalating military activity and so prevent it from developing into general war or any other military activity that might encourage superpower intervention.[93] Operative Israeli military activity was at its source reaction to and reprisal for Egyptian breaches of the cease-fire, accompanied by a policy of refraining from any initiative that might lead to escalation of military activity along the canal.[94] The belief was that to reimpose the cease-fire, it would be enough to direct heavy artillery strikes at Egyptian strongholds along the canal and against sensitive targets vital to the Egyptians from the civil and economic standpoint. Operational military activity was therefore limited to artillery counterstrikes, directed at silencing the Egyptian artillery and against Egyptian economic and civilian installations along the canal. These counterbombardments were intended to show the Egyptians the cost of their military activity, not only from the military standpoint but also from the economic and civilian standpoint.[95]

When the Egyptians increased their military activity along the canal in the second half of April and sent commando groups on raids on the eastern bank, the Israeli opinion grew that artillery defense was not enough to reimpose the cease-fire. The central dilemma of the decision makers in Israel was how to put an end to the Egyptian breaches of the cease-fire and still preserve the limited character of belligerent activity along the canal. This dilemma was especially acute for internal reasons and also

because of the circumstances surrounding military relations between Egypt and the rest of the Arab States. The first signs were
beginning to appear of anxiety among the Israeli public over the
large number of casualties being suffered along the canal as a
result of the Israeli army's failure to impose the cease-fire on the
Egyptians. There was also the feeling that the war had no aims of
any importance from the Israeli point of view.[96]

On the other hand, Israeli policy makers reached the view
that Israel's defensive strategy could be interpreted as military
weakness and this would be liable to tempt the Egyptians to try
general war. The need grew to find a military initiative that
would deter the Egyptians from starting a general war.[97] The
military action adopted for this purpose, in addition to continued reinforcement of the strength of the Bar-Lev Line and artillery counterstrikes, was not new. It was a reversion to an earlier type of reaction that had been judged effective in the past:
reprisal raids in-depth in Egypt against targets considered sensitive from every point of view—military, economic, and psychological. The considerations weighed by the political and military
leadership of Israel in their choice of reprisal actions intended to
deter the Egyptians from general war, reimpose the cease-fire,
and even bring the war to a real close were described by Ezer
Weizmann (at the time Chief of Operations on the General Staff)
in his book, *Thine the Sky, Thine the Land.*

A country with a strong regular army, which has only recently defeated
its foes in a war of movement excellently waged, if it chooses to fight by
means of commando raids and not to make use of its full strength, does
so for one of two reasons or both together: either it does not believe it
can make use of its strength to the full extent and in all its forms, or else
it does not wish to, from the deluded belief that this or that commando
action will solve the problem.[98]

These calculations combined led to the adoption of the "policy of reprisals": on the one hand, anxiety over possible escalation of the war that made it necessary to refrain from more escalatory military means such as air raids, and on the other hand,
lack of insight into Egypt's war aims and a mistaken evaluation
of Egyptian readiness to pay the full price for carrying on with

the War of Attrition. Israel misjudged Egypt's readiness and ability to take the reprisals, a readiness proved among other things by the government's evacuating the population of the canal towns and resigning itself to the destruction of the economic installations along the canal. The first target chosen for the Israeli reprisal policy was once more Naj' Ḥamādī, a choice based on the effectiveness of the first raid on Naj' Ḥamādī at the beginning of November 1968. The belief that the second Naj' Ḥamādī action would produce the same results as the first (and stop the War of Attrition) testified to the Israeli misperception of Egyptian aims and misjudgment of the effectiveness of means capable of producing a change in those aims. The reprisal policy was in fact something of a confession that Israel did not know what to do in this unaccustomed war situation. In spite of their being an operative success, the reprisal actions were not capable of smashing the Egyptian war effort because the price they cost the Egyptians was too low in comparison with the sacrifices the Egyptians were prepared to make in a protracted war of attrition. Ezer Weizmann had this to say of the reprisal actions: "They are no more than pinpricks as far as the Egyptian army is concerned. They spread the fame of Zahal in the world, they provide some sweet consolation for the Israeli public, but they are not and cannot be decisive in war and they are no solution to the war of attrition—they don't bring it to an end or even damp it down." [99]

With the increase of Egyptian belligerent activity along the canal and in the form of repeated commando raids, the question again arose of how to deprive Egypt of the military initiative and compel her to observe the cease-fire without risking serious escalation. These aims had not been served by the defensive strategy adopted heretofore, including the reprisal actions. The army and the Israeli public were increasingly demanding that the defensive strategy be called off and new, bold initiatives be adopted in order to break down the Egyptian army's increasing self-confidence. This demand was expressed mainly through the columns of the press.[100] Early in May 1969 Dayan raised the possibility of abandoning the defensive for the first time.

I favor the defensive stand, but if the Arabs keep on with this war it is very doubtful whether we can let it stay a defensive one from our point of view. In the same way as a people that does not want war can be dragged into one just because the other side declares war, an army that wishes to stay on the defensive can be dragged into an offensive war just because war is being waged against it. War has dynamics of its own. Its purpose is victory, and it is impossible to be victorious only by maintaining a defensive posture.[101]

This was said as part of the effort to deter the Egyptians, as a signal to them that in spite of Israel's (and Egypt's) vital interest in keeping the war in low profile, this Israeli interest depended on the existence of certain conditions. Dayan did not spell them out in detail, but what he meant was that if Egypt was not ready to keep belligerent activity under control, Israel was likely to break out of the confines that Egypt wanted to impose on the war. Dayan signaled an additional warning to the Egyptians in the same sense in another speech a week later.[102]

Dayan's words marked formal recognition of the difficulties of the defensive stand, but he still saw clearly that the war could not be ended with a single counterstrike because this would mean serious escalation.[103] Thus the immediate conclusions were still basically defensive—to organize for a static and protracted war but at the same time to try and deprive the Egyptians of the initiative in the conduct of the war by a degree of escalation that would produce expansion of the war. At the end of this first phase of the war, the Israeli leadership was still, in fact, of the opinion that the desired degree of escalation could be kept within the category of static war of attrition, i.e., they could effect a gradual escalation of military activity without changing the essential character of the war.[104]

Military Activity in the First Phase

Military activity, between March 8 and July 20, was limited and local along the length of the Suez Canal (except for the Israeli commando raids deep into Egypt). Both sides wanted to keep a low profile because they shared the fear of general war. Despite the flat contradictions between their respective politico-strategic aims, their basic common interest at this stage was to avoid general war. The preference for limited war was really a matter of both sides having no alternative. While Egypt had to give the preference to a narrowly controlled use of force because of her strategic inferiority (absence of capability to develop a general military option), Israel also preferred a war situation of limited use of force as a lesser evil. Once it became clear that there was no possibility of maintaining the cease-fire, Israel preferred controlled use of force for fear of a complete breakdown of strategic stability in her relations with the Arab States. Thus both sides feared a general war, but in this first stage the fear was asymmetrical. Israel was the side with the higher stake in the status quo and therefore greater fear of the political changes liable to follow from an overall war—intervention by the superpowers and imposition of a political solution. Despite its strategic superiority, Israel was apprehensive that full use of her superiority would mean an end to the political status quo that depended on the non-intervention of the superpowers in the Israeli-Arab conflict as a whole and in the Israeli-Egyptian conflict in particular. Intervention by the superpowers was thought more likely to occur in a general war, given the existence of superpower interests in the region. Egypt's fear of general war, on the other hand, was weaker than Israel's since the Egyptian strategy in the war was one of manipulating the political and strategic limitations that prevented Israel from initiating a general military option. Moreover, the Egyptian leadership thought it had reason to assume that if Israel were nevertheless to decide for a general military option, the USSR was likely to intervene in order to prevent Israel from defeating Egypt.

The asymmetry of fears in the first phase enabled Egypt to impose the type of war it wanted—static, prolonged, and characterized by artillery activity and by commando raids on the eastern shore. This was the type of war that Egypt had an interest in waging, with Israel constrained to accept it both from unwillingness to expand the fighting and from failure to clearly perceive what were Egypt's aims and intentions in waging this type of war. At this stage, therefore, the development of military activity was determined by the Egyptians in line with their operative plans. These provided for massive artillery bombardments, the aim of which was to soften up the Israeli line and inflict the greatest possible damage; and sending over commando units that would be given cover and assistance by continued artillery fire.

The Israeli reaction was mostly in line with the characteristic activity of counterartillery fire. From mid-April on, Israel began to carry out commando raids deep into Egypt as a counter to the Egyptian commando units' penetration on the eastern shore and the general increase in Egyptian military activity. With most of the military activity concentrated along the canal, Israeli raids deep into Egyptian territory constituted a breach of the local character of the war (its arena being the canal), the character that the Egyptians were interested in maintaining. Operationally, the targets aimed at by Egyptian military activity were Israeli military targets along the canal. The Egyptian attempt to limit the targets to military ones only failed in the first stage. Israel did concentrate on military targets but did not refrain from also hitting Egyptian economic and civilian targets. This failure to agree on targets at this early stage of the war was due to changes in delimiting front line targets and to changes in military deployment along the canal. The Egyptian front line included economic and civilian targets as well as "purely" military ones, while the Israeli line consisted of military targets only. Thus Egypt's concentrating on purely military targets was a concomitant of the absence of civilian or economic targets on the Israeli line. It must be assumed that if Israeli nonmilitary targets had existed along the canal, the Egyptians would have acted against them too or else would have arrived at an understanding to be observed mutually to refrain from hitting civilian and economic targets.

It was the nature of the military deployment along the canal that gave the Egyptian superiority in artillery its outstanding advantages. Israel turned Egyptian economic and civilian targets into "hostages" in order in some measure to restore the balance that was otherwise in Egypt's favor. In the very first days of the war, Israeli fire was directed at vital Egyptian objectives along the canal—the fuel tanks and refineries in the Suez and also Egyptian shipping in the Gulf of Suez. The Israeli view was that it would be possible to deter Egypt from utilizing her strategic advantages by raising the price that she would have to pay for breaches of the cease-fire. By means of inflicting heavy damage on Egyptian civilian and economic activity along the canal, Israel hoped to be able to force Egypt to renew the cease-fire.[105] This hope was largely based on past experience of relations with Egypt—the success of Israeli countermeasures after the sinking of the destroyer *Eilat* and after the artillery incidents late in 1968, countermeasures that put a stop to Egyptian military activity at the time.[106]

The fact that Egyptian economic and civilian targets were in close proximity to or actually on the Egyptian front line made it technically difficult to delimit military activity, especially since the Egyptians put part of their artillery emplacements close to these targets. Though the Egyptians attempted to delimit the targets, they realized from the first that it would not be possible to exclude the economic and civilian installations along the canal from the list of targets, both because of their proximity to the front line and also because Israel had hit these installations in the past.[107] Nonetheless, the Egyptians were not prepared to be reconciled to the addition of economic and civilian targets to the objectives aimed at by Israel, and they threatened reprisals against Israeli urban and civilian centers.[108] If these threats were not carried out, it was not only due to the technical difficulty of hitting Israeli centers but also because of Egyptian fears of setting off a chain reaction of reprisals and counterreprisals from which Israel would gain more than Egypt, given the proximity to the front line of the Egyptian civilian centers.[109] The Egyptian threats were apparently intended to calm Egyptian public opinion rather than to deter Israel.

At this stage, activity in the air was limited, compared with what happened later in the war. The Egyptians refrained from putting in their air force, because they judged it was not yet ready to confront the Israeli Air Force.[110] Israel refrained from putting in its air force from the conviction that to do so would be escalatory and counterproductive.[111]

Interaction between Military and Political Activity in the First Phase

Interaction between military and political activity was characteristic of the War of Attrition as a limited war. Interaction developed in the course of the war between the military activity on
the canal and the diplomatic activity of the superpowers that
concerned themselves with the affairs of the region.

The interaction between the two types of activity flowed
from the politico-strategic concepts of the two belligerents. The
two local actors, Egypt and Israel, saw the war as a means to
achieving their political aims. Military activity was seen by both
sides as likely to further the desired political solution or to block
the unwanted political solution. The existence of intensive diplomatic activity on the part of the superpowers served as a convenient arena for both sides' maneuvers in military initiatives.
The relative success or failure of these military moves determined the nature of the diplomatic activity in the different
phases of the war.

In the first phase, from March to December 1969, the diplomatic moves of the superpowers were mostly made under the influence of the local actors. The local sides attempted to get the
diplomatic initiatives changed in the directions they wanted;
how far they succeeded in this was the chief test of the success
of their military moves. In the next period, after the intense
Israeli bombings and Soviet military intervention in the actual
fighting, the war was progressively globalized. The Soviet military involvement—and the fears aroused as a consequence for
the stability of the system of superpower relationships—increased the influence of the superpowers over the military
moves of the local actors in the region.

The character of the diplomatic moves changed with the
changing nature of military activity in the region. In the first
phase of the war, the diplomatic initiatives were directed toward finding a solution for the Israeli-Arab conflict, and more
especially the Israeli-Egyptian conflict. The escalation of the war
from the end of 1969 on—the intensified Israeli bombings and
the direct Soviet intervention that was their consequence—

produced a change in the character of the diplomatic initiatives of the superpowers. The political solution that was the focus of diplomatic moves in the course of 1969 gave way to what were seen as the immediate objectives to be aimed for in the system of international relations—preventing confrontation between the superpowers and increasing the stability of superpower relationships. A cease-fire and limiting arms deliveries to the region were seen as objectives connected with the stability of relationships between the superpowers. Furthermore, the political solution was seen as possible only after other serious obstacles had been overcome—escalation prevented, military activity reduced in scale, and arms deliveries to the region limited. The first objective was a cease-fire. Unless and until all these aims were achieved, the political solution was seen as out of reach.[112]

The Two-Power and Four-Power Talks
In the first phase of the war, the two main forums for the talks that took place between the superpowers on the Middle East crisis were in New York—the four-power talks in the United Nations and the two-power talks between representatives of the United States and the Soviet Union (U.S. Assistant Secretary of State Joseph Sisco and Soviet Ambassador Anatolü Dobrynin). The two-power and the four-power talks began on April 3, 1969, against the background of the first weeks of the War of Attrition. The aim of the talks was defined to assist the sides in the conflict to reach a measure of political settlement that would lead to a solution of the conflict (given the failure of the parties to the conflict to reach any political settlement at all).[113]

Boths sets of talks were conducted under American restrictions to the effect that they must aim not at imposing a solution but at encouraging the states in the region to begin talks themselves with the help of the superpowers under the tentative setup designed for this purpose.[114] The feeling in general was that the talks were a race against time, that the flare-ups along the canal indicated the possibility of a new war, and that the results of the talks would affect future military moves.[115]

The first contacts in the two-power and four-power talks

concentrated on the attempt to reach a general formula for the political solution, a formula that would be acceptable to the superpowers and also to their local clients. There are no official details available on the content of the talks between the two superpowers, but it would appear that they were conducted on five main issues: the question of reaching a contractual settlement between the sides, the extent of an Israeli withdrawal, the question of Jerusalem, the question of the refugees, and the question of freedom of transit and shipping in the straits of Tiran and the Suez Canal.[116]

Following renewed contacts between the superpowers in March, April, and May, on May 26 the United States transmitted to the USSR a plan for Egyptian-Israeli settlement. The plan included "contractual agreement," frontiers that do not reflect the conquest and negotiations between the parties to determine the specific boundaries. This plan was thought to represent a compromise between the views of the two on the questions at issue.[117]

At one stage the American compromise plan was accepted by the USSR to be submitted to its Egyptian client. Gromyko visited Cairo from June 10 to 13 for the purpose of transmitting the details of the plan to Abdel Nasser and reaching a coordinated Egyptian-Soviet stand on the plan.[118] The visit ended in failure as the Egyptian leadership was opposed to the American proposals. The Soviets believed that the Egyptian refusal left an opening for further negotiation, but the attitude of the Egyptians was mainly the result of their successes in the War of Attrition.[119] Their success in imposing the kind of war they wanted and in carrying out their operational program according to plan led them to the conviction that they could secure a better political settlement than that put forth in the American proposal. They acted on the assumption that their military moves were achieving the objectives and that continuation of military pressure along the canal would get them a better political settlement.[120]

A better political settlement did not mean contractual agreement nor a separate Egyptian-Israeli deal, and it insisted on a package including all the Arab parties. It emphasized a timetable for Israeli withdrawal from all the conquered territories and opposed any discussions on the subject of boundaries. The USSR accepted the Egyptian view and, according to Heikal, the two sides agreed to reject the American proposals but nevertheless to maintain contact with the United States. Egypt made this continued contact conditional, however, on her previous consent to any further proposals that might be formulated by the superpowers.[121] This was brought out in the joint communiqué issued at the end of Gromyko's visit. The USSR made clear its full support for the just fight of Egypt to remove the results of aggression (at this stage the fight was mainly a military one) and Egypt declared her intention to go on striving to secure a political settlement based on the UN Security Council Resolution 242.[122]

The rejection of the American proposals marked Egypt's success in giving the contacts between the superpowers the direction she wanted; this success sprang from her ability to exploit the American plan as a test of Egyptian-Soviet relations. Since at this stage the Egyptians judged the American plan contrary to their interests, the USSR was obliged to weigh the importance of its relations with Egypt within overall Soviet interests in the region against its efforts to stabilize its system of relations with the United States. The rejection of the American plan demonstrated the Soviet grant of priority to relations with Egypt over relations with the United States.[123] With the USSR's rejection of the American proposals and its hardening attitude expressed in its reverting to its stand prior to the two- and four-power talks, the situation was back to the starting point of the talks in March and April.[124] In fact, a deadlock had been created and the talks were suspended. The four-power talks closed on July 1, after fifteen meetings had been held between the representatives concerned.[125]

The failure of the first round of diplomatic moves showed the superior capacity of military moves to determine the stand taken by the sides to the conflict. The Egyptian military successes brought about the failure of the contacts between the two superpowers and this failure led to a certain change in the nature of the contacts. The American Secretary of State William Rogers hinted as much at his press conference of July 2, 1969. The tense situation along the canal was now accorded greater importance than in the first months of the war. It was felt that to secure a cease-fire was more vital than to work for a political settlement since the continued war along the canal could get out of control and turn into a general war.[126]

Israeli Attitudes on Superpower Diplomatic Initiatives
Since the end of the Six-Day War Israel was opposed to the talks and diplomatic initiatives for reaching a peace settlement in the region on a number of grounds. First, such moves ran counter to the principle of direct negotiation between Israel and the Arab States. Second, the talks were liable to lead to an imposed solution under which Israel would have to pay the price in full (withdrawal from territories) without securing any acceptable resolution of the political conflict. Third, two of the countries taking part in these talks—the USSR and France—were hostile to Israel.[127]

Faced with the decision of the superpowers to hold talks among themselves, together with increased Egyptian military activity along the canal, Israeli policy makers were confirmed in their view on the link between Egyptian military activity and the deliberations in the two- and four-power talks. From the beginning, Israel had been convinced that Egypt's aims in "warming up" the canal front were mainly political and meant to point up the danger threatening the strategic stability of the Middle East in order to pressure the superpowers into imposing a political settlement acceptable to Egypt. The Israeli leadership had refrained from escalating its military activity along the canal in order not to provide positive feedback in support of Egyptian and Soviet efforts to stress the connection between belligerent and diplomatic activity. In statements to the media, the Israeli leadership stressed that Egypt's efforts were directed to causing international panic and that they should be treated as deliberately misleading propaganda.

Israel defined the situation along the canal as a limited "warming up" of the front, as incidents or local flare-ups, and not as signs of a "downward descent toward general war."[128] The Israeli line was that the Middle East was not a powder keg and hence there was no danger in the region of confrontation between the two superpowers.

The four powers have met together and declared that the situation is unbalanced, that the Middle East is a powder keg, and that they are liable to be forced into a war with each other, a world war, and this supposedly entitles them to arrange matters here and recommend settlements. All this is based on exaggeration. There is no prospect of large-scale clashes hereabouts and *ipso facto* no prospect of a clash here between the United States and the USSR.[129]

Moreover, the superpowers themselves caused increased tension in the region by the very fact of their deliberations, strengthening the Arab reliance on the connection between military activity and talks between the superpowers.

It is impossible not to remark that systematic breaches of the cease-fire occur in increased numbers and gravity precisely when the four-power talks are being held; impossible not to conclude that the rulers of the Arab countries have actually been encouraged in their hopes that the more they step up aggression during the four-power talks, even if this does not serve any real military purpose, the better their prospects of emerging with political gains. We do not mean to accuse the United States or Great Britain, not even France, of intentionally encouraging aggression against us. But we are bound to make them face the consequences that we have to suffer on those grounds. The four-power deliberations have not produced any lessening of tension nor deterred aggression, have not produced a more moderate and responsible attitude on the part of the Arab States nor helped create a climate of peace. The fact is that precisely while the four-power talks proceed, the Arab leaders have thrown off all restraint on the front.[130]

4 Egyptian Strategy Breaks Down

ON JULY 20, 1969, the Israeli Air Force was put in as an active military element in the war, marking the change that now began in the character of the war between Israel and Egypt. The two outstanding features of this change were escalation of the war and the breakdown of Egyptian strategy. The Israeli decision to start a measure of escalation of the war was the product of a number of basic factors in combination: (a) changed Israeli perception of the nature of Egypt's war aims; and (b) rising Israeli losses in the months May, June, and July 1969.

The decision to change the Israeli strategy in the war and to extend the war was mainly a result of changed Israeli perceptions regarding Egypt's war aims. At the beginning of the first phase of the war, the Israeli leadership had seen Egyptian war aims as very limited, but now, at the end of this first phase, these aims were judged to be considerably less limited. At the end of the first phase, the war of attrition being waged by the Egyptians along the Suez Canal came to be seen not only as a strategy for wearing down Israel, but as part of a larger Egyptian plan intended to prepare the ground for a crossing of the canal in the summer of 1969 and establishing a bridgehead on the eastern bank of the canal. The increase in Egyptian activity on the canal in the months of June and July was what led the Israelis to modify their judgment. The frequency and intensity of the Egyptian artillery bombardments along the canal, the rise in the number of raids by Egyptian commando units, and the penetration of Egyptian planes over the Sinai combined to strengthen Israel's suspicions that Egypt's intentions were not confined to "warming up" the front, destroying the Bar-Lev Line, or wearing Israel down, but were directed toward carrying out a wider military operation with less limited aims.[1]

With the closing of the first phase of the war, the Israeli leadership judged that Egypt was liable to accept the dangers involved in extending war as a result of mistaken evaluation on her part of the relation of forces between Israel and Egypt. The strategic and tactical advantages of the Egyptian military deployment along the canal on the one hand, and on the other the restraint exercised by Israel in the first months of the War of Attrition were seen as the principal factors making an Egyptian widening of the war possible.[2] Consequently, as early as the summer of 1969 the Egyptians were considered likely to attempt a wide military action that would include a canal crossing. Even though crossing the canal was adjudged a limited military operation and the Israeli leadership continued to hold the view that Egypt was not capable of conquering the Sinai by force, it was thought that the crossing would have wider political aims.[3] The evaluation was that the Egyptians intended to cross the canal in regiment strength or even with several regiments (in any case, a limited military force) in order to establish a bridgehead on the eastern shore and to impose a cease-fire that would sanction the existence of the Egyptian bridgehead. A limited Egyptian success in a canal crossing would be enough to produce a real shift in the territorial, political, and military status quo by means of diplomatic initiatives imposed by the Powers.[4]

The rise in Israeli casualties was very influential in determining the change in Israeli strategy in the war. In the three months of May, June, and July 1969, Israel suffered 194 casualties in the war along the canal, 53 of them fatal. (In July, the number of Israeli casualties reached 108—77 wounded and 31 killed.) Half of the total casualties in these months were wounded by Egyptian artillery fire. As in the past, so too now the sensitivity to losses of the Israeli public and leadership was a dominant factor in the overall politico-strategical calculations of Israeli policy makers.[5] Just as in other limited wars (Korea and Vietnam) internal constraints at home had their influence on the

Israeli decision to expand the war. There was much internal opposition to taking a high rate of losses for the sake of the limited aims—imposition of the cease-fire on Egypt—of this static, prolonged war. This opposition among both the public and the leadership helped to produce readiness to break out of the defensive strategy that had mainly guided Israel's reactions in the first months of the war.[6]

The new evaluation of Egyptian aims led to the formulation of new Israeli aims. The politico-strategic Israeli aim of continuing to insure the existence of the territorial, political, and military status quo was still the overall purpose of Israeli policy makers, but the threat to the maintenance of this aim was now seen as larger than had been thought, in light of the new evaluation of Egyptian aims. Israel's fundamental aim in the second phase of the war was to prevent the Egyptians from executing their plan of crossing the canal, or at least to disrupt the Egyptian timetable by means of military proof that Egypt lacked the military capability to carry through the plan.[7] This Israeli aim was formulated differently at different times: preventing escalation of Egyptian military activity along the canal; preventing the local, limited war from degenerating into a more general war; or "escalating for the sake of deescalation."[8] Other Israeli aims at this stage were to reduce the number of casualties, counter the Egyptian military initiative along the canal, and impose a renewed cease-fire or at least a significant dampening of Egyptian belligerent activity.[9]

From Defensive to Offensive Strategy

Reevaluation of Egyptian war aims and consequent formulation of new Israeli aims necessarily involved a change in Israeli military strategy. The defensive strategy adopted in the first phase of the war was now seen as inadequate to prevent the Egyptians from carrying out their plan of crossing the canal or even disrupting their timetable.[10] The new military strategy had to measure up to the Egyptian military challenge and also had to take the following principles into account:

(a) refraining from serious escalation of the war along the canal,
(b) not seriously worsening relations with the USSR,
(c) preserving Israel's ties with the United States, both politically and with regard to Israel's security,
(d) preventing a flare-up of fighting on the other fronts—Jordan and Syria, and
(e) maximizing economy of men and equipment, especially planes.[11]

These five principles were supposed to be the guidelines for Israeli strategy in the second phase of the war that lasted from July 20 to the end of December 1969, but in the course of this phase some of these principles were hardly adhered to, especially with regard to their political import.

The new Israeli war strategy was a limited offensive one, resting principally on the combination of two elements: a new one—the utilization of the air force as an active military element in the war, and an old but improved military element—frequent commando raids, on a larger scale than previously, deep into Egyptian territory. Basically the new strategy was designed to block the planned Egyptian crossing of the canal, but it was also intended to put an end to Egyptian military activity or to reduce it in very considerable measure.

The Decision to Send in the Air Force
Even before the Israeli leadership's reevaluation of Egyptian aims, large-scale utilization of the air force had been proposed. When the Egyptians intensified their bombardments, Ezer Weizmann, Head of Operations on the Israel General Staff and a former commander of the air force, raised the proposal to put the air force into action against Egypt. His opinion was that the defensive strategy adopted by the IDF from the beginning of the War of Attrition had proved ineffective. He called for utilizing the full power of the IDF "not only in order to end the War of Attrition, which is important in itself, but to block the road for the Egyptian army on its way to harder and more serious wars."[12]
When he failed to convince the military and political echelons of

the need to "make serious use of the IDF to put an end to the War of Attrition," Weizmann tried to persuade them to "make serious use of the air force" in order to deal "painful blows" that the Egyptians would really feel.[13]

Weizmann's proposals were rejected by the top echelons, both military and political.[14] Putting in the air force was seen from the start as highly escalatory. The best testimony to this was the fact that up to July 20, Israel had deliberately refrained from using the air force. The calculations behind this restraint were mainly political ones—uncertainty as to USSR and U.S. reactions and uncertainty over the possibility of the local, limited war developing into a general one, with all that this meant for the *status quo*, which it was judged vitally important to keep in being.

Even at this stage the opinion held was that strong military pressure should not be brought to bear on Egypt, since the USSR would not allow serious escalation to Egypt's detriment, given the increasing Soviet involvement and large-scale investments there.[15]

The Minister of Defence, Moshe Dayan, was the main opponent of the use of the air force on the Egyptian front. Dayan's view was that the air force should only be put in if there were "no choice," in view of its escalatory significance, that is to say, only in very serious military situations such as an Egyptian attempt to cross the canal, even with limited forces, or the development of Egyptian military plans for general war. In situations like these, putting in the air force would in effect be a preemptive strike directed against definitely extreme Egyptian actions.[16]

Dayan's views were shared by other Israeli defense leaders, Chief of Staff Bar-Lev, and the air force people themselves with Commander Mordekhai Hod at their head. The air force people strongly opposed putting in the air force on account of the Egyptian missiles system along the canal, unless the IDF were to have at its disposal other means capable of neutralizing the Egyptian missiles system.[17] There was also uncertainty as to the tactical effectiveness of bombing Egyptian ground targets such as infantry, gun, and mortar emplacements.

It was only when the Israeli leadership and Dayan at its head were fully convinced that the Egyptians were preparing to carry out their plan for a canal crossing in mid-1969 that the decision was reached to put the air force into action. Though this step was still considered escalatory and dangerous in view of the prevailing uncertainty over possible Soviet reactions, what finally settled the issue was the judgement arrived at that there was "no choice." Once Israel decided that an Egyptian crossing of the canal had to be prevented by military means, she had only two military alternatives at her disposal in mid-1969: a large-scale land operation launched on the front, to include crossing the canal in order to hit the Egyptian military forces deployed along the canal, or else a limited use of the air force to hit this deployment. In these circumstances, the second alternative was judged to be less escalatory and involving less of the political and military dangers of any and every escalation.[18]

The decision in favor of limited utilization of the air force was also taken in the belief that the key to any Egyptian plan for crossing the canal must be air superiority in general and on the canal in particular. It was thought that any Egyptian canal crossing operation must necessitate sending up the Egyptian Air Force in the opening phase of the crossing so as to "soften up" the Israel line and prevent the Israeli Air Force and armor from disrupting the crossing. This led to the conclusion that the best way to disrupt the Egyptian plan for the crossing was to prove to the Egyptians that their air force not only did not enjoy local air superiority along the canal but was not capable of carrying out its task even in the most limited canal crossing operation. The Israeli Air Force had demonstrated its absolute air superiority over the Egyptian Air Force in the Six-Day War; what was not proposed was to prove Egyptian air inferiority in spite of the existence of the Egyptian missiles system. If the Egyptians were shown that the Israeli Air Force held air superiority, they would be "persuaded" to refrain from attempting their canal crossing operation and perhaps even to reduce the level of Egyptian military activity along the canal without Israel's having to escalate the war still more seriously.[19]

Aims and Significance of Utilizing the Air Force—
the Israeli Concept
In the judgment of Israeli policy makers, their decision meant an escalation of the war. Therefore, throughout the period from July 20 to the end of December 1969, they tried to make clear to the public why Israel had had to drop defensive strategy and opt for a limited escalation. Their line was to present their decision as a "no choice" situation; in the light of their evaluation of the dangers of the Egyptian canal crossing plan, they had decided to face the dangers of escalation involved in putting in the air force. But they also tried to show that the process of escalation begun by Israel would in the end lead to anti-escalatory developments. This apologia was based on political calculations—uncertainty regarding Soviet and American reactions and also uncertainty over the possible development of the war into a general one, in spite of the evaluation that the relation of forces between Israel, Egypt, and the Arab States ruled out this possibility.

Chief of Staff Bar-Lev coined a term to characterize Israel strategy at this time: "escalation for the sake of deescalation."

The use of this concept (escalation) is a matter of definition. If what is referred to is the use of the means of warfare, such as for example putting aircraft into action in the fighting on the canal, this does perhaps involve some escalation because a weighty additional factor has been put in. But if what we are speaking about is not the means of warfare but the state of the hostilities in a situation of confrontation between ourselves and the Egyptians, then the introduction of an additional means of warfare does not necessarily aggravate the situation. For example, I am prepared to say that putting planes into action currently on the canal is "escalation for the sake of de-escalation," an increase of activity for the purpose of securing a reduction of activity.[20]

Israel's other aims were also stressed: preventing Egypt from waging general war and getting her to reduce her military activity along the canal. Israel hoped to prove to Egypt by means of punishing strikes by the air force that Egypt was not ready for general war. While Egypt kept up her constant military activity along the canal she would have to pay for it dearly.[21] Moderating

Egypt's uninterrupted belligerent activity would also, it was believed, reduce Israeli losses.[22] By putting in the Israeli Air Force,
the Israeli policy makers also hoped to deprive Egypt of the military initiative and free themselves from the War of Attrition that
Egypt had imposed on its own terms. They hoped to reverse the
process and impose war on Egypt under the conditions that
Israel wanted.[23]

On the operative level, the aims of utilizing the air force
were: to extend the area of the fighting along the canal to oblige
Egypt to spread out her forces and thin the massive Egyptian
concentration along the canal,[24] to wipe out the antiaircraft defense system along the canal (ground-to-air missile launching
sites, antiaircraft guns, and radar installation)[25] to open an air
corridor and create "open skies" for Israeli Air Force penetration
in depth, and to force the Egyptian Air Force to fight under un-
equal conditions (with the antiaircraft defenses destroyed), and
so undermine its security and limit its activity in the air.[26]

From the beginning on July 20 to the end of December 1969,
three main phases can be distinguished: (a) July 20 to 28: limited
input aimed at blocking the possibility of a canal crossing; (b)
August 13 to 19: limited input aimed at moderating Egyptian
military activity; (c) September 9 to end of December: less limited input, aimed at imposing a cease-fire on Egypt.

In the first phase, the main task of the air force was to get the
Egyptians to give up their canal crossing plan. This was what
Dayan called "the Battle for the Canal," i.e., "the battle with the
Egyptians trying to cross over the canal."[27] The addition of the
air force on July 20 was limited to securing this aim. Because of
the projected dangers of escalation with all its implications, the
air action focused on a limited and narrow area in the northern
sector of the canal, from Qanṭara north. This sector was thought
to be the same sector from which Egypt planned to launch the
canal crossing. It was also chosen in the belief that there was
only one missile site there and relatively few antiaircraft guns,
and that the conditions of the terrain—thickets and water channels—would insure that the bombing achieved its aim, given the
difficulties the Egyptians had there in digging themselves in
properly.[28]

Targets for bombings were focused on posts and strong-points of the Egyptian armed forces deployed in the zone adjacent to the canal, SA-2 missile sites, artillery emplacements, commando bases, radar stations, and gun and mortar sites. In the course of the bombings in this phase, ground-to-air SA-2 missile sites were taken out, as were gun emplacements, radar stations, tanks, and tank posts. This first phase ended on July 28. It was assumed that the basic aim of the bombings had been secured, i.e., that by then Egypt had to put off her plans for crossing the canal. Other reasons for marking a pause were a desire to test the reaction of the superpowers to the degree of escalation, as well as a certain astonishment over the force and effectiveness of the blow that had been struck.[29]

The halt in the bombings permitted a certain degree of recovery on the part of the Egyptians, who learned to adjust to the limited bombings and then continued with their war of attrition.[30] There was no air action from July 28 to August 12. The fighting was confined to artillery exchanges, light arms, and mortar fire.

The second phase began on August 13 and continued until August 19. The Egyptian recovery and the increase in Egyptian artillery fire led to the second round of air force bombings. In this phase, the air force activity was described as a reaction to Egyptian artillery fire. It was also called "linked response"— every time the Egyptians started a heavy artillery bombardment, Israel considered herself free to send in the air force against the Egyptian artillery positions.[31] In this phase began what Dayan called "the battle for the battle for the canal," that is, "the battle in which the Egyptians tried to smash our strongpoints so as to be able to wage the real battle for the canal after that."[32] In other words, Israel once again focused on the Egyptian War of Attrition, now that the immediate danger of a canal crossing had been warded off. The aim now was to bring about a moderation of Egyptian activity. In this phase, air action was transferred to the Gulf of Suez region as well as to the central sector of the canal, and was directed mainly against the Egyptian artillery. Nevertheless, the IDF was not yet thinking in terms of continuous air warfare on the Egyptian front. It had not yet concluded that the air force was Israel's best and most effective answer to the Egyptian War of Attrition. Utilization of the air force was still conceived of in very limited terms since the policy makers were guided by their wish to prevent continued escalation of the war.[33]

It was because of the relative ineffectiveness of the "linked response" system that Israel embarked on the third phase that began on September 9 and continued up to the end of December. From September on, Israel stopped putting in the air force as linked response and went over to a new strategy "counterattrition" or "wearing down the wearers down"—systematic pounding of the entire Egyptian front along the canal and the Gulf of Suez, intended eventually to impose a cease-fire on Egypt or to considerably moderate Egyptian activity. From this point on, the air force had the major role in the War of Attrition.[34]

In this third phase the air force strikes were heavier and more intensive than in the previous phases, but action was still strictly limited to the length of the canal (including the Gulf of Suez) and no strikes were made on targets behind the front.[35] At first the air activity centered on the western shore of the Gulf of Suez, but later it was extended to additional sectors of the gulf and different sectors of the canal. The basic aim of this wave of bombings, the longest phase of the three, was to take out the entire Egyptian antiaircraft system and to secure absolute air superiority over the canal and deep into Egyptian territory. By securing absolute air superiority, the Israelis wanted to deter the Egyptians not only from undertaking the canal crossing operation, but also from going on with the War of Attrition once the Egyptian rear was exposed to further counterblows. Besides bombing the Egyptian antiaircraft defense system, the air attacks centered on Egyptian artillery emplacements. By the end of the third phase, Egypt was left without any effective defense against Israeli air superiority along the Gulf of Suez and the canal.[36]

The Effectiveness of Utilizing the Air Force

Beyond any doubt, sending in the Israeli Air Force (IAF) on July 20 blocked the Egyptian plan for a canal crossing or at least disrupted its timetable. According to the Israeli evaluation, the Egyptian plan was meant to be carried out in mid-July and the air force action certainly caused it to be put off for the time being or even indefinitely. From the end of July, the Israeli policy makers judged that the aim of blocking the canal crossing had been secured, and this marked the end of the first phase of utilizing the air force.[37]

By putting in the air force, Israeli policy makers hoped to moderate Egyptian belligerent activity on the front, and principally to reduce the massive artillery bombardments that were the main cause of rising Israeli casualties on the canal during the preceding period.[38] It was thought that the Egyptians would be obliged to thin out their forces on the front so there would be fewer men and units to serve as targets for the planes; in this way Egyptian artillery activity would necessarily be reduced. Strikes at the artillery emplacements and at munition dumps would also help to secure this result.[39] These aims were only achieved up to a certain point.

To examine how effective the air force action was in securing these results, we have compiled a few simple statistics. Belligerent activity on the canal has been examined throughout the whole first period of attrition, from March to December 1969. This ten months period has been divided—March to July and August to December—up to the introduction of the IAF and after it.[40] Belligerent action has been divided into three main classes—light arms fire, artillery fire, mortar fire—and the recorded frequency of incidents of each kind.

In the period from March to December 1969, 4,110 different incidents were registered (including air and sea actions and commando raids), an average of 411 incidents per month or 13 per day. On examination of the intensification of belligerent activity, the main criterion for which is *quantitative*, it appears that in the period from August to December it was more intensive than March to July, in spite of the introduction of the IAF. Incidents in the months August to December numbered 2,561 as against 1,549 from March to July, i.e., 62 percent of all belligerent activity from March to December 1969 took place in the months August to December.[41] To put it differently, belligerent activity from August to December was 65 percent higher than from March to July. If we recall that the data before us were published by the IDF and that they refer only to belligerent activity initiated by Egypt, it is evident that putting in the air force not only did not reduce belligerent activity (quantitatively) from August to December, but on the contrary intensified it to a marked degree (see table 4.1).

When the effect of the IAF actions on the types of Egyptian belligerency is examined, some interesting findings emerge. Comparison of the two periods shows considerable differences in the frequency of the types of activity (light arms fire, artillery bombardments, mortar shelling). Artillery incidents constitute 48.8 percent of all belligerent activity in the March to July period (light arms fire—43 percent, and mortar shelling—only 3.4 percent); then the percentage of artillery incidents declines to only 19.3 percent of all incidents from August to December. IAF action was of course the main reason for this drop in the frequency of artillery fire incidents. In this respect, the IAF had a very considerable degree of success. This can be shown still more clearly by comparing the intensity of artillery fire incidents in the periods immediately before and immediately after the air force was put in—June and July as compared with August and September. June and July were months of intensive artillery fire:

Table 4.1 Numbers of Incidents Initiated by the United Arab Republic Along the Israeli-Egyptian Front, March to December 1969

Month	Total Incidents	Daily Average	Percent of Total
March	84	2.7	2.0
April	475	15.8	11.7
May	231	7.5	5.6
June	404	13.5	9.8
July	355	11.5	8.6
August	515	16.6	12.5
September	448	14.9	10.9
October	642	20.7	15.6
November	495	16.5	12.1
December	461	14.9	11.2
Total	4110	13.4	100.0

SOURCE: IDF spokesman, MER (1969–70), p. 167.

77 percent of all belligerent incidents in June and 58 percent in July. (This partial decline was probably the effect of IAF action during the last ten days of July.) As against this, August and September showed the lowest intensity of artillery incidents since March: 14 percent of all belligerent incidents in August and only 12.5 percent in September (see table 4.2).

The success of the IAF in reducing artillery fire also emerges clearly in table 4.3: 60 percent of all the 1,250 incidents of artillery firing in 1969 occurred between March and July. The percentage of artillery incidents was also considerably reduced in August and September (the first months after the air force was brought in) calculated as percentage of the total artillery incidents for the whole of 1969: 6 percent in August and only 5 percent in September.

As already stated, however, the reduction in the number of artillery incidents did not produce a reduction in the total of all incidents. On the contrary, there was a striking quantitative intensification. The reason for this is mainly the significant rise in other types of firing—by light arms and mortars. The most significant rise was in mortar shelling, from 3 percent between March and July to 30 percent between August and December. The rise in light arms fire was less striking, from 43 percent to 48 percent (but the absolute number of small arms fire incidents almost doubled from 660 to 1,229). In the months of August and September, precisely when there was a marked decline in artillery fire incidents, a striking rise in light arms fire and mortar shelling occurred (44 percent of all incidents in August were light arms, 41 percent mortars), compared to June—when only 19 percent of all incidents were light arms fire and mortar shelling, and July—when the percentage was 37 percent.

The marked rise in incidents of light arms fire and mortar shelling was apparently caused by the mobility of these arms systems on the one hand, and on the other by their presenting restricted targets for strikes by the IAF as opposed to artillery emplacements and tanks. Moreover, the IAF focused mainly on wiping out the artillery fire sources.[42]

The increased scale of Egyptian belligerent activity (quantitatively) in spite of the IAF bombings was also a sign of Egypt's

Table 4.2 Numbers of Incidents Initiated by the UAR Along the Israeli-Egyptian Front, March to December 1969 (Breakdown by Months and Type of Incidents)

Month	Mortar Shelling No.	%	Light Arms No.	%	Artillery No.	%	Other No.	%	Total Incidents No.	%
March	—	—	71	84.5	6	7.2	7	8.3	84	100
April	1	0.2	282	59.4	169	35.6	23	4.8	475	100
May	1	0.4	157	68.0	63	27.3	10	4.3	231	100
June	4	1.0	71	17.5	311	77.0	18	4.5	404	100
July	47	13.3	85	23.9	207	58.3	16	4.5	355	100
August	209	40.6	225	43.7	72	14.0	9	1.7	515	100
September	187	41.7	186	41.5	56	12.5	19	4.3	448	100
October	165	25.7	345	53.7	117	18.2	15	2.4	642	100
November	110	22.2	231	46.7	136	27.5	18	3.6	495	100
December	95	20.6	242	52.5	113	24.5	11	2.4	461	100
March–July Total	53	3.4	666	43.0	756	48.8	74	4.8	1549	100
Aug.–Dec. Total	766	29.9	1229	48.0	494	19.3	72	2.8	2561	100
Total	819	19.9	1895	46.1	1250	30.4	146	3.6	4110	100

SOURCE: IDF spokesman, MER (1969–70), p. 167.

Table 4.3 Numbers of Incidents Initiated by the UAR along the Israeli-Egyptian Front, March to December 1969 (Breakdown by Months and Type of Incidents)

Month	Mortar Shelling No.	%	Light Arms No.	%	Artillery No.	%	Other No.	%	Total Incidents No.	%
March	—	—	71	3.6	6	0.5	7	4.8	84	2.0
April	1	0.1	282	14.9	169	13.5	23	15.7	475	11.7
May	1	0.1	157	8.3	63	5.0	10	6.9	231	5.6
June	4	0.5	71	3.7	311	24.9	18	12.3	404	9.8
July	47	5.7	85	4.6	207	16.6	16	11.0	355	8.6
August	209	25.6	225	11.9	72	5.7	9	6.2	515	12.5
September	187	22.8	186	9.8	56	4.5	19	13.0	448	10.9
October	165	20.2	345	18.2	117	9.4	15	10.3	642	15.6
November	110	13.4	231	12.2	136	10.9	18	12.3	495	12.1
December	95	11.6	242	12.8	113	9.0	11	7.5	461	11.2
Total	819	100.0	1895	100.0	1250	100.0	146	100.0	4110	100.0

SOURCE: IDF spokesman, MER (1969–70), p. 167.

capacity for speedy adjustment to the new military element introduced into the battle array. "The Egyptians are getting used to
living with the bombings and are not letting up in their war of
attrition," said Ezer Weizmann.[43]

The air force's success in reducing artillery fire was of great
significance, since artillery fire was the dominant component in
the Egyptians' system of operational calculations in starting the
War of Attrition. The qualitative and quantitative superiority of
the Egyptian artillery in the months March to July was the outstanding feature of belligerent activity in those months. From
August to December the Egyptian artillery was still an important
component in the fighting, but not to the same extent as in the
previous months. Artillery fire continued in the months August
to December but there were no longer the massive bombardments there had been in the months March to July.[44]

Sending in the air force did not bring about a significant
reduction of Israeli casualties. In the months from August to
December, the number of casualties (killed and wounded) was 48
percent of the total casualties in the whole period of March to
December (245 out of 515). There was also no significant decline
in relative distribution of killed and wounded as a result of the
air force actions (see table 4.4). Of those killed, 46 percent (65
out of 140) and of those wounded 48 percent (180 out of 375)
were casualties from August to December. The ratio of dead to
wounded did not change either (see table 4.5).

It must be remembered that it is extremely difficult to say
what the number of Israeli casualties might have been if the
IAF had not been sent in. The upward trend of the casualty figures in July (93 casualties—25 killed; 68 wounded) might have
been maintained if we assume that Egyptian belligerent activity
would have continued to increase in scale and might even have
led to a canal crossing. The air force blocked this possibility
and may in fact have saved Israel very heavy losses.[45] There was
a significant reduction in casualties after July, but then the figure
for July was exceptionally high, above the average for both
March to June and August to December. The effect of the bombings was seen chiefly in the reduction in the number of casualties inflicted by Egyptian artillery fire, which had been the main

Table 4.4 IDF Casualties on the Egyptian Front, March to December 1969

Month	Artillery Incidents Casualties			Overall Casualties		
	Wounded	Killed	Total	Wounded	Killed	Total
March	24	4	28	29	7	36
April	13	10	23	34	21	55
May	16	8	24	30	15	45
June	15	—	15	34	7	41
July	43	15	58	68	25	93
Total March–July	111	37	148	195	75	270
August	24	3	27	55	13	68
September	10	10	20	30	16	46
October	14	4	18	47	11	58
November	5	3	8	29	12	41
December	7	6	13	19	13	32
Total August–Dec.	60	26	86	180	65	245
Total March–Dec.	171	63	234	375	140	515

SOURCE: IDF spokesman, MER (1969–70), p. 172. These figures do not include Israeli losses suffered in the course of Israeli-initiated reprisal attacks.

Table 4.5 Overall IDF Casualties on the Egyptian Front, March to December 1969

March–July		August–December		Total		
No.	%	No.	%	No.	%	
270	100	245	100	515	100	Total
75	28	65	27	140	27	Killed
195	72	180	73	375	73	Wounded

SOURCE: IDF spokesman, MER (1967–70), p. 172.

cause of the losses from March to July. The air force reduced the number of casualties from this source. From March to July, 55 percent of all casualties were from artillery fire (49 percent of those killed and 57 percent of those wounded), while from August to December casualties from artillery fire were only 35 percent of the total (40 percent of all those killed and 33 percent of those wounded). Thus the drop was greater in the proportion of those wounded than those killed (see table 4.6). The fact that the overall reduction in casualties was limited was mainly due to the increase in other types of Egyptian belligerent activity—light arms fire and mortar shelling.

Thus sending in the air force only partially achieved the aim of reducing casualties. It may indeed have prevented a rise in the rate of losses that might have occurred otherwise, but it only brought about a limited reduction of losses as compared with the preceding period.

The third phase of activating the air force achieved two things—"counterattrition" and robbing the Egyptians of the initiative in the fighting. The initiative passed over to the IDF. The strategy of the "limited offensive" or "attrition in the air" secured quite impressive results both strategically and operationally. In the sphere of strategy, Israel forced the Egyptians to abandon the idea of the canal crossing and to concentrate on the War of Attrition. Thereupon the IAF was sent in to deprive the Egyptians of the initiative as well in the War of Attrition. Strategically speaking, wiping out the Egyptian air defense system made it clear to both Israel and Egypt that the initiative in the fighting on the canal had passed over to the IDF. Egypt was forced to seek an answer to the absolute Israeli air superiority along the line of the canal, the whole rear being left without any protection against the IAF.

Operationally speaking, the turning point was reached when the air force, serving as flying artillery, succeeded in reaching something like a draw with the Egyptian artillery. Sending in the air force largely counterbalanced the Israeli inferiority in artillery. This found practical expression in the reduced Egyptian

Table 4.6 IDF Casualties on the Egyptian Front in Artillery Incidents as Percentage of Total Casualties, March to December 1969

Months	Wounded	Killed	Casualties
March–December	45.6	45.0	45.4
March–July	56.7	49.3	54.8
August–December	33.0	40.0	35.0

SOURCE: IDF spokesman, MER (1969–70), p. 172.

artillery activity. From the operational viewpoint the sum of the air actions was the wiping out of the Egyptian air defense system along the canal-line, including all of the estimated eight to twelve Egyptian SA–2 missile launching sites on the canal front.[46] An indefinite number of radar sites and antiaircraft guns were also taken out[47] and numerous artillery pieces and other war material were destroyed.[48] It appears that up to November 1969 the Egyptians had over 1,000 casualties, most of them from aerial bombing.[49] Also as a result of the massive IAF bombings, the Egyptians began to thin out their forces and reduce their artillery activity because of hits on artillery emplacements. Because of the loss of the air defense system, the Egyptian Air Force lost a considerable number of aircraft in the period from July 20 to the end of December 1969. In attempting to prevent the Israeli bombings or to reply in kind by bombing the Israeli line, the Egyptian Air Force lost thirty-eight planes (in fights in the air and from ground antiaircraft fire).[50]

As part of the strategy of counterattrition, Israel continued to carry out commando-type raids deep into Egyptian territory, but these raids differed in character from those in the earlier phases. From July 19 on, with the raid on Green Island, up to the end of December, Israel carried out ten raids deep into Egypt. Most of these were directed against military objectives, unlike the commando raids of the first phase directed against economic and civilian objectives. Nevertheless, the raids deep into Egypt were still limited in scope, apart from the raid by the armed forces (see table 4.7). Most of these raids centered on the Gulf of Suez area. In most instances only limited casualties and damage were caused, except for the armored forces raid and the capture of radar equipment in the raid at the end of December. In spite of their operational success, these raids were not capable of substantially affecting Egyptian determination to go on with the War of Attrition. As before, raids of this nature could not produce major strategic results.

Cease-Fire Imposed on Egypt
Once it was clear that Egypt had put off its plan for crossing the Suez Canal, it became Israel's principal aim to send in the air

Table 4.7 Balance Sheet of Israeli Commando Raids: July–December 1969

Date	Area Raided	Target
July 19	Green Island in Gulf of Suez	Fortified military position
August 27–28	Nile Valley (near Manqabād village, 8 km. west of city of Asyūt)	Central military camp
September 7–8	Ra's Sādāt (20 km. south of Suez city)	Egyptian naval base
September 9	Western shore of Gulf of Suez (a 50 km. stretch of coast northward from Ra's Abū Daraj to Ra's Za'farāna)	Military posts and bases
October 20–21	Western shore of Gulf of Suez (in Abū Daraj area)	Egyptian military transport
October 24–25	Upper Egypt (in area of Qirnā village)	Civilian installations
October 27–28	Gulf of Suez (Road Ra's Za'farāna-Ra's Ghārib)	Egyptian military transport
December 18–19	Ṣāliḥiyya region (30 km. west of Suez Canal)	Military camp
December 22–23	Red Sea—Port of Safāga	Egyptian naval base
December 26–27	Gulf of Suez—Ra's Ghārib	Egyptian post

SOURCE: IDF spokesman, MER (1969–70), pp. 156–66.

force to impose a cease-fire on Egypt. It was judged that this could be achieved by destroying the Egyptian air defense system and by constant counterattrition. By securing decisive air superiority Israel would deter the Egyptians not only from attempting to go on with the idea of a canal crossing but also from continuing the war, since otherwise she would be dealt still heavier blows. Decisive Israeli air superiority was meant to serve as an

Character of Raid	Results
Attack on military post (direct encounter)	Egyptian losses: 25 killed, heavy damage to military installations; Israeli losses: 6 killed, 10 wounded
Heavy mortar shelling (indirect encounter)	Losses on Egypt (no figures) no Israeli losses
Attack on Egyptian torpedo boats (indirect encounter)	2 Egyptian torpedo boats sunk (3 Israeli soldiers killed in accidental explosion on return to base)
Combined armor and armored infantry with air force assistance (direct encounter)	Strike at many and variety of military installations: naval radar, air radar unit, over 20 shore guns, buildings, artillery, tanks, and transport; Egyptian losses: over 200 killed; Israeli losses: 1 killed and 1 wounded.
Ambush on high road (indirect encounter)	Egyptian losses: 3 killed, damage to vehicles; no Israeli losses
	11 Egyptian civilians taken prisoner; no Israeli losses
Ambush on high road (indirect encounter)	Egyptian losses: 3 killed, damage to vehicles; no Israeli losses
Mortar shelling of military camp (indirect encounter)	No firm data on Egyptian losses; no Israeli losses
Mortar shelling of naval installations (indirect encounter)	No firm data on Egyptian losses; no Israeli losses
Attack on post and removal of new Egyptian, Soviet-made radar installation (direct encounter)	Egyptian losses: 2 killed, 4 taken prisoner, loss of radar installation; no Israeli losses

NOTE: All raids were small-scale with the exception of September 9 which was somewhat larger, and December 26/27.

indication of Israel's future intentions if Egypt did not stop the fighting.

Egyptian strategy in the war broke down with the destruction of the Egyptian air defense system and the initiative passed to Israel, but this still proved insufficient to impose a cease-fire on Egypt. The limited action of IAF was not capable of bringing the war to an end, but only of moderating it. As long as Israel went along with the war's remaining limited and a static war of attrition, the use of offensive military means such as the IAF could secure only partial results. Despite Israeli air superiority, Egypt still had the benefit of massive deployment along the canal. In order to bring the war to an end by military means, Israel would have had to give up her limited offensive strategy for an unlimited one and be ready to pay the full military and political price involved. In the course of August and September, the Israeli policy makers came to realize that limited operation of the air force would not end the war, but only moderate it.[51]

Even those who had been in favor of sending in the IAF saw that limited action could not end the war or even significantly moderate it. In Ezer Weizmann's opinion, the reason was mainly that the air force was sent in as an isolated component in the fighting instead of as an integrated component; only a combined input of large-scale armored forces together with the air force would be capable of ending the War of Attrition. What was needed to end the war, he believed, was large-scale action on the ground to conquer areas on the western shore of the canal and get control of Port Said, together with still more numerous and more powerful air raids.[52] Late in 1969 the decision went against a land action of this kind and against more and larger-scale bombing because these moves were judged too escalatory.[53] Given the impossibility of ending the war by more serious escalatory deployment, continued utilization of the air force was seen as the only means available to Israel to partially offset Egypt's strategic advantages though it could not neutralize them completely.

The Politico-Strategic Results
of Sending in the Israeli Air Force
In evaluating the politico-strategic results of sending in the Israeli Air Force, it is necessary to distinguish between the first two phases of the air force action and the third phase. In the first two phases (July to August), the decision to send in the air force represented an escalation of means, while in the third phase (from September on) there was escalation of the aims of the fighting. Sending in the IAF was intended in the first phase to block

an Egyptian canal crossing, and it did bring about a postponement of the plan and thus prevent an extension of the war. This
phase was characterized by "escalation for the sake of deescalation," a term coined by Chief of Staff Bar-Lev. Given the impossibility of preventing an extension of the war by any means other
than a limited military offensive, the Israeli decision was a result
of no alternative. Any other military initiative was liable to have
been more escalatory.

The second phase of "linked response" in August was also
escalatory as regarded military means, but these were the only
means available to Israel to counterbalance Egypt's strategic advantages. In view of Israeli artillery inferiority, sending in the
IAF as "flying artillery" was a means of reaching something
like a "draw" in the War of Attrition.

In the third phase, Israel went beyond the aims it had set in
the two previous phases. Israel tried to break down the Egyptian
strategy by changing the nature of the war altogether. This was
expressed in the concentrated, systematic pounding of the Egyptian air defense deployment. Wiping out the Egyptian air defense
signaled to the Egyptians not only Israel's transition to "attrition
against attrition" but also her intention to assert her absolute air
superiority along the Suez Canal front and deep inside Egypt as
well. In fact, the Egyptian air defense system along the canal was
meant not only to neutralize the Israeli Air Force at the front but
also to insure the rear, since it was realized that the Egyptian Air
Force could not accomplish this. Once Israel secured air superiority, there was no stopping the process of escalation and Egypt
was left with no alternative but to end the war. Given Israel's
absolute strategic superiority (that had in effect restored the situation to what it had been on the eve of the War of Attrition), if
Egypt were to go on with the war it would mean ending it with
yet another defeat. Egypt had overestimated the political and
strategic limitations preventing Israel's expanding the war; when
she realized her mistake she set about trying to bring in the
USSR as the best way to stave off another defeat. Israel's securing
absolute air superiority also reinforced the danger of widening
the war still further from the very fact of the increased temptation
to exploit that strategic superiority in order to end the war.

The Israeli evaluation that the political constraints were less serious at the end of the third phase than they had been adjudged on the eve of sending in the IAF, together with the fact that the IAF had not succeeded in ending the war by means of limited action, opened the way in January 1970 for a widening and intensification of IAF bombings.[54] It was precisely apprehension over the possible widening of the war that led proponents of limited war theory to issue warnings against securing absolute air superiority in a limited war.[55] Even if this view refers to a limited war between superpowers, it also holds for limited wars between local actors that are not superpowers. The War of Attrition between Israel and Egypt clearly confirmed this theory. Israeli air superiority opened the way for still more serious escalation of the fighting.

Attrition—From Tactics to Strategy

The Egyptian leadership had been of the opinion that Israel would refrain from sending in its air force for both political and military reasons, and the change of tactics took them by surprise.[56] The Egyptians tried to divine the ulterior aims of the move and to weigh their own policy accordingly. At first they thought that the addition of the Israeli Air Force opened a new phase in the fighting along the canal, and that it marked a serious step in escalation of the war on Israel's initiative. They saw that a change had taken place in Israel's defensive strategy and that Israel was now preparing to react against Egypt with an offensive strategy. The Egyptian leadership considered that four factors had made Israel change her defensive policy:

First, the failure of Israel's defensive strategy, based mainly on a static deployment—the Bar-Lev Line.[57]

Second, Israel's failure to adjust to a war of attrition, a type of war not suited to the IDF and Israeli war tradition. By its nature as a static and prolonged war, it deprived the Israeli army of its preeminent strategic advantages—surprise, mobility, and capacity to carry the fighting into enemy territory. Moreover, since Egypt held the military initiative because of her strategic and tactical advantages in a war of attrition, Israel had no way of exploiting her specific strategic advantages except by escalation.[58]

Third, rising Israeli losses in the first phase of the war, the destruction of the Bar-Lev Line, and the lowered morale of the Israelis at the front and in the rear. (In a static, prolonged war of attrition characterized by a high rate of wearing down of manpower and material resources, Israel was not capable of holding out for a long time, given her human and material limitations.)[59]

Fourth, the Israeli belief that the War of Attrition was simply prefatory to a large-scale Egyptian attack, meant to include a canal crossing.[60] The calculations that impelled Israel to choose the air force as the main instrument in its offensive strategy were seen as based on the political and military limitations that prevented her from adopting a more general military option.[61]

The air war was seen as giving Israel strategic advantages such as surprise, concentration, and speed of movement; hence freeing her from static warfare, prolonged attrition, and full mobilization over a long period.[62] Other advantages accruing from sending in the air force were Israel's ability to exploit her strategic superiority and to utilize her limited manpower resources more efficiently (since she had manpower available for this type of warfare, i.e., two first class airmen for every aircraft), thus reducing the number of lives lost.[63]

Though Israel's military strategy in sending in the IAF was seen as limited in character, her politico-strategic aims were not. It was thought that she wanted to bring down the Egyptian regime and substitute one that would more readily accept the peace terms or would maintain the territorial, political, and military status quo until the Arabs did agree to Israeli peace terms.[64] On the purely strategic level, Israel wanted to make use of her strategic advantages in limited war to secure results comparable to those that could be attained by a general war. It was apprehension over the political results of general war that induced Israel to try to utilize her advantages in limited war. The Egyptians still believed that Israel would refrain from going beyond the bounds of a war of attrition, but that she would try a limited offensive strategy to turn the Egyptian War of Attrition into an Israeli war of counter-attrition to force Egypt to moderate her belligerent actions, or to stop the war completely.[65]

Within the bounds of this limited offensive strategy, Israel set the following aims: to destroy the Egyptian army or deal it very heavy blows before it could complete its preparations for the decisive battle of liberation (the canal crossing and conquest of the Sinai);[66] to force the Egyptian High Command to decide to disperse the Egyptian concentrations on the canal front in order to ease the military pressure on the Bar-Lev Line and so deprive the Egyptians of the strategic advantages involved in their deployment there;[67] to deprive the Egyptian army of the military initiative and show the Egyptians that the battle would rage everywhere and not be limited to the front where the Egyptians enjoyed clear military superiority; to wear down the Egyptian High Command by constant attrition in order to deter it from planning and preparing future military operations; and to create a wide breach in the Egyptian air defense in order to hit objectives deep inside Egypt whenever Israel decided to do so.[68] By wiping out the Egyptian air defense system Israel also wanted to insure absolute air superiority and thereby reduce the danger of a possible Egyptian attack.[69]

The Egyptians also saw psychological significance in the utilization of the Israeli Air Force and in the raids deep into Egyptian territory (the armored forces raid and the seizure of radar equipment at Ras Ghārib). The aim was psychological attrition of Egypt, undermining of morale on the Egyptian front and in the rear and on the inter-Arab front as well. Sending in the IAF was seen as developing Egyptian and inter-Arab public opinion that all the efforts at Egyptian reconstruction over the previous two years could not counter Israel's military superiority. Israel still had military preeminence and the proof thereof was the freedom of action enjoyed by the air force and the commandos to strike anywhere at any objective they chose. The destruction of Egypt's air defense only made this superiority more tangible. From the inter-Arab viewpoint, the air actions were meant to prove that Egypt, the strongest Arab country, not only could not fight a war of liberation, but could not even wage a war of attrition.[70]

Nonetheless, the Egyptian leadership judged that Israel could not secure her aims solely by means of war in the air. In spite of Israel's absolute air superiority, she could only achieve limited results. (American bombing in North Vietnam, though less limited than the Israelis', also had been unable to achieve more than limited results.) As long as Israel did not initiate a general war that would have to include a Suez Canal crossing—and this Israel could not do because of military and political constraints—the air war would necessarily have limited results. (Air action was seen as possessing qualities of general war, from the point of view of continuity in time, but focusing on military targets only with the exclusion of the air defense system in a limited geographic sector displayed qualities of limited war.)[71]

Up to the time of complete destruction of their air defense system at the end of December, the leadership believed that in certain circumstances Egypt could prevent Israel from achieving her aim of imposing an air war of attrition: first, by not dispersing the large Egyptian forces along the canal, forces that were the basis of her strategic advantage in the fighting on the canal (an axiom accepted by Israel); second, strengthening the internal front by preparing the public to face the possibility of an additional extension of the front by Israel; and third, disrupting Israel's plans and frustrating her intentions by continuing to impose a war of attrition on land (not in the air), a static war contrary to Israel's kind of warfare.

The entry into action of the Israeli Air Force from July 20 on brought about a substantial change in Egyptian planning. The original four-stage Egyptian plan was blocked at its third stage—a limited canal crossing by regular forces preparatory to a large-scale crossing. IAF action forced the Egyptians to give up all thought of an immediate canal crossing and to concentrate on continuing the War of Attrition.[72]

The Egyptian canal crossing plan, based on securing local air superiority along the canal, could not be carried out once the Israeli Air Force asserted its absolute superiority over the Egyptian air force. The wiping out of the Egyptian air defense system assured this superiority in even larger measure.[73] In the first days of IAF action the Egyptian conclusion already took shape to the effect that the operation of crossing the canal would have to be abandoned for the time being, given the changed strategic situation on the canal front. Indications of this are found in the speech by Abdel Nasser on July 23, the Egyptian Revolution anniversary. It was in this speech that Nasser coined the term "war of attrition" (ḥarb al-istinzāf), and for the first time publicly explained the strategic implications of this kind of war.[74] The Egyptian plan for a crossing was not canceled outright, but was indefinitely postponed.[75]

In contrast to the period from March to July when the Egyptians treated attrition as a matter of tactics, after July attrition was given more strategic significance. The Egyptian effort (even if only as a matter of rhetoric) to turn attrition from a tactic into a strategy was in fact a confession of failure. In the first phase of the war, the Egyptians had not gained any real, solid achievement. When the IAF now demonstrated Israel's strategic superiority afresh, the military options available to Egypt were more limited than they had been at the beginning of March. Attrition remained the only available strategy, under worse conditions than at the beginning of the war. Attrition presented in the guise of strategy was intended for internal consumption and inter-Arab needs—as proof of Egypt's iron determination to go on with the war despite the worsening situation. In other words, the Egyptian leadership found it necessary to explain to the Egyptian people and to the Arab world why the War of Attrition had to be continued even though it had so far proved ineffectual. Moreover, on the operational level attrition was still being waged in the same fashion as in the preceding months and it was therefore necessary to affirm that significant changes were turning attrition as tactic into attrition as strategy.

From the end of July 1969, the Egyptian leadership assisted by the Egyptian and Arab media began presenting a whole series of arguments aimed at convincing people that the War of Attrition was the strategy best suited to Egypt. Most of this argumentation had already been put forward during the first phase of the war when attrition was being used as a tactic. Thus, for example, it was stressed again that the War of Attrition secured both strategic and tactical advantages for Egypt as opposed to the strategic and tactical disadvantages under which Israel labored in this kind of warfare. The differences in human and material re-sources and in specific arms systems and their manner of deploy-ment were once more underlined.[76]

Important differences between tactical and strategic attrition are found in three dimensions—time, the connection between the War of Attrition and the final stage of "liberation" (recon-quest of the Sinai and the occupied territories), and in the stress laid on the conditions supposed to insure the success of the war. Attrition as strategy is a prolonged war, one that may go on for years as opposed to attrition as tactics, which is thought of as lasting a matter of weeks.[77]

A war of attrition even when considered as strategy is not the final war, not the battle for liberation. Just as in the tactical phase (March to July), strategic attrition is a phase connected with the battle of liberation, but since it is on the strategic level it is therefore liable to be protracted. After the plan for the canal crossing had been postponed for an indefinite period, it was nec-essary for purposes of internal and inter-Arab propaganda to stress the link between the phases of attrition and liberation, even when the distance between the two phases increased con-siderably.[78]

The Egyptian leadership stressed that if attrition were to be an effective strategy (i.e, one not liable to suffer reverses in the first phase), certain fundamental preconditions must be pro-vided:

(1) The "confrontation elements" (i.e., Syria, Jordan, Iraq, and the PLO) must be mobilized for the war with attrition nec-essarily chosen as their common strategy. Attrition on all fronts would increase the pressure on Israel and thereby ease Israel's pressure on Egypt.[79] In the first phase of tactical attrition, Egypt needed the confrontation elements mainly at the canal crossing stage.

(2) All the military activity carried on as part of attrition must be directed by a guiding political concept (a war of attrition being at bottom a political strategy).[80]

(3) Although regarded as a limited strategy, a war of attri-tion demands mobilization of the entire economic, diplomatic,

and military potential of all the Arab countries. (The importance of all-Arab assistance for the Egyptian war effort was more evident from July on than in the preceding months, a fact that testifies to Egyptian military and economic difficulties.)[81]

(4) A war of attrition necessitates a military strength equal to that of the enemy. The intention was to secure Egyptian military superiority in the least possible time. Increased Soviet military assistance and the creation of a second front were more vitally necessary than in the first phase.[82]

(5) A war of attrition demands superior determination and dedication to the aims for which it is fought, will power and decisiveness in persisting for a long time and at all costs. This was to prepare the internal front for a protracted war involving heavy losses.[83]

(6) A war of attrition, though limited, is not always absolutely under the control of the warring parties and is liable to escalation of aims and means. Egypt had to control the development of escalatory action and keep the initiative in the conduct of the war, withholding it from the enemy. (Egypt had to initiate escalatory action and prevent Israel from doing so.) Control of the conduct of the war also would insure that Egypt would not prematurely be dragged into a general engagement. (In such a war Egypt would be deprived of her strategic and tactical advantages.)[84]

In strategic terms attrition is also defined as an indirect strategy in contrast to a direct strategy. It is seen as the strategy of all the people fighting for their freedom, based on evading or postponing direct operations and refraining from general battles. This strategy is intended to achieve the same ends as direct strategy, not by decisive victory in the field (as in direct strategy), but by a cumulative series of small victories over a long period. In other words, the aim of a war of attrition as strategy is to secure concrete results such as Israeli withdrawal, without getting into a total war.[85] On the operational level, a war of attrition as strategy is intended to cause the heaviest possible losses by striking hard at Israeli manpower, in the hope that the differences in manpower resources would cancel out Israel's strategic superiority.[86]

Egyptian attempts to give form and substance to attrition as a strategy did not lead to any real gains. Not only was no second front opened to ease the pressure on Egypt, there was no increase in economic aid to Egypt from the Arab States. Since there were no substantial changes on the operational level, Egypt's strategic and tactical advantages that had proved effective as long as the Israeli Air Force was not utilized to counter them were much diminished. Egyptian aims in the war now underwent a further change. Not only was the plan for crossing the Suez Canal postponed, but the effectiveness of the War of Attrition was so reduced that there was doubt whether it could be kept going at all. The points of strategic importance on which so much stress had been laid were mainly a matter of cosmetic cover-up, a make-believe role that Egypt had recourse to in order to hold out against the Israeli air war of attrition without any real means of neutralizing IAF actions. Instead of waging a war of attrition with offensive aims, Egypt was now obliged to work out a defensive strategy for herself that would be dependent on the reestablishment of a more effective air defense system.

Breakdown of Egyptian Strategy and the Rogers Plan

The Israeli Air Force action from July 20 on reactivated the diplomatic initiatives, rejected by Egypt at the end of May, that were now perceived to be useful.[87] Attempts to renew diplomatic contacts were made on Soviet initiative, such as Gromyko's contact with Rogers at the United Nations General Assembly in September 1969. It was apparent that the introduction of the IAF in the warfare on the canal had not gone against American interests. Lack of U.S. opposition and even silent acquiescence to IAF action can perhaps be explained by the fact that in spite of the escalatory significance of the IAF move, this produced a renewal of talks between the superpowers.

If Egyptian military successes had not been countered, it would not have been possible to establish further constructive contacts. The Soviet feelers in September 1969 showed the failure of Egypt's military effort. The Soviet move to renew contact with the United States in the Gromyko-Rogers talks in New York on September 22, 26, and 30 resulted mainly from Egyptian signaling, but they indicated Soviet readiness to renew contact. Furthermore, in the communication from the Egyptian Foreign Minister Riyād to the American State Department, Egypt agreed to accept the pattern of the "Rhodes talks" as a formula for indirect contacts between the parties to the conflict.[88]

The Egyptian signals for the renewal of the contacts gave real impetus to the diplomatic moves. As a result of these signals, Foreign Minister Gromyko and Rogers agreed to renew the four-power talks (though they did not fix any date) as well as the two-power talks, that were seen by both of them as preferable to and more important than four-power talks.[89] Gromyko and Rogers even agreed that the contacts between the two superpowers, now renewed at Egypt's suggestion, should follow the pattern of the earlier two-power talks, i.e., they should take place between Dobrynin and Sisco.

The two-power talks were renewed on October 17 and led to the drafting of a new U.S. plan, later called the "Rogers Plan." This American plan was presented to the USSR at the meeting between Sisco and Dobrynin on October 28, 1969. Like the U.S. plan at the end of May, the Rogers Plan took the form of a compromise proposal theoretically sponsored jointly by the two superpowers. It was specifically framed to solve the Egyptian-Israeli conflict in all its main components.[90] The plan itself was made public six weeks later, on December 9, 1969, by U.S. Secretary of State Rogers.[91] It accorded first priority to settling the Egyptian-Israeli conflict; a plan for settling the Jordanian-Israeli conflict was presented by Rogers at a later stage. Settling the Egyptian-Israeli dispute was considered of decisive importance because of the centrality of Egypt in the regional system and because of the increasing scale of military activity on the canal.[92] The plan was presented to the USSR as a joint compromise proposal inspired by the Sisco-Dobrynin talks, but the USSR took care not to identify itself with the American plan, which was being given detailed treatment in the world press. The Soviet attitude was guided mainly by the desire to preserve good relations with Egypt.

The two local players, Israel and Egypt, knew of the existence of the Rogers Plan before it was formally made public by Rogers in his speech six weeks later.[93] Israel's policy makers saw the plan as running counter to practically all the principal aims of Israeli foreign policy as framed after the Six-Day War.[94] The formal publication of the plan created a sense of crisis in the government of Israel.[95]

The Israeli government convened a special session immediately after the publication of the plan by Rogers on December 10 and rejected the plan outright.[96] In its communiqué of December 11, the government condemned the talks between the superpowers, describing them as assisting the Arab States to step up their acts of aggression. The war of attrition along the canal was called the central point of the interaction that the Arabs discerned between military action and political activity. By the very fact of holding talks and keeping up the contacts between them, the superpowers strengthened the basis of the Arab view.[97]

The United States presented its plan for a political settlement between Israel and Jordan a week later, on December 18. This plan, which was called the "Yost Document" after the American representative at the four-power talks, Charles Yost, was transmitted to Israel on the same day through the Israeli Ambassador to the United States, Yitzhak Rabin. The Yost Document was in fact the direct continuation of the Rogers Plan and the two documents together represented a new American policy in the Middle East.[98] The government of Israel reacted immediately, rejecting the Yost Document as completely as it had the Rogers Plan (session of December 22).[99] The Knesset ratified the government's policy on the Rogers Plan and the Yost Document on December 29.[100]

Abdel Nasser also rejected the American plan outright in his speech of November 6 before the National Assembly, defining the United States as Enemy Number One of the Arab States.[101] This attitude at least in part reflected the failure of the Egyptian military moves on the canal, with the Israel changeover to a strategy of counterattrition against Egypt. Earlier Egyptian views that the desired political solution would only be achieved in the course of military successes still held, but Israel's military superiority led to recognition that the diplomatic initiatives were working against Egypt now, given her inferior military situation; therefore what was needed was not new diplomatic initiatives, but a military response to Israel's superiority.[102] This came out clearly in Abdel Nasser's speech of November 6 calling for continuation of the war against Israel.

Concrete indications of the way Egypt would direct its next military moves were, first, the Egyptian attempt to acquire weapons systems from the USSR of a higher degree of sophistication than formerly, in order to neutralize Israeli Air Force superiority, and, second, the attempt to create a united front of the Arab States for the war against Israel, which would produce an active second front in the east as well as financial support for the Egyptian war effort. On December 9, an Egyptian mission left for Moscow, headed by Anwar Sadat (head of the Egyptian National Assembly), Minister for War Fawzī, and Foreign Minister Riyāḍ.[103] The delegation had meetings with Soviet policy makers Brezhnev, Kosygin, Podgornyi, Ponomarev, Gromyko, and Grechko. Though the visit was described as very successful, the USSR did not agree at this stage to meet the Egyptian request for more sophisticated weapons systems.[104] The Soviets called for a continuation of diplomatic efforts to find a solution, but at the same time they backed the Egyptians in rejecting the Rogers Plan.[105] On December 23, Ambassador Dobrynin informed U.S. Secretary of State Rogers of the Soviets' formal rejection of the Rogers Plan.[106] The long delay in handing over the Soviet answer was apparently connected with the Soviets' desire to know the results of the Arab summit meeting, the Rabat Conference, which convened on December 20 at Egypt's request.

The Rabat Conference ended in failure from the Egyptian point of view, since the other Arab States rejected the Egyptian proposals for a more general war on Israel financed by the oil-rich countries.[107] The rejection of the Rogers Plan by all the parties involved—Egypt, Israel, and the Soviet Union—led to another impasse in the diplomatic moves. The main reason for the failure of diplomacy at this stage was again the link with the military situation.

The successes recorded by the Israeli Air Force between July and December 1969 were the source of the failure of the diplomatic efforts.[108] The Israeli military superiority that had been demonstrated by the air force action also led to a renewed hardening of attitude on Israel's part. The Israelis believed that it was now possible, by increasingly severe military blows, to force Egypt to accept the cease-fire and a continuation of the political and military status quo.[109] In this situation the diplomatic initiatives were unwelcome to both Israel and Egypt, though for different reasons. Israel did not want the diplomatic initiatives because they did not accurately reflect her politico-strategic position in the region (since she was called upon to return to the situation that preceded the Six-Day War). Egypt considered the diplomatic initiative undesirable in view of her strategic inferiority, even though the proposals came near to the Egyptian stand.[110] The Israeli concept of the war developed in a manner parallel to the Egyptian concept. A solution to the conflict had to reflect Israel's politico-strategic position, with her strategic superiority beyond challenge.[111]

It was in fact the Egyptian rejection of the Rogers Plan that led to the Soviet rejection. Once the Soviets' client in the region rejected the plan, it became impossible to impose it on Israel. The rejection put an end to the two-power talks, though contacts between the superpowers also took place in the course of 1970. The initiative for closing down the two-power talks came from the American side,[112] and the talks formally ended on July 1. The failure of the two-power talks led to the decision to revive the four-power talks; these started up again on December 2, 1969. In the last few days of the year no less than six meetings were held.[113]

The four-power talks were renewed on French initiative, for the French believed that they could bridge the American and Soviet positions in the forthcoming meetings.[114] The communiqué issued by the representatives of the four powers after the first meeting once more stated that the aim of the talks was "to assist in establishing a just peace in the Middle East on the basis of United Nations Security Council Resolution 242, confirmed in all its component parts."[115] The communiqué further stressed the increasing tension in the Middle East, calling it serious and a threat to international peace.

5 Israel Imposes Its Strategy

THE ISRAELI DECISION to carry out air raids deep inside Egyptian territory created a new stage in the War of Attrition and in the annals of the Arab-Israeli conflict. The escalation that then took place led to significant changes, not only in Egyptian-Israeli relations, but also in the relations of these two countries with their respective patron superpowers—the United States and the Soviet Union, and also in the interaction between the Arab-Israeli conflict and the conflict between the superpowers. Special interest is attached, therefore, to the political and military considerations behind the Israeli decision. The main problem is what induced the Israeli policy makers to come to such an escalatory decision, given the fact that the Israeli political and military concept had been basically defensive and prudent ever since the Six-Day War; and even more so in the first stages of the War of Attrition.

The Israeli decision, which so definitely meant escalation of war objectives, was the outcome of changes in Israeli views concerning the interaction between political and military calculations in the conduct of the war. In contrast to the first period of the war (March to December 1969), which was characterized by the preference accorded political over military considerations, Israel now chose to put military considerations before political ones. This choice was mainly the outcome of the strategic gains secured earlier. The air superiority that Israel had assured itself in its destruction of the Egyptian air defense system—an operation that was, in fact, the first indication of the priority of military considerations—provided Israel with an opportunity that was both militarily and politically unique. The decision to send bombers deep into Egyptian territory was intended to exploit Israel's strategic superiority and translate the military gains into political ones. It was thought that the strategic superiority asserted by Israel at the end of 1969 would enable it to "teach the Egyptians a lesson" for having started the War of Attrition and would also bring the war to an end by deciding the outcome both militarily and politically. It also appeared to be an opportunity to prevent the imposition of a political settlement not to Israel's liking.[1]

When military calculations became dominant, the political constraints that had characterized Israel's behavior in the first stage of the war were *ipso facto* less weighty and readiness to incur risks in the political sphere rose sharply.[2] The decision to bomb Egypt "in depth" was reached by stages. The proposal originally came from the military command. Ezer Weizmann, Head of the General Staff Operation Division, brought the proposal forward as early as September 1969. The considerations he advanced were basically military ones, i.e., the poor results of previous escalatory measures were due to the limited Israeli Air Force input. Weizmann believed that the effectiveness of the IAF as a means for deciding the war was a function of more significant escalation. The military command proposed three alternatives: to initiate a large-scale land operation and to capture the western shore of the canal, especially between Qantara and Ismailia; to initiate a limited operation and to capture the area between Qantara and Port Said; or alternatively, to step up air raids in scale and in depth, i.e., to continue to rely on the air force as the main arm of the fighting but to change from a limited offensive strategy to a less limited offensive strategy. The first two alternatives were rejected in the light of the following evaluations: (a) the superpowers' political constraints, (b) no operational possibility for a large-scale land offensive because of lack of military means for this purpose (at that time the IDF had no bridges for a canal crossing), (c) probable losses in a canal crossing estimated at over a thousand, (d) insecurity that the operation would reach its objectives. The third alternative, IAF raids deep inside Egypt, was agreed to be less escalatory, in view of the political constraints and in view of operational possibility and projected losses.[3]

The Operation Division at the military command worked out three more alternative plans for in-depth raids in Egypt. The first alternative was a full operation of the IAF against military and economic targets until the political and military objectives were achieved, regardless of time limitations. The second alternative was full operation of the IAF against military and economic targets for a limited time (a few weeks) and according to well-defined stages, until the political and military objectives were achieved. The third alternative was partial operation of the IAF against a limited selection of military targets according to sub-sequent military and political developments without any former planning. The first two alternatives were rejected by the military command before they were suggested to the government because of political and military constraints (i.e., the IAF could not at-tempt a prolonged and massive operation). The third alternative was adopted by the military command and was submitted for consideration by the government.[4]

In the last months of 1969, when the army had worked out definite plans for in-depth bombing in Egypt, the proposal was discussed on the political level as well, but it was never really given proper consideration by the government as a whole or by the Ministerial Defense Committee. Discussion of the idea in government circles was postponed until after the elections to the Knesset that were due to take place at the end of October 1969. The postponement was in itself an indication that the govern-ment took a very serious view of the escalatory implications of the proposal and chose to pass the responsibility for the decision on to the new government that would be formed after the elec-tions. It was not only a question of avoiding responsibility; to make a decision at this point would have meant tying the hands of the new government as well. Serious discussion of the pro-posal began after the formation of the new government of "na-tional union" in December 1969.[5]

The new government was, in fact, composed of the same ele-ments as the one that had preceded the elections, but the Knesset elections gave formal, democratic legitimization to a government that had been set up under the pressures of the circumstances surrounding the Six-Day War. The proposal to bomb deep inside Egypt was raised in the new government on account of the same military considerations that had led Ezer Weizmann to make the proposal in September 1969. It seemed clear that limited Israeli Air Force raids had not been sufficient to get the Egyptians to honor the cease-fire. It was believed in Israel that Abdel Nasser and the greater part of the Egyptian population were not aware of what was happening at the front, nor of the turning point reached as a result of the destruction of the Egyptian air defense system. In spite of the destruction of the canal cities and the tremendous exodus of some 750,000 refugees to inner Egypt, as well as the heavy blows dealt the Egyptian forces on the canal, the Egyptian leadership showed no signs of readiness for a cease-fire and/or any significant moderation of belligerency.[6] The rise in Egyptian belligerent activity on the canal in October and December 1969 despite the destruction of the Egyptian antiaircraft system, together with the Egyptian rejection of the Rogers Plan, indicated that the Egyptians were determined to go on with the war.[7]

The Israeli policy makers reached the conclusion that the best way to put an end to the war and secure an acceptable political settlement was to make Israel's strategic superiority really felt—to expand military action, in other words. Since a large-scale or limited land operation had to be turned down because of its escalatory implications, IAF raids deep inside Egypt were agreed on as a less escalatory option.[8] The arrival of the Phantom aircraft from September 1969 on played its part since the Phantoms made the decision operatively feasible.[9]

Israel's Political Aims

Israel's political aims in deciding on in-depth air raids were, to get the Egyptians to end the War of Attrition by threatening to weaken or overthrow Nasser's regime, and to prevent the imposition of a political solution against Israel's wishes. Israel was opposed to the Rogers Plan, but the fact that the USSR and Egypt rejected it was interpreted by Israel as pressure on the United States to impose a political solution that would be better than the Rogers Plan from the Egyptian viewpoint. Israel sought a swift military decision in the War of Attrition simply because protracted war threatened the strategic stability of the region. If the criterion for reaping political gains was military success, then an Israeli decision for the protracted War of Attrition would free the United States from the need to give way to Soviet-Egyptian pressure and impose a political solution in line with Egyptian interests.

Behind the Israeli decision on in-depth raids there was also the assumption that Nasser was a main factor in the continuation of the Arab-Israeli conflict. Hence his overthrow (or even his being weakened) would be likely to open the way to political settlements with the Arab States and with Egypt in the first place. This view marked a revolution in Israeli thinking on the nature of the Egyptian-Israeli conflict since it had long been believed, at least up until the Six-Day War, that Nasser was the only leader capable of reaching a political settlement with Israel. What altered the Israeli view was Nasser's behavior during the critical period preceding and leading up to the Six-Day War and during the period from the end of the Six-Day War until the War of Attrition. The continued existence of the Nasser regime was now seen as frustrating any possibility of a peaceable settlement between Israel and the Arab States. For the first time in the annals of armed confrontation between Israel and the Arab States, Israel aimed at threatening the opponent's regime as a means of ending the conflict and not at total destruction of the enemy forces.

The aftermath of the Six-Day War should have given the Israeli government a clear indication of Nasser's standing, but the Israeli leadership failed to accurately evaluate the staying power of the Nasser regime. The Israeli leadership thought that in order to threaten the overthrow or the weakening of the Nasser regime, it was necessary to carry the war into Egypt. It was assumed that the difference between a war like the Six-Day War, fought in the Sinai far from Egyptian population centers and a war taking place near Egyptian civilians' homes was very considerable. In-depth raids were seen by the Israeli leadership as an effective way of showing the Egyptian public something of the serious results that could be brought about by continuing the war initiated by Nasser. The raids were intended to sow distrust between the Egyptian people and Nasser. For the first time the Egyptian public would see with its own eyes that for years Nasser had been leading them to their ruin. It was hoped that the Egyptian people would try to find a way out of the sufferings of the War of Attrition and the continuation of the Arab-Israeli conflict by overthrowing or weakening Nasser's regime. The Israeli leadership saw a positive coordination between their exerting increased pressure by means of painful blows dealt inside Egypt, and Egypt's showing increased readiness to end the war.[10]

The first indications of this train of thought are found in what Moshe Dayan said in mid-1968: "If we want to and if we have to, we can bring them down through the civilian population. . . . The distance to Cairo today is 100 kilometers and that puts it within easy reach. Our being in the Sinai enables us if need be *to strike terror into the hearts of the Arabs of the cities. This means that if we want to, we can break the Arab will to fight.*"[11]

In the public pronouncements of Israeli policy makers the stress was, however, on the military importance of the in-depth raids, in order to minimize their escalatory significance from the political viewpoint as much as possible.[12] In their various public utterances, Israeli policy makers denied that the in-depth raids were intended to bring down the Nasser regime (mainly because of the escalatory implication of this aim), but nevertheless they did not hide their hope that this is what would, in fact, happen. They explicitly stressed that if the raids indirectly achieved this goal they would not regret it, since Nasser's regime was the worst possible for Israel. The following list presents the main pronouncements by Israel's policy makers on the relation between the in-depth raids and the overthrow of Nasser.

(1) Abba Eban, Foreign Minister (in *Ha'aretz*, January 2, 1970):

Our actions are carried out on the basis of calculations of Israel's security, and we do not fix any political goal with respect to its effect upon the [Egyptian] regime. An Egyptian failure in the security sphere would necessarily result in undermining faith in the Egyptian regime. After the raids at the end of September 1969, we heard of a fairly strong shakeup of the regime. In the West people tend to say that Nasser is a negative figure, but there is no guarantee that whoever would take his place would be any better or more convenient from Israel's point of view. All the same, I am of the opinion that the possibility of peace with Egypt will be improved if the Egyptian people are blessed with a different regime. It is my belief that if Nasser changes his tune and comes forward to negotiate with us, we shall of course enter into negotiations with him, but from the point of view of history and common sense, the likelier assumption is that it would be easier for a different regime to take such a step. Nasser has been burdened with this inheritance of war for the last twenty years, but more especially since 1967. Peace will require a process of [the Arabs'] confessing [their] sins—something not very often done by weak Arab regimes. A new regime would be free, in spite of criticism from its predecessor, to seek a way out of the dilemma it is caught in. As for myself, from the Israeli point of view, I do not accept the expression, "worse than Nasser." He is utilizing the whole of his hostile capabilities against Israel, and if this is a limited one, it is simply because his power is limited. If there is a new regime, Egypt will have less influence in the Arab world and this will represent an improvement with regard to us.

(This was said before the raids, but it shows that the subject was raised in the course of reaching decisions.)

(2) Moshe Dayan, Defense Minister (Government Press Office, January 13, 1970):

The in-depth raids hurt the regime . . . but this development is a side effect and not the goal.

(3) Golda Meir, Prime Minister (in Davar, January 16, 1970):

We shall not go into mourning if Nasser falls, but our Air Force operations are not intended to achieve this purpose. But if it also brings about a change of government in Egypt, we shan't waste any tears over it, but it's not a political aim of ours, and I don't know if Nasser's successor will be any better than he is, but I don't think he can be much worse. And that also holds good for Egypt. He's the one who's wrecked his people and its land. His influence in the Arab world is a threat to peace.

(4) Golda Meir, Prime Minister (in the *Jerusalem Post,* January 18, 1970):

I would not waste any tears if Abdel Nasser were knocked out of power. However, the deep penetration raids were not aimed at pushing him out of power, but at cutting him down to size. The proximity of the raids to Cairo has driven home the truth not only to Abdel Nasser, but to the entire Egyptian people, who have to know in what direction their leader is dragging them!

(5) Abba Eban, Foreign Minister (to Israel Broadcasting Authority [*IBA*], in *Daily Report* [*DR*], January 20, 1970):

The Egyptian people itself has to decide about the regime as well as the chances of achieving peace. . . . If a new Egyptian regime were established, there would be a 50 percent chance [for peace] as compared to zero now.

(6) Israel Galili, Minister Without Portfolio (in *Davar,* January 23, 1970):

No successor to Abdel Nasser could be any worse a ruler than he is.

(7) Moshe Dayan, Defense Minister (Government Press Office, to IBA January 28, 1970; in *DR,* January 29, 1970):

. . . not to cause the downfall of Abdel Nasser, but rather to bring the truth about the regime in Egypt to the Egyptian people, to speak to them directly, to tell them, "Listen, people of Egypt, your leaders are not acting for your good. What they say about your chances of destroying Israel is not true."

(8) Golda Meir, Prime Minister (in *Ha'aretz,* March 2, 1970):

The attacks by our Air Force deep inside Egypt are not intended to reach the Egyptian capital or to bring down Nasser's regime. It is not we who are responsible for his being Egypt's ruler and we have not taken it on ourselves to overthrow him. That is the task of the Egyptian people. I can't say we shall weep over it if he does fall.

(9) Golda Meir, Prime Minister (in *Ha'aretz,* March 17, 1970):

It is not our purpose to overthrow Nasser. It isn't we who elected him president.

(10) Haim Bar-Lev, Chief of Staff (in *Davar*, May 13, 1970):

It is not our purpose to change the Arab regime.

(This was said after the in-depth raids had stopped.)

(11) Golda Meir, Prime Minister (in *Bamahaneh*, June 5, 1970):

What would happen if Nasser were to disappear? It couldn't be worse. I think things couldn't be worse for Egypt. Nasser is bad for his own people in the first place, but that's their business. And what could be worse for us than someone who is making war on us all the time? At all events, it's not a problem that should worry us because it isn't we who declared war on Egypt and we aren't continuing the war in order to get rid of Nasser. But if somebody wants us not to defend ourselves with all the strength we have because if we do, heaven forbid, then Nasser is liable to fall—well, that's something we can't accept. But apart from that, we haven't done a thing against Nasser.

(This was said after the in-depth raids had stopped.)

(12) Abba Eban, Foreign Minister (in *Ha'aretz*, June 5, 1970):

I said I should not weep if Nasser fell. But that is not our task nor the purpose we are fighting for. The government never adopted a doctrine of overthrowing Nasser by Israeli military pressure, and now even less so.

(This was said after the in-depth raids had stopped.)

Israeli Evaluation of External Constraints

The Israeli government judged from the start that its decision to carry out in-depth air raids was escalatory, both strategically and politically, since such raids went beyond the narrow limits of the politico-strategic relations between Israel and Egypt. It was necessary to examine the connection between in-depth raids and the political and strategic interests of the superpowers in the region. Evaluating the superpowers' possible reactions was part of the process of deciding whether or not to carry out the raids. The decision had been reached that in-depth raids could effect a sub-

stantial change in politico-strategic relations between Israel and
Egypt, but adequate means were not available for reaching a
more general evaluation of the politico-strategic interaction between the environment of the Arab-Israeli conflict and that of the
inter-superpower conflict. As a result, Israeli policy makers
failed to reach a reasoned evaluation of the prospective reactions
of the two superpowers to the in-depth raids.[13]

The Soviet Attitude
The key question in the process of reaching the decision was
how the Soviet Union would react to the Israeli attempt to bring
about the collapse of the Nasser regime or to weaken it to a
marked degree. In contrast to the close diplomatic ties between
Israel and the United States, which made it far easier to
thoroughly clarify the American attitude (though this was not
done), the absence of diplomatic ties between Israel and the Soviet Union made it very difficult to reach a reasoned evaluation
of the Soviet attitude. The government lacked adequate means
for tackling this question. In his research on the Israeli security
concept, Dan Horowitz writes: "The national security conception
was not adequate to provide a proper way of framing strategy in
face of the threat of Soviet intervention. The Israeli security conception was evolved in the context of the Arab-Israeli conflict,
which made it reasonably possible to translate strategic problems
directly into military terms."[14]

It was, in fact, two leading ministers in the government,
Moshe Dayan and Yigal Allon, who evaluated the Soviet attitude
in the light of their individual sets of beliefs and hopes. The difference in outlook of the two men in their evaluation of the Soviet attitude centered around the main question: is the Soviet
Union liable to intervene directly in the Arab-Israeli conflict by
military means, and if so, in what circumstances will she intervene? The two men's views on this subject were already known
long before the proposal to carry out in-depth raids. Vice-Premier
Yigal Allon was inclined to view the prospect of Soviet military
intervention in the Arab-Israeli conflict as highly unlikely, given
certain considerations. First, the Soviet Union must be apprehensive lest her intervention develop into global confrontation with

the United States. Second, the Soviet Union must have accurate information on Israel's strength and must be aware that Israel would be prepared to go on fighting even in the event of Soviet intervention. Third, since the end of World War II the Soviet Union had been careful not to get directly involved in any war or to intervene militarily anywhere (except inside the Communist bloc: Hungary, 1956; Czechoslovakia, 1968). Fourth, if the Soviet Union were to take upon itself the main burden of the war, then it would have to send an armed expeditionary force to the Middle East region not much smaller than the American expeditionary force in Vietnam; this would simply be inconceivable.[15]

Despite all these considerations, Yigal Allon thought that Israel should nevertheless not take a lighthearted view of the Soviet presence in the Middle East and should refrain from providing a solid pretext for partial Soviet intervention. Israel should not be deterred from utilizing any means of defense it found necessary, but all the same, in planning future operations the Soviet factor should be taken into account among the overall considerations.[16] In-depth raids were not adjudged by Yigal Allon as creating a situation in which the Soviets were liable to intervene. He thought the Soviet factor important in the whole set of calculations bound up with the plan for the raids, but not one that should deter Israel from utilizing the opportunity now open to her to undermine or overthrow the Egyptian regime.[17]

From the outset, Defense Minister Moshe Dayan presented a very cautious position regarding the Soviets. During the Six-Day War he had expressed serious apprehensions of Soviet intervention in the fighting. His hesitations over the conquest of the Suez and the Golan Heights were connected with his views on the dangers of an eventual confrontation with the Soviet Union. About everything concerning the Soviet attitude, Dayan showed a deep caution that at times seemed to the other policy makers almost mystical.[18] Dayan believed direct military intervention by the USSR in the Arab-Israeli conflict far more likely than it seemed to Yigal Allon. Although the USSR was not formally allied with Egypt and not under any explicit obligations toward her, nevertheless the structure of Soviet-Egyptian relations and the nature of Soviet interests in the Middle East (mainly in

Egypt) were such that the possibility might well arise that "if it wants to, when it wants to, and insofar as it wants to, [the Soviet Union] will contend that it is under an obligation to come to the aid [of Egypt]." [19] Dayan said that repeatedly. "Thus neither is there any possibility of contending with any certainty that the USSR will not in any situation or in any circumstances send military forces into action against Israel, whether directly or indirectly." [20] He thought the Soviet Union would indeed be liable to intervene in a situation where Israel tried to overthrow Nasser's regime or inflict a crushing new defeat on him. Given the Soviet investment in Egypt, with that country the pivot of Soviet involvement in the Middle East, the USSR could not acquiesce in attempts to overthrow Nasser. [21] Dayan rejected Yigal Allon's argument that the USSR was disinclined to intervene except in countries with which it had a continuous land link and which were members of the Warsaw Pact. The historic fact that the Soviet Union had not so far intervened overseas was not necessarily proof that she would not do so in the future. Furthermore, the contention that the USSR lacked the technical capability to intervene in the Middle East was devoid of all foundation. For a country the size of the USSR, said Dayan, there are no technical problems, only political ones. If the Soviet Union were to decide to intervene, it would basically be a political decision. Technical considerations would be no obstacle. [22]

In Dayan's opinion, the Soviet decision had already been made to intervene directly in certain circumstances; the question was whether the in-depth raids would turn this possibility into a reality. Dayan thought that if the aim of the raids were to overthrow Nasser, then they would of necessity accelerate the Soviet decision to intervene directly in order to prevent his fall. [23] Nonetheless, Dayan supported the decision to carry out the in-depth air raids. Like everyone else in the government, Dayan wanted to utilize the military option as long as it was available, i.e., to realize strategic gains up to the point of Soviet military intervention. [24]

Where did the Prime Minister stand on this key issue? In an interview with the *Ha'aretz* correspondent, Amos Elon, in July 1970, Golda Meir contended that the possibility that in-depth raids "might bring in the Russians" did not seem very real to the government. This feeling was based on hearing "opinions from all the responsible factors. . . . All information was weighed carefully." [25] The "responsible factors" she referred to were the military intelligence people. They judged that, given the limited nature of the in-depth raids, these would not be enough to produce real military intervention in the fighting by the USSR. Even if there were intervention, it would be limited in principle and would not go so far as to endanger the existence of the state of Israel. In reaching the decision to carry out the raids, this evaluation by military intelligence was of importance in reducing the pressure of the constraints related to the Soviet Union. Mrs. Meir declared in her interview: "Had we known that this could help the Russians to reach the canal region, would we have considered such a possibility? The answer is that we would have considered it, but it never occurred to anyone then. . . ." From this it would seem that Mrs. Meir accepted the optimistic view that in-depth air raids would not lead to Soviet intervention in the war. [26] It emerges in her memoirs, in any event, that the government did realize that the raids might bring about Soviet involvement, [27] but the decision was weighed in the context of the Arab-Israeli conflict and not in the Israeli-Soviet context nor on the plane of the superpower conflict.

The concept of "we and the Egyptians" and not "we and the Russians" was based on the judgment that it was possible to make real military and political gains in the Egyptian-Israeli context. The belief that the Soviets would not intervene even if Abdel Nasser fell or if his regime were undermined was more in the nature of wishful thinking than a reasoned evaluation of the complex relationship between Egypt and the USSR, or of Soviet interests in the Middle East in general and in Egypt in particular. The government was inclined to think that Israel could take the risk of carrying out the in-depth raids. Even if these provided a sufficient pretext for Soviet military intervention, the severe limitations the Soviet Union would face in reaching a decision to intervene were likely to considerably reduce the danger of their doing so effectively. What the government failed to realize was that a very limited Soviet military intervention would be enough to insure the continued existence of the Egyptian regime and to neutralize the real effects of the raids.

The U.S. Attitude

In the process of reaching the decision to carry out the in-depth raids, what very largely made the decision possible was the Israeli evaluation that the United States was not opposed to them, an evaluation based on the judgment of the Israeli Ambassador to the States, Yitzhak Rabin.[28] Rabin thought that the United States would not oppose the raids and might even give them silent support. He believed that an identity of interests had been created between the United States and Israel on their attitudes about the Nasser regime, and he therefore advocated exploiting this identity of interests in order to utilize the possibility of weakening or overthrowing that regime. These opinions were based on three assumptions:

First, the Americans were concerned about the future of their interests in the Middle East and especially in the pro-American Arab States, Jordan and Saudi Arabia, as a result of Nasser's strengthened position in the Arab world. They thought the Egyptian ruler had regained much of the prestige lost in the Six-Day War. The overthrow of the royal regime in Libya in September 1969 and the fact that Nasser had succeeded in convening the Arab summit conference in Rabat (even though he did not win its support) were seen as clear indications of his resurgent political strength in the Arab world. The interaction between the need to secure American interests in the Middle East and recognition of Nasser's standing in the Arab world, an interaction that had characterized the American attitude at the end of the 1950s and in the early 1960s, was seen by Rabin as still holding good at the beginning of the 1970s.

Second, the Americans were concerned over the increased Soviet involvement in the Middle East and they saw Nasser as more responsible than anyone else. A change of the Nasser regime could help limit this involvement.[29]

Third, during the early stages of the War of Attrition, the Americans had not expressed any objection to Israeli military action on the Egyptian front, including the destruction of the Egyptian air defense system, in contrast to the concern displayed by them over Israeli military action against Jordan and Lebanon. If the Americans did not actually encourage escalation against Egypt, they did not explicitly oppose it either.[30] The U.S. agreement to supply Phantom aircraft to Israel was itself an additional indication. If the Americans had in fact opposed Israel's military activity in the Egyptian sector, they would not have supplied military means such as the Phantoms.

In sum, Rabin's view was that in these circumstances of identity of interests with the United States, Israel should take advantage of the available option. He relied on impressions gained in conversations with persons in the top echelon during his stay in Washington.[31] He believed that the American need to decrease the threats to their interests in the Middle East was met in the short run by making Israel the defender of American interests in the region. But was this desirable from the American point of view? It would certainly increase American isolation in the Arab world and it was doubtful whether the United States was interested in this in the long run. Moreover, the Americans were really more concerned about the danger of confrontation with the Soviet Union, given the rising escalation in the Middle East, than about Nasser's renewed strength in the Arab world. Israeli efforts to overthrow or weaken Nasser were not only unlikely to decrease the threat to United States interests in the Middle East, but were even calculated to increase it since the Soviets would extend their involvement in Egypt and the Middle East in order to prevent the weakening or overthrow of the Nasser regime which would increase the danger of superpower confrontation.

Rabin's views on the lack of United States opposition to in-depth raids which he expounded to the government during his visit to the country on December 21, 1969 certainly influenced the decision to carry out the raids.[32] Even if Rabin had correctly evaluated short-term U.S. policy, the Israeli government ought to have given thought to possible changes in conditions that might lead the United States to stop supporting the raids. Would the Americans be prepared to support them in the event of direct Soviet military intervention? Would they intervene to neutralize the prospective dangers to Israel from Soviet intervention? These were the questions that were later seen to be crucially important, but it was not properly gone into in the course of reaching the decision on the in-depth raids. The Israeli policy makers in fact disregarded superpower relationships and failed any thorough evaluation, either on the global plane or on the Middle Eastern plane, or else they failed to understand them. The doubts raised by Moshe Dayan at the end of 1967 regarding U.S. support of Israel in case of Soviet intervention in the war had lessened very considerably by January 1970.[33] There was no formal or general U.S. statement to Israel regarding Soviet military intervention, but Israeli policy makers thought this support was more certain than it really was. It must be inferred that Rabin's opinion regarding the American attitude, together with the evaluation that real gains could be secured by in-depth bombing, facilitated these optimistic conclusions.

The Decision Is Carried Out

The Israeli Air Force raids began on January 7 and continued until April 13, 1970. Generally speaking, two main phases can be distinguished by the criterion of the areas hit and the targets in those areas. In the first phase (January–February), the IAF raids focused near Egypt's main cities—Cairo, Ismailia, Inshāṣ, and Ḥilwān; the targets were mainly large military camps. In the second phase (March–April), the raids focused on the Nile Delta; the main targets were SA-2 missile sites and radar stations (see table 5.1). Most of the raids (27 out of 36) were carried out in January and February. The sharp drop in the number of raids in March and April and their concentration on different areas and targets were almost certainly due to the beginning of direct Soviet military intervention. The setting up of SA-3 missile sites manned by Soviet personnel near Egypt's cities, which began in the second half of March, led to a change in the areas attacked from army camps near the large cities to SA-2 missile sites and radar installations in the Nile Delta.

Egyptian Perception of the Israeli Strategy

The top echelon in Egypt had no difficulty summing up the political and military significance of the new Israeli strategy. They saw the in-depth air raids as intended not only to end the War of Attrition, but also as leading to a strategic and political solution of the prolonged crisis in Egyptian-Israeli relations. The Egyptian leadership judged that Israel intended to utilize its strategic superiority in order to impose a political solution that would represent fundamental Israeli interests, i.e., perpetuate the cease-fire lines reached after the Six-Day War by legitimizing them in a political settlement. The Egyptians thought the Israelis intended to achieve this basic aim by overthrowing the Nasser regime. Nasser's various pronouncements and Heikal's articles in *Al-Ahrām* explained the new Israeli aims behind the strategy of in-depth raids. In an interview in April 1970, Nasser said: "What the Israelis and the protégés of the West are doing . . . is driving us to despair until the Arabs give me up and the people of Egypt overthrow me."[34]

In the same vein, Heikal pointed to the connection between a collapse of the Nasser regime and Israel's success in imposing a political settlement: "Everyone in Israel is constantly saying that Nasser must go and soon, and this will be the first step to a solution that will satisfy Israel."[35] The Israeli raids, in Heikal's view, were intended to humiliate Nasser and show his regime to be powerless in the face of Israeli might. In this way Israel hoped to cause a split between Nasser and the Egyptian people and prepare the way for his overthrow.[36]

The Egyptians analyzed the strategy of the in-depth air raids as an Israeli attempt to use an apparently limited military strategy—air attrition—in order to achieve less limited aims. In view of the military and political constraints operating against developing a total strategy, they concluded that Israel preferred a military escalation that at least appeared to be limited.[37] In fact, the in-depth raids constituted a serious escalation of the war from both the military and political viewpoints. From the military viewpoint, the Israeli extension of the front of belligerency and

Table 5.1 Deep Penetration Air Raids by the Israeli Air Force in 1970

1970	Place	Proximity to Major Towns	Nature of Target *
Jan. 7	Inshāṣ	30 km. NE of Cairo	Military camps
	Tall al-Kabīr	50 km. W of Ismailia	Large camps, incl. hq. of Suez Canal front
	Dahshūr	13 km. SW of Ḥilwān	EAF stores
Jan. 13	Tall al-Kabīr	50 km. W of Ismailia	Large camps, incl. hq. of Suez Canal front
	Khankā	20 km. NE of Cairo	Military camps, incl. EAF stores
Jan. 16	Area of Suez-Cairo Road		Military camps
Jan. 18	Huckstep	20 km. E of Cairo	Major supply bases
	Jabal Ḥawf	5 km. N of Ḥilwān	Military bases, including equipment and ammunition stores
Jan. 23	Huckstep	20 km. E of Cairo	Major supply bases
	Ḥilwān Camps	4 km. N of Ḥilwān	Military camps
Jan. 28	Ma'ādī	10 km. S of Cairo	Military camps
	Dahshūr	13 km. SW of Ḥilwān	EAF stores
Feb. 2	Balṭīm	NE delta region	Military camps
	Manqabād	8 km. W of Asyūṭ	Military camps and hq.
Feb. 6	Janadla	15 km. S of Asyūṭ	Military camps, incl. ammunition dumps
	Tall al-Kabīr	50 km. W of Ismailia	camps inclu. hq. of Suez Canal front
Feb. 8	Inshāṣ	30 km. NE of Cairo	Military camps
	Ḥilwān Camp	4 km. N of Ḥilwān	Military camps
Feb. 12	Khankā	20 km. NE of Cairo	Military camps including EAF stores
	Dahshūr	13 km. SW of Ḥilwān	EAF stores
	Jabal 'Uwaybid	N of Suez-Cairo Road	Radar station
Feb. 17	Dahshūr	13 km. SW of Ḥilwān	SA-2 missile sites
	Ḥilwān Camps	10 km. SE of Ḥilwān	SA-2 missile sites
Feb. 26	Cairo-West Air Base	30 km. W of Cairo	SA-2 missile sites
	Duḥmays	NE delta region	SA-2 missile sites
Mar. 6	Damyāṭ	N delta region	Radar station
Mar. 12	Jabal 'Uwaybid	N of Suez-Cairo Road	Radar station
Mar. 13	Manṣūra	NE delta region	SA-2 missile site
Mar. 23	Balṭīm	NE delta region	Radar station
Mar. 31	Manṣūra	NE delta region	SA-2 missile site
Apr. 3	Manṣūra	NE delta region	SA-2 missile site
Apr. 8	Ṣāliḥiyya	30 km. W of Qanṭara	Unspecified military targets

1970	Place	Proximity to Major Towns	Nature of Target *
Apr. 13	Not given	30 km. E of Ḥilwān	Unspecified military targets
	Manzila	NE delta region	Unspecified military targets

SOURCE: MER (1969–70), p. 148.
  * According to Israeli and western sources.

the inclusion among the targets of not purely military ones shifted the front from the Gulf of Suez and the Red Sea to deep inside Egyptian territory and turned the whole of Egypt into a battlefield. The Israeli escalation was not total only to the extent that it was not meant to wipe out the Egyptian armed forces, but instead to break Egypt's will to fight by bringing the war home to Egypt itself.

The new Israeli strategy was also sometimes called "psychological strategy" or "psychological warfare." It was seen by the Egyptians as intended to upset the preparations for a large operation against Israel by attacking the morale of the Egyptian army and by convincing the Egyptian masses (after failing to convince the political leadership) that military confrontation with Israel was very damaging and dangerous, not only on the front but also within the country.[38] The real effect of the raids was meant to be not military but psychological—to arouse fears and apprehensions and implant a lack of faith in the capacity of the armed forces, and moreover to sow distrust and dissension between the political leadership and the public.[39]

The Egyptian leadership believed that the strategy of the in-depth raids had been worked out before its execution in cooperation with the Americans and had received their concurrence. In their view, there were two main reasons for the U.S. support of the Israeli raids. First, the United States feared weakening its position in the region as a result of the efforts to promote inter-Arab unity, as manifested in the Arab summit meeting in Rabat at the end of 1969 and in the Egyptian-Libyan-Sudan rapprochement. By intensified air raids, Egypt thought the United States hoped to weaken Egypt's position in the Arab world and thereby reduce the danger of an anti-American bloc in the region,[40] and to force Egypt to accept the Rogers Plan (which Egypt had rejected) or a political settlement along the lines of the Rogers Plan, or to reestablish the cease-fire agreement.[41] All the same, the Egyptians did not say outright that the Americans wanted Nasser overthrown because the United States saw him as an obstacle to the expansion of American interests in the region.[42]

According to Heikal, there was full coordination between Israel and America on the escalation process behind the in-depth raids, even to the point of fixing the areas and the targets raided.[43] The practical indication for American support for the raids was seen in the continued supply of planes to Israel, the main operational arm: "The United States gave its approval for Israel's use of the Phantoms for the raids deep inside Egypt. . . . Israel could not have acted without the clear consent of the Americans, since if the United States wanted to bring pressure to bear on Israel regarding the use of the Phantoms against Egypt . . . it would have stopped the permit to export."[44] Moreover, since Israel and Egypt were fighting a war of attrition, it was obvious that the supply of Phantom planes was directed against Egypt.[45] Heikal even asserted that there was agreement between Israel and the United States on the length of time the raids would continue. Israel promised the United States to stop the in-depth raids within a definite length of time, on the assumption that the aims of both Israel and the United States in carrying out the raids would have been achieved by then.[46]

The Egyptian Decision to Invoke Direct Soviet Military Intervention

Egypt meant to utilize the threat of direct Soviet military intervention in the fighting as the basis of its attrition strategy, and even to put the threat into effect to neutralize situations where Israel might decide to extend the war. A situation of this kind developed gradually. When Israel sent its air force into the fighting and especially when it began to destroy the Egyptian air defense system, it became clear to the Egyptian leadership that Egypt was incapable of confronting Israeli strategic superiority and that they would soon have to turn to the USSR with an urgent call for help.

The destruction of the Egyptian air defense system along the canal left the Egyptian leadership with three possible courses: to stop the war, to accept the Rogers Plan, or to go on with the War of Attrition. The first course was rejected outright; it would have meant going back to the starting point, to the situation as it was before the beginning of the war. The second course was also rejected as a way of ending the war; though the Rogers Plan was closer to the Egyptian peace conditions than to those of Israel, it was rejected precisely because of Egypt's inferior strategic position. To accept the plan was seen by the Egyptian leadership as surrender to an imposed political settlement. In these circumstances, the third course was in fact the only way. But the decision to go on with the war in the face of Israel's strategic superiority was suicidal. In order to be able to continue the war, Egypt had to find a way to neutralize Israel's superiority. For this it needed direct, even if limited, Soviet intervention in the fighting to prevent Israel from reaping the fruits of her strategic achievements.

On December 9, 1969, Nasser sent a delegation to Moscow to try to secure concrete Soviet assistance. The delegation was headed by Anwar Sadat, head of the Egyptian National Assembly (and Vice President of Egypt from December 20, 1969). The other members were Maḥmud Riyāḍ, the Foreign Minister, and Muḥammad Fawzī, the Minister of Defense. The delegation's aim was to obtain deliveries of more sophisticated arms, mainly the improved MIG-21 (MIG-21J), in order to challenge the Israeli Phantoms. The delegation's efforts did not succeed; even though the Russians showed understanding of Egypt's military needs, they refused to make any real commitments.[47]

The Israeli Air Force in-depth raids that began on January 7, 1970, led to the final Egyptian decision to invoke direct Soviet intervention in the War of Attrition. It was now clear to the leadership that Israel was preparing to translate its strategic achievements into political ones. In the very first phase of the in-depth

raids, Nasser decided to visit Moscow himself, in spite of being
ill, and this sufficiently indicates how deeply apprehensive he
was about these raids, which he believed were intended to bring
about the collapse of his regime.[48]

Nasser's secret visit to Moscow took place on January 22; he
was accompanied by Defense Minister Fawzī and Information
Minister Heikal.[49] Details concerning the aims of Nasser's jour-
ney to Moscow and its results have long been public knowledge.
In his book The Road to Ramadan, Heikal largely confirms what
was already known. Nasser's immediate aims were to bring
about an easing of the Israeli pressure on Egypt and to put a stop
to the in-depth raids by setting up a more sophisticated Egyptian
antiaircraft defense system than the one that had existed previously.[50] The previous network, based mainly on SA-2 missiles,
had proved ineffective in neutralizing the IAF.[51] Nasser demanded that the Soviets supply Egypt with a new missile system
of the SA-3 type, judged capable of standing up well to Israel's
Phantoms and Skyhawks. By demanding SA-3 missiles, Nasser
intended to bring about direct Soviet military intervention in the
War of Attrition; since Egyptian personnel trained to operate the
SA-2 missiles were not capable of operating the new missile system, there was really no point in getting SA-3 missiles without
Soviet teams to operate them.[52] But Nasser's demand for Soviet
teams was not based solely on technical grounds; it can be assumed that he was fully aware of the great political importance
of having Soviet personnel operate the missiles. The SA-3 missile
system was certainly meant up to a point to serve as a military
deterrent to the IAF (fear of aircraft losses), but it would also
have the additional effect of political deterrence. Israel would be
faced with a very serious political situation and would have to
decide whether to risk military confrontation with the Soviet
Union.

The Egyptian demands turned out to have even more serious
implications. According to Heikal, Soviet army personnel,
headed by Defense Minister Grechko, made it clear that it was
not only a question of the teams to operate the missiles, but that
these were only one link in the chain of a complex defense system that also needed planes manned by Soviet airmen. Since

Nasser was demanding immediate air defense, this meant that besides the SA-3 missiles and the Soviet teams to operate them, the USSR would have to lend Egypt Air Force flights. Involvement of this type seemed sufficiently serious to the Soviet policy makers; their first response was hesitant and negative.[53] It can be assumed that from the outset Nasser appreciated the serious difficulties with which he confronted the USSR when he demanded a sophisticated air defense system. In order to gain his ends he had to put the Russians in a dilemma; they had to accept the political and military risks involved in satisfying his demand for direct Soviet military intervention in the fighting or face the danger of witnessing the collapse of Nasser's regime and the establishment of a pro-Western regime in Egypt, with all that implied for Soviet interests in the Middle East. In this connection, Heikal quotes Nasser's warning to the Soviet leaders: "I shall go back to Egypt and I shall tell the people the truth. I shall tell them that the time has come for me to step down and hand over to a pro-American president. If I cannot save them somebody else will have to do it. That is my final word."[54]

Securing Soviet consent was in fact Egypt's real achievement in the War of Attrition. The Soviet response not only enabled Egypt to go on with the war and incur less risk in doing so, but also opened the way to securing the political settlement Egypt needed to counterbalance Israel's strategic superiority.[55]

The Israeli Strategy Proves Counterproductive

To judge the effectiveness of the strategy of in-depth air raids, one must consider two questions: Did Israel achieve its aim? and did the politico-strategic results that Israel secured by sending in the IAF serve its politico-strategic aims? The results of the in-depth raids were in fact the opposite of what the Israeli strategists had hoped to achieve. Not only did the raids fail to achieve Israel's aims; they produced results absolutely contrary to what had been Israel's politico-strategic aims ever since the Six-Day War. One of the main objectives behind the stragegy of in-depth raids was Nasser's overthrow, but not only was his regime not undermined, since the Six-Day War it had never been as secure as it became during the period of the raids. Nasser succeeded in exploiting the raids to reinforce Egyptian solidarity and strengthen popular identification with the regime.[56] He furthermore succeeded in exploiting them in order to get expanded Soviet military intervention—one of the main objectives behind the Egyptian political strategy of attrition, thus not only insuring the Egyptians against defeat, but also securing a certain strategic equilibrium and opening the way to an end to the war under better politico-strategic conditions for Egypt. Increased Soviet military involvement in Egypt and Soviet willingness to militarily intervene on Egypt's behalf was certainly in the sharpest possible opposition to Israel's strategic aims.

Israel now had to accept the U.S. cease-fire plan under conditions that were worse from her point of view. Israel's failure with the in-depth strategy was due to erroneous evaluation of conditions that could lead either to Soviet intervention in the war or even more to the mistaken view that the strategy would make it possible to decide the war, both strategically and politically. The in-depth raids were indeed an effective means of attrition against Egypt, but not a means to defeat her. To control the outcome of a war strategically, there have to be large-scale military operations with combined air and land action.[57] The military history of the last forty years proves that air raids deep inside enemy territory are not enough to decide the outcome of a war. The air raids on Germany in World War II and U.S. raids during the Vietnam War, though they were directed against enemy civilian-industrial targets, did not bring about a military decision. To strategically decide the war, the Allied armies in World War II had to win on land, even if their air raids did make a very considerable contribution. Ezer Weizmann upholds this argument. He writes,

Instead of seeing the Air Force as one of the components in the fighting and putting in land forces and armor on a significant scale in order to crush the Egyptian front with all its artillery and missiles, they entrusted the entire task to the Air Force alone and saw this as the sole solution, while the land forces continued to dig themselves in. What was needed was a land operation on a significant scale that would have a wide and deep impact.[58]

The in-depth raids did not even succeed in moderating Egyptian belligerent activity or reducing Israeli losses to any marked extent, two of the declared aims of the Israeli policy makers in the strategy of in-depth raids. A comparison of Egyptian belligerent activity in the peak months of the raids (January–February 1970) with that in the preceding months (November–December 1969) bears witness to this (see table 5.2). (The months March–April have not been included in this comparison, although the raids went on in those months because then the Soviet military intervention in the fighting altered the scale of Egyptian belligerent activity.) In the months January–February 1970, there were, it is true, signs of a drop in the scale of Egyptian belligerent activity (13 percent) in comparison with the months November–December 1969 (956 incidents of all kinds initiated by the Egyptians from November to December as against 829 from January to February), but this drop is hardly significant since the Egyptian activity was in fact more serious than before, i.e., there was more artillery fire and mortar shelling and consequently a lower proportion of light arms fire. From November to December 1969, there were 473 light arms fire incidents, while from January to February there were only 306, a reduction of 35 percent; but mortar shelling and artillery fire incidents increased from 454 between November and December to 482 between January and February, i.e., a rise of 6 percent. A comparison of the distribution of incidents in the whole period reveals an interesting picture: between November and December, light arms fire incidents constituted 50 percent of all the Egyptian-initiated belligerent activity; artillery and mortar incidents were only 47 percent (mortars 21 percent, artillery 26 percent). A substantial change took place from January to February; light arms fire incidents dropped to 37 percent of the total, while artillery and mortar fire incidents rose to 58 percent of the total Egyptian belligerent activity (25 percent mortars, 33 percent artillery).

Table 5.2 Egyptian Belligerent Activity, November 1969–February 1970

	Light Arms	Mortars	Artillery	Other	Total
Nov.–Dec. 1969					
Number	473	205	249	29	956
Percent	49.5	21.4	26.1	3.0	100
Jan.–Feb. 1970					
Number	306	207	275	41	829
Percent	36.9	25.0	33.2	4.9	100

SOURCE: IDF spokesman, MER (1969–70), p. 167.

The increased artillery and mortar fire activity between January and February 1970 (in spite of the Israeli in-depth raids) produced a significant rise in the number of Israeli losses in comparison with the period preceding the in-depth raids. Between January and February there were 87 Israeli casualties (dead and wounded) as a result of Egyptian-initiated belligerent activity, as compared with 73 between November and December 1969 (i.e., a rise of 19 percent). This significant rise was caused by the increase in the number of wounded (from 48 between November and December, to 64 between January and February), a rise of 33 percent, while the number killed fell from 25 between November and December to 23 between January and February. From the distribution of casualties between wounded and killed, it appears that a change for the better (see table 5.3) took place in January–February (26 percent of the casualties dying as against 34 percent in November–December).

The rise in the number of casualties between January and

Table 5.3 Israeli Casualties, November–December 1969 and January–February 1970

	Wounded	Killed	Total
Nov.–Dec. 1969			
Number	48	25	73
Percent	65.8	34.2	100
Jan.–Feb. 1970			
Number	64	23	87
Percent	73.6	26.4	100

SOURCE: IDF spokesman, MER (1969–70), p. 172.

February was mainly the result of the increased activity of the Egyptian artillery: 35 of the 87 Israeli casualties between January and February were wounded by Egyptian artillery fire (40 percent of all casualties), against only 29 percent of all Israeli casualties between November and December (21 out of 73).[59]

Effect of the Air Raids on the War

The in-depth air raids unquestionably effected a most serious escalation of the War of Attrition, both militarily and politically. Even if the war continued to be a limited war of attrition, it went beyond previous bounds. With the air raids deep into Egypt, many of the limitations that had characterized the war in its first period, March–December 1969, necessarily disappeared. In the months January–April 1970, it was in many respects a new war, since the in-depth raids started substantial changes in the character of the war, both politically and militarily. First, a significant escalation in the political aims of the belligerents took place as a result of the changed interaction between political and military considerations in the behaviors of Israel and Egypt. From the situation at the start—limited and defensive political aims (defense of the military and political status quo)—Israel shaped aims that went far beyond the political aims characteristic of a limited war. The Israeli aims in the strategy of in-depth air raids—breaking the Egyptian's political and military will to go on with the war by threatening Nasser's overthrow—were without question aims more characteristic of a total war than of a limited war. Even if the military means for achieving these aims were relatively limited, they were not limited enough to prevent the conviction that Israel now had more general political aims. Moreover, even if, as her leaders at times declared, Israel did not intend to bring about the defeat of Egypt or the overthrow of the regime, her adversaries, Egypt and the USSR, were convinced that Israel's war aims were in fact more general than they had been; hence for them the concept of the war necessarily became more general and not limited. What Israel really wanted was to utilize the characteristics of a limited war to secure more general aims. The Egyptian decision to invoke Soviet intervention in the fighting was also unquestionably a political and military escalation of the war. Even though the primary aim behind the efforts to cause Soviet military intervention was to deter Israel from going on with the in-depth raids and to counterbalance Israeli strategic superiority, Egypt hoped in securing this intervention to be able to realize the option of a more general war at a later stage in order to secure the liberation of the Sinai.

Second, the in-depth air raids produced concrete changes from the purely military point of view. The war was no longer local—limited to the canal front, but expanded so that a large part of the territory of Egypt became a frontal region. The targets also changed. They were still basically military, but they now included military targets that were not first-line targets and not directly involved in the war (Israel's concentration of air raids between December and January, on army camps at a distance from the front line).

6 Soviet Military Intervention

IN DISCUSSING THE FACTORS that brought about Soviet military intervention in the war, a central problem is the connection between the Israeli in-depth raids and the Soviet intervention. There are, broadly speaking, two main arguments. One is that there was no direct connection between the two events, since the Soviet decision to intervene in the war had taken shape even before the air raids. The other argument is that the Israeli in-depth raids were, in fact, what brought about the military intervention of the USSR, since this intervention only took place after Israel initiated the in-depth raids.

The conclusion reached in this study is that a distinction must be drawn between the Soviet decision to intervene in the War of Attrition as a matter of principle and the moves made to put the decision into operation. The question is not only when the Kremlin decided to intervene in the war, but at what moment the decision was put into operation. From the facts at our disposal we conclude that although the decision for intervention in the war was made in principle before the Israeli in-depth raids, i.e., without any connection with them, the raids helped bring about operative implementation of the decision. Once the Soviet leaders put their decision into effect, their intervention went further than just ending the raids, but this in itself is not necessarily sufficient to contradict the assertion that it was the raids that brought about the operational execution of the decision to intervene. This study concludes that the Soviet leadership framed its decision for intervention as a matter of principle even before the

War of Attrition. The Soviet decision to intervene was fundamentally based on the perception that the USSR could not tolerate having Egypt's suffering another defeat in a war with Israel like the defeat inflicted by the Six-Day War. An Egyptian military defeat in a future war would seriously endanger the Nasser regime in Egypt. A change of the Nasser regime and possible subsequent change of other pro-Soviet regimes in the region would seriously affect Soviet standing and investments in Egypt and the Middle East. If Egypt were likely to face defeat, the USSR would have to consider directly intervening to prevent it.[1]

During the period between the Six-Day War and the War of Attrition, the Russians took steps to influence Egypt against starting a new war with Israel, and they stepped up their diplomatic activity in order to put an end to the crisis by diplomatic means. When the Egyptians did start their War of Attrition, the USSR did everything it could to secure maximum control of Egyptian military activity, to reduce as much as possible the number of war situations in which the Soviet Union would be bound to directly intervene in the fighting. By physical presence in Egypt and by restriction to defensive those arms supplied to Egypt, the USSR hoped to prevent the Egyptians from starting an escalation of the war that would be liable to produce an escalatory response from Israel.[2] When the Israeli Air Force was sent in (July 20, 1969 on), the process that led to the operative effect of the Soviet decision to prevent a future Egyptian defeat was triggered. The Soviet leadership saw that fuller utilization of the IAF had made a substantial change in the strategic balance between Israel and Egypt. As long as the War of Attrition remained a ground war, Egypt succeeded in exploiting her strategic superiority that accrued to her from the difference in the strategic deployment of Israeli and Egyptian forces along the canal, with a view to attaining certain military and political ends. But once the War of Attrition became an air war, Israeli air superiority changed the strategic balance. The Soviet judgment was that Egypt could not hold out in an air war of attrition for any length of time, and in the second half of 1969 they therefore stepped up arms deliveries.[3] They also gradually began assuming responsibility for Egypt's air defense, as indicated by their increasing military presence in the country.[4]

The Soviet government, however, was not yet of the opinion that the new strategic situation called for direct military intervention. The view that intervention was necessary began to take shape after the IAF destroyed the Egyptian antiaircraft system, including the SA-2 missiles, along the canal.[5] The elimination of the Egyptian antiaircraft defense was the turning point, for it was this more than anything else that proved Israel's real strategic superiority in the War of Attrition. Only a counterweight to this air superiority could prevent Israel from affirming her strategic superiority. In October 1969, the Kremlin begain to contemplate sending pilots to Egypt in order to counterbalance Israel's absolute air superiority.[6] The crucial question is whether the Kremlin would have put into effect the decision to intervene if, after wiping out Egypt's antiaircraft, Israel had stopped the escalation it had initiated. In other words, if Israel had refrained from carrying out air raids deep inside Egyptian territory, would the Soviets have put their decision to intervene into effect? Israeli policy makers contended after the event that the Kremlin put the decision to intervene in the war into effect after the elimination of the Egyptian antiaircraft system and before Israel began the in-depth raids, for they saw how very badly Egypt was doing in the war.[7] According to them, the Kremlin informed the Egyptian delegation that visited the USSR in December 1969 (before Nasser's visit to Moscow at the end of January 1970) that they had decided to set up an SA-3 missile system in Egypt.[8] The main evidence supporting this contention is that the digging of Egyptian missile sites was observed before the in-depth raids began.[9] The destruction of the Egyptian antiaircraft defense system was clearly an important factor in the Soviet decision to go ahead with military intervention as previously planned, but the fact remains that the decision was only put into effect after the Israeli in-depth raids, and even then only after the Soviet leaders realized that there was no way of reaching an agreement with the United States to put an end to the Israeli in-depth raids.

For the Soviet leaders, the Israeli in-depth raids provided a very real indication that Egypt was facing a fresh military defeat. Their judgment that Nasser could not hold out if the raids continued was reinforced by Nasser's visit to Moscow in the second half of January 1970.[10] They promised Nasser in the course of this visit that they would come to his aid, but they did not keep their word until the end of February 1970. In the month that elapsed between Nasser's visit to Moscow and the delivery of SA-3 missiles to Egypt, the Kremlin tried renewed diplomatic efforts to persuade the United States to put a stop to the Israeli in-depth raids and thus save the Soviet leadership from having to intervene directly.

From the outset, the Kremlin fully appreciated the escalatory implications of direct military intervention in the War of Attrition even if only on a limited scale and hoped to get the Americans to appreciate the full implication of the Soviet undertakings in Egypt.[11] The Russian diplomatic efforts reached their peak on February 2 with the note sent by Kosygin to the leaders of the Western powers, Presidents Nixon and Pompidou and Prime Minister Wilson.[12] The note expressed the concern of the USSR over the continued Israeli air raids and blamed the United States for the deteriorating situation, since the raids were made possible by the delivery to Israel of American Phantom planes. Kosygin warned that in the absence of U.S. and Western efforts to curb Israel, the USSR would be obliged to supply Egypt with all the arms needed to resist the in-depth air raids.[13]

Following Kosygin's note, the Soviet media launched a large-scale campaign to make clear the gravity of the Middle East situation and to warn that if the Israeli in-depth raids continued, the USSR would be forced to step up deliveries of defensive arms to Egypt to insure that country's defense.[14] Kosygin's note and the propaganda campaign to persuade the Americans to curb their ally in the region were also intended to politically prepare the ground for Soviet military intervention in the war if the Americans did not respond. The U.S. reply (February 4, 1970) to Kosygin's note did not leave the Russians much choice; President Nixon urged them not to damage the American-Soviet understanding regarding non-intervention in the conflict on the part of the superpowers. The U.S. reply reiterated the proposal that an agreement be reached between the superpowers on a limitation of arms deliveries to the region and warned that if the Soviet Union rejected this proposal, the United States would be obliged to continue supplying arms to Israel.[15]

Nixon repeated this warning to the Soviet Union a fortnight later when addressing the Congress on U.S. foreign policy (February 18): "The United States would view any effort by the Soviet Union to seek predominance in the Middle East as a matter of grave concern. . . . Any effort by an outside power to exploit local conflict for its own advantage or to seek special position would be contrary to that goal." [16]

The Americans hoped that these two warnings from President Nixon would deter the Soviet Union from direct military intervention. This hope was based more on persuading the Russians of the worthiness of observing the "rules of the game" between the superpowers inside and outside the Middle East than on the Soviet government's political dilemma in the face of the continued in-depth raids. The Americans did not correctly evaluate the full extent of the Soviet undertakings in Egypt and the importance to the Kremlin of the credibility, for the sake of Soviet status and interests in the Middle East, to be attached to these undertakings.[17] The Israeli in-depth raids challenged the Russians' willingness to defend their client. For the Kremlin, Nixon's reactions were clear proof that the Americans were not prepared to put a stop to the in-depth raids and that they were desirous of insuring Israel's strategic superiority. In this situation the Russians had no choice, from their point of view, but to take action themselves to curb Israel.[18]

Aims and Development of Soviet Military Intervention

The primary and immediate aim of the Soviet military intervention in the war was to insure the survival of the Nasser regime in Egypt. The Soviet government hoped to achieve this by stopping or limiting the Israeli in-depth raids. But once they decided to intervene, they wished to secure additional aims as well. They wanted to restore the strategic balance on the Suez Canal front, to be able to go forward with their diplomatic efforts fo find a solution to the Middle East conflict while holding the best possible bargaining cards.

The Soviet government sought to attain these ends by setting up an improved antiaircraft defense system in proximity to
the canal, facing the central and southern sectors of the front at a
depth of 15 to 30 kilometers from the canal, comprising SA-2 and
SA-3 missiles, antiaircraft guns, and improved radar installations.[19] This system was to serve two main purposes—to put an
end to the in-depth raids or curb them very considerably and to
create a strategic balance on the canal front. In order to accomplish those aims, the Egyptians began a blitz construction
operation in February 1970 to build the physical infrastructure of
the antiaircraft installations, but Israeli reconnaissance planes
spotted their mechanical equipment at work. Although the purpose of the Egyptian activity was not clear at first, the decision
was made to have the Israeli Air Force destroy the new Egyptian
constructions and sabotage the work.[20] From the beginning of
March, the IAF systematically bombed the construction sites
and prevented an Egyptian antiaircraft system from being installed near the canal.[21] It was almost certainly this failure of efforts to build the antiaircraft defense infrastructure that led to a
change in Soviet plans. The Russians apparently decided to concentrate first on blocking the in-depth raids and to put off tackling the strategic balance on the canal. To put an end to the
in-depth raids or to curb them as far as possible, they installed missile systems manned by Soviet crews near three main vital points
inside Egypt: Cairo, Alexandria, and the Aswan Dam. When this
was completed, they found means to install an antiaircraft system near the canal in order to counterbalance Israeli strategic superiority on the canal front.

Delivering, manning, and operating the SA-3 missile systems
apparently began at the end of February 1970.[22] The first news of
the missiles—their delivery and installation and their Soviet
crews—was published in the *New York Times* on March 19.[23]
The paper reported that a large quantity of SA-3 missiles had arrived with numerous Soviet personnel to operate them. The
paper estimated their number at about 1,500 and also reported
on the possibility of the USSR's sending Soviet Air Force planes
to defend the new missiles against Israeli air attacks. The missiles were installed at the three central points—the Cairo area,

the Alexandria area, and the Aswan Dam. The installation of these three missile systems was mainly of political significance. Demonstrating the Soviet presence in these places was a signal to Israel to stop the in-depth raids or to very considerably limit them. By raising the threshold of political constraints for Israel, the USSR hoped to considerably curb Israel's military activity deep inside Egypt. These signals were indeed speedily recognized. Israel stopped bombing in the proximity of Cairo and the in-depth raids were slowed down, though not altogether stopped. In order to altogether stop the Israeli in-depth raids, the Russians would have had to demonstrate their presence in the air as well. The active participation of Soviet pilots in the Soviet defense deployment in Egypt was intended precisely to achieve this aim.

The Israeli Attitude

There were two distinct stages in the Israelis' settling on their attitude to the Soviet military intervention in the fighting: up to April 18, the date of the clash between Soviet and Israeli pilots; and from April 18 to the end of the War of Attrition. Up to April 18, the Israelis focused on assessing the significance of the installation of the missiles in Egypt and the manning of the sites by Soviet crews. After April 18, Israeli attention centered on the increased Soviet intervention in the war (the appearance of the pilots and the renewed attempt to install the Egyptian antiaircraft defense system along the canal).

The news that the USSR was delivering SA-3 missiles to Egypt and that Soviet crews were manning the missile installations came as a great surprise to the Israeli government—inevitably so, since the Israel view had all along been that the USSR was prepared to acquiesce in the Israeli in-depth raids. The continuation of the raids throughout a relatively long period—over two months—without any strong Soviet reaction had lessened the fear of Soviet military intervention in the fighting.[24]

The framers of Israeli policy were now obliged to reconsider the question of the connection between the in-depth raids and the Soviet direct military intervention in the fighting. Was it in fact the in-depth raids that led to the Soviet military intervention? And now that the Soviet intervention was an established fact, how would it develop if the raids continued? As to the first question, the Israeli policy makers were all agreed that there was no necessary connection between the in-depth raids and the Soviet direct military intervention. Opinions were divided, however, on the second question. Defense Minister Moshe Dayan was of the opinion that although the Soviet military intervention had not been caused by the in-depth raids, to continue the raids would nevertheless be liable to spur the Russians to expand their intervention and the raids should therefore be restricted.[25] Dayan saw the installing of the SA-3 missiles and their manning by Soviet crews as the first stage in the "Sovietization" of the Egyptian war machine, though he did not believe that the USSR would send in its own planes and pilots; he nevertheless thought that cutting down the Israeli in-depth raids would to some extent curb increased Soviet intervention.[26] On March 22, 1970, only three days after the *New York Times* reported the installation of the SA-3 missiles in Egypt, Dayan appeared on Israeli television to say that the government would limit the in-depth raids and would not attempt to assert Israel's strategic superiority *everywhere* in Egypt. All the same, Dayan made it clear at this early stage of Soviet intervention that Israel would not agree to reduce her strategic superiority on the canal. Dayan hoped to be able in this way to reach some sort of understanding with the Russians on fixing limits to belligerent activity, to avoid possible clashes with the Russians and persuade them not to extend their intervention in the fighting given Israel's willingness to set herself limits.[27] Dayan realized that this in itself might not be enough to insure that the Russians would in fact refrain from stepping up their intervention. He saw that the Soviet military intervention had created a new politico-strategic situation that went beyond the bounds of Israel's ability to stand up to it on her own. Only the United States could prevent the Russians from extending their intervention, he said, and already at this stage he wanted to confront the United States with the grave implications of the widening Soviet activity in Egypt:

Since Israel is dealing not only with the SA-3's but with the Soviets, I want to state in all simplicity that we have no capability for an all-out confrontation with the Soviet Union. If the USSR decides to enter into the Middle East conflict 'fully' and if the USA fails to restrain it and refuses to help Israel, we shall be in a very difficult situation.[28]

Vice Premier Allon did not agree with Dayan's assessment of the situation. He appreciated the gravity of the installation of the Soviet missiles in Egypt, but he did not think that this should be considered "Sovietization" of the war. He contended that the Soviet military intervention was limited in nature and that there was no prospect of large-scale Soviet intervention in the fighting, given the political and military constraints inhibiting the USSR.[29] Allon was of the opinion that this limited Soviet military intervention did not necessarily oblige Israel to change her policy of in-depth raids. He was even opposed to Dayan's demand that the United States be confronted with the gravity of the situation; he thought it might do more harm than good. As a result of the Vietnam War the United States feared a military confrontation with the USSR in the Middle East and this was liable to spur her to make political concessions to the Soviets and the Arabs at Israel's expense. The danger of military confrontation with the USSR had to be avoided at all costs. Allon therefore judged it vital for Israel to reassure the White House.[30]

Though Dayan's views were not shared by all his fellow Ministers, the government did as he proposed and limited the in-depth raids. Israel did not abandon the raids but concentrated them in the northeast area of the delta and reduced their frequency. The targets were also changed from army camps to missile sites and radar installations, selected with great care.[31] When it became clear at the beginning of April 1970 that Soviet interceptor planes were defending the missile sites and various places deep inside Egypt, Dayan was prepared to stop the raids entirely. Speaking on April 9, he said,

We make no pretension to behave in the skies over Cairo as if they were our own. We are not bound to insure conditions for ourselves that will enable us to weave back and forth in the airspace over Cairo, Alexandria, or Aswan as if they were our skies. But *we are bound to insure our military capacity to hold the cease-fire line along the canal for as long as the fighting continues.* If a cease-fire prevails, so much the better. But if the Egyptians decide to renew the war, *a situation must prevail where we can hold the cease-fire line. And this hold on the cease-fire line demands action in the air and for this we have to insure that our planes can operate there. It is not Cairo, it is the cease-fire line, and I stress the distinction.* Moreover—perhaps it is too optimistic an assumption—but I not only hope, I believe that this distinction between Cairo and Aswan and Alexandria on the one hand and the canal region on the other also exists for the Russians. Since it is the Egyptians who made the decision to renew the fighting along the line, contrary to the Security Council decision to which the USSR was a party, the Russians are in no hurry to put in soldiers of their own. But for our part *we have to avoid getting into escalation and we must limit the fighting as far as possible. Action that is necessary for holding the cease-fire is one thing,* and what goes on in other parts of Egypt is something else again. I hope that this policy will insure our avoiding not only formal involvement in war with the Soviet Union, but also the physical necessity of harming Soviet soldiers and Soviet soldiers' opening fire on our planes. *I hope it will be possible to find a modus vivendi of this kind on the cease-fire line.* [32]

Thus Dayan was again proposing an agreed limit to air activity, in order to insure that the Russians would not extend their intervention in the fighting. Dayan was prepared to pay a higher price, i.e., to put an end to the in-depth raids, in order to get the Russians to respect Israel's strategic air superiority in the canal zone and to refrain from attacking there in conditions of a continuing war of attrition.

The Israeli in-depth raids stopped on April 13, 1970.[33] Their end bore witness that Dayan had done his part in the agreement proposed by him for delimiting military actions. The question was whether the Russians were prepared to accept his proposal to refrain from expanding their intervention. The Soviet answer came on April 18, only five days after the end of the in-depth raids, when the first clash in the air took place between Soviet and Israeli pilots.[34] Thereby the Russians for the first time made it plain that they would not be satisfied by the ending of the in-depth raids and were not prepared to agree to delimit bounds to military action. In Israel the view gained ground that the Russian aims in the fighting went beyond neutralizing Israel's strategic superiority in the canal zone (as well as in the rest of Egypt) and depriving Israel of the strategic advantages she had secured in the War of Attrition (by sending in its air force and destroying the Egyptian antiaircraft system along the canal).[35] Israel's strategic superiority on the canal insured that Egypt would not be able to expand the War of Attrition or secure significant gains in a continuing war of attrition on the ground. Furthermore, this strategic superiority insured Israel against any shift in the political and military status quo against her wishes.[36] In the last months of the War of Attrition, preserving strategic superiority on the canal became basic politico-strategic aim and even turned into the "red line" in politico-strategic relations with the USSR. Dayan's efforts prior to April 18 to have lines drawn with Russian acquiescence delimiting military action had the purpose of preventing clashes with the Russians and insuring Israel's strategic superiority on the canal. Even though these efforts had failed, the same aims were now the cornerstone of Israeli strategy. When Israel saw that it was receiving no politico-strategic return on the concession it had made in order to satisfy the USSR—ending the in-depth raids—it had no alternative but to present the Russians with a new "price list." In the last months of the War of Attrition, Israel's declared policy stressed that it would not be deterred by fear of military confrontation with the USSR in the event of a Soviet attempt to intervene in the fighting in the canal zone (along the front line) or to breach the cease-fire line laid down after the Six-Day War (the political and strategic status quo), but it would continue to refrain from aggressive air action deep inside Egyptian territory.[37] For the first time since the beginning of Soviet intervention in the fighting, Israel presented limitations to the USSR, a breach of which would necessarily lead to a military clash between Israel and the USSR. Two such limitations were basically geographical—no operational action by planes and pilots in the air space over the front (30 to 40 km. from the canal line), and no installation of antiaircraft systems of any kind—mainly SA-3 missiles—on the western bank of the canal. These limitations were based on the assumption that failure to accept these geographical limits on military action would undermine Israel's strategic superiority on the canal.[38]

Israel's declared readiness to confront the Russians in given strategic conditions was based on the assumption that the scale of Soviet intervention in the fighting—and hence the U.S. reaction to that intervention—would be directly influenced by Israel's readiness to fight in defense of what it defined as its primary interest. By presenting its policy as one of no choice, Israel meant to deter the Russians in some measure from deepening their involvement in the war and to make them responsible for any clashes that might occur in the future, as well as to pressure the Americans into increasing their efforts to persuade the Soviet Union to limit its intervention. This policy was clearly stated by Israeli policy makers in the last months of the War of Attrition. Thus in May 1970, Dayan twice declared: "We have to be ready to fight physically on the cease-fire lines, even *in conditions of Soviet involvement in Egypt, since no other force will fight our war for us. If we possess the readiness to fight, then maybe other nations—including perhaps the United States—will be likely to help us."* [39] And again:

> *If we do not fight, no one will come to our help, we shall not get the Phantoms, and tomorrow the Russians will already be installing SA-3 missile sites on the canal, if they discover that this does not involve their pilots clashing with ours.* We are not going to rush to meet the Russian pilots, but if there is a line we shall fight on that line. We cannot allow ourselves anything less than this, and on this basis alone can we have any *prospect of getting support at some stage from others as well and hope that the Russians will calm down and be deterred and not press things to the point where we shall have to fire at them and also bring down their planes.* [40]

The expression, "Israel isn't Czechoslovakia," occurred more than once in the speeches of Israeli policy makers to stress Israel's determination to defend the cease-fire line even at the price of a clash with the Russians. [41]

Trying to Bring Israeli and U.S. Policies into Line

After the clashes in the air on April 18, the matter of getting together with the Americans became a basic consideration in

Israeli policy. The opinion now held was that Israeli determination to fight on the cease-fire line was not itself enough to affect Soviet behavior. It was thought that only a firm American stand against Soviet intervention in the fighting would influence the conduct of the USSR.[42] Israeli policy makers judged that in order to secure a firm American reaction it was necessary to convince the United States that not only Israeli interests, but also basic American interests in the Middle East were liable to be affected by increased Soviet military intervention in the war.[43] As long as the Soviet intervention was limited to installing SA-3 missiles, the Americans were not convinced that this degree of involvement really constituted a grave danger to American and Israeli interests. The Americans apparently accepted the Soviet contention that the aim of their involvement was to put an end to the in-depth raids. As opposed to Israeli contentions, the American version was that the in-depth raids had led to the Soviet involvement and that Israel bore the main responsibility for this.[44] More than this, the Americans even held that the installation of missiles and their manning by Soviet personnel did no real harm to the balance of forces at Israel's expense, and they refused to renew deliveries of the Phantoms.[45] The American decision to continue holding up delivery of planes to Israel arose from the desire to bring pressure to bear on Israel to end the in-depth raids and also to signal to the Kremlin that the United States was prepared to take action to curb Israel.[46]

The appearance of Soviet pilots in the arena was seen by Israeli policy makers as additional convincing proof that the Soviet intervention was aimed at securing politico-strategic gains beyond putting an end to the in-depth raids.[47] Israel now asked the United States to adopt a policy that would deter the Soviet Union and to change its line on renewing arms supplies to Israel.[48] The U.S. reaction to both the new disclosures and on the scope of Soviet involvement in Egypt was absolutely contrary to Israeli expectations.[49] It went no further than political statements by heads of the administration that were hardly any stronger than President Nixon's warnings before the increased Soviet intervention.[50] There was no change in U.S. policy regarding the Phantoms. On April 29, 1970, President Nixon did order a reappraisal of political and military aspects of the Middle East situation in the light of the new phase of Soviet involvement, but he postponed renewing deliveries of Phantoms until after the completion of the reappraisal.[51] This postponing of the supply of Phantoms put the Israeli government in an embarrassing enough situation because it was interpreted as a devaluation of U.S. support for Israel, when what had been hoped for was massive political and military support.[52] Before the in-depth raids, Israeli policy makers had been sure of the effectiveness of U.S. deterrence and of the credibility of U.S. support of Israel if a situation should arise where the Russians decided to intervene in the war. This certainty now gave way to serious doubts. The Israeli Ambassador to the United States, Yitzhak Rabin, said at this time:

> If there is one thing the western world is apprehensive about, it is a confrontation between the superpowers, and if there is one thing the American public doesn't want today and seeks to avoid with all its power, it is the risk of a nuclear world war. A dangerous situation is seen in the Middle East today, the possible focus of developments that are liable to lead to such a war. Hence there is more weighing up and more caution over taking steps, whether in the field of help to Israel of all kinds or whether in political contacts in the international arena, with the aim of seeking every way to prevent the danger of war even if this is detrimental to Israel's interests. . . . The United States is under no formal obligation to come to the aid of Israel, even if the latter is attacked by the USSR. Without going into the causes, the state of Israel has no prospect today, in the present state of affairs in America, of receiving any American support or pledge of this kind. There is no prospect of the United States issuing a warning that a blow directed against Israel will be seen as a blow at the United States.[53]

Even so, the Israel assessment was that if Israel were to be attacked by the Russians, the United States would not leave her as their prey. It was not at all clear, however, what "not leaving Israel as prey" really meant. If it meant U.S. intervention in a clash between Israel and the USSR on the cease-fire line (according to the Israeli definition) or U.S. non-intervention so long as Egyptian and Soviet forces advanced to the 1967 frontiers,[54] it suddenly became evident that it was not at all clear what U.S. support of Israel really signified and in general what were the conditions in which Israel could expect real American intervention to help her. In these circumstances, Israeli policy makers could only hope that Russian uncertainty regarding the prospective U.S. reaction would constitute the main deterrent to an expansion of the Soviet intervention; they could not expect more than that.[55] Contacts between Israel and the United States gave no help in clarifying what was involved in U.S. support of Israel, nor did they help clarify what were Soviet intentions. In essence, the United States contended that if Israel were to adopt a balanced policy on belligerence, i.e., to fight only on the cease-fire line, to exercise maximum restraint in the face of Soviet provocation, and to make more flexible pronouncements regarding the political settlement, the danger of a clash between Israel and the USSR could be reduced.[56] At the precise moment when Israel expected a firm U.S. reaction in the face of Soviet intervention, the Americans went to great trouble to bring the war to an end as the only way of reducing the danger of superpower confrontation in the region.

Countering the In-Depth Raids and Counterbalancing Israeli Air Superiority

Early in May 1970, the Russians began to put the second phase of their intervention in the war into operation.[57] They apparently judged that unless and until Israel was deprived of her air superiority on the canal, there was no possibility of putting an end to the war or settling the Middle East crisis. Continued Israeli strategic superiority on the Suez Canal meant permanent maintenance of the military and political status quo for Israel.[58] The Soviet aim was to restore the War of Attrition to its level before the strategic process initiated by Israel's destruction of the Egyptian antiaircraft defense system and in-depth raids. By setting up an improved antiaircraft system on the canal, they hoped to neutralize Israeli air superiority and enable Egypt to conduct a land war of attrition, exploiting its strategic and tactical advantages in such a war.[59] With its air superiority neutralized, Israel would modify its stand and Egypt would be able to agree to end the war in a better strategic bargaining posture. The loss of a limited number of planes and a rise in Israeli casualties would be enough to convince Israel that it could not maintain its strategic superiority indefinitely and to let Egypt feel that it had reduced its air inferiority. The American decision to hold up plane deliveries to Israel was interpreted by the Russians as a sign of American willingness to bring a moderating influence to bear on Israel.[60] The Soviet military intervention in the last months of the War of Attrition was marked by efforts to restore strategic balance on the canal. Soviet military involvement acquired noteworthy dimensions at this stage (see table 6.1).

The first attempts to construct an antiaircraft network on the canal front, later dubbed "the SAM-Box," began early in May after the renewed artillery offensive on the canal. This time the Egyptians tried a new system initiated by the Soviets. The idea was to carry out a blitz operation and prepare the missile sites in a matter of days. The Egyptians hoped to defend the workers and the missile installations with the help of antiaircraft guns.[61] The Israeli Air Force reacted swiftly. During the first twenty days of May (except May 12), the IAF carried out 43 attacks on the Egyptian construction efforts—20 on the central sector, 17 on the southern sector, and 6 on the northern sector.[62] Scores of antiaircraft guns were destroyed in the raids and hundreds of Egyptian workers were wounded. This Soviet-Egyptian effort was blocked like the previous one. The Russians renewed the attempt

Table 6.1 Estimated Soviet Military Presence in Egypt: January–September 1970

Date	Pilots	Missile Personnel	Others	Total Personnel	SA-3 Missiles	Planes	Air Bases
January 1	0	0	2,500–4,000	2,500–4,000	0	0	0
March 31	60–80	4,000	2,500–4,000	6,560–8,080	22	0	1(?)
June 30	100–150	8,000	2,500–4,000	10,600–12,150	45–55	120 MiG-21J	6
September 30	150	10,000	2,500–4,000	12,650–14,150	70–80	150 Mig-21J	6

SOURCE: *Strategic Survey for 1970* (London: Institute for Strategic Studies, 1971), p. 47.

to set up a missile network in the proximity of the canal at the beginning of June. This time they tried a new method—"missile ambushes." They brought in isolated missile pads near the canal during the night and camouflaged them well. They opened missile fire on Israeli planes from time to time and afterward kept silent in the hope of not being spotted.[63]

But this method also failed. IAF planes discovered three missile launch-pads that had been brought to the canal and destroyed them.[64] The turning point in the Soviet-Egyptian effort to set up a missile network on the canal came in the second half of June, when an entirely new Soviet plan was devised. The plan depended on the constraints of the geographical delimitation that the Americans imposed on the Russians. On the second of June, after the failure of the earlier Soviet attempts to set up a missile network in the proximity of the canal, the United States warned the Soviet Union (in a talk with Dobrynin held by Rogers and Sisco) not to try to set up a missile network in the proximity of the canal any nearer than 30 kilometers from it. The Americans acquiesced in limited Soviet involvement in Egypt and were concerned about checking the Israel in-depth raids, but they saw that if the Russians succeeded in installing a missile network on the water line, this would indeed secure them outstanding strategic advantages. Israel's strategic superiority would be gone, not only on the canal front but also deep into the Sinai, since the missile network would also cover part of the Sinai air space. To give their warning due weight, the Americans made it clear that any Soviet attempt to breach the geographical limit would be considered a direct challenge to the United States, which would oblige a direct response.[65]

The new Soviet plan for installing the missiles was carried out successfully in conformity with these limitations, and the main characteristics and even most of the details were known to Israel a few days after the plan was completed.[66] According to Israeli sources, the new elements in the Soviet plan were first, speedy introduction of the missile pads in a single night, without any continuous solid infrastructure built to receive them. In the past, the Egyptians had installed the missiles in trenches prepared at fortified, fixed sites, the main parts of which were concrete. When the IAF planes spotted the work in progress, they did not allow the Egyptians to finish and reach the stage of installation. In the new system, the missile pads were not put into fortified points but spread out in the open; the launching installation was slid into place in a ditch which could be prepared relatively quickly, and there the launcher and the missile were set up.

Second, the missile sites were concentrated in a narrow geographic sector in the central sector of the canal, along a strip of only about seventy kilometers, not along the whole front. The network was installed in an area resembling a rectangle on the map, parallel to the canal and west of it. This rectangle stretched lengthwise from the zone opposite Ismailia in the north to the Suez-Cairo highway in the south. Across the width of the rectangle, the nearest missile sites were at a distance of about twenty-three kilometers from the canal and the furthest ones at a distance of about fifty to fifty-five kilometers from the canal.

Third, the antiaircraft network was densely crowded together. Contrary to what had been done in the past, the antiaircraft network was not constructed on the principle of a defense line, but in a dense, crowded deployment. There had been sixteen SA-2 missile sites in Egypt in the past, scattered along the canal front from Port Said in the north to the Suez in the south. The new network was much denser. In this rectangle, seventy kilometers from north to south and some thirty kilometers from east to west, there were concentrated ten to fifteen SA-2 missile sites and at least two SA-3 missile sites. The SA-3 missiles, mixed into the new network, were put at the rear of the rectangle at a distance of about fifty kilometers from the canal, their function being to provide additional cover for the SA-2 missile sites.

Fourth, the missile sites were disposed in an unprecedented fashion. Instead of being installed in a linear manner, so each site was covered only by its neighbors in the line, they were now grouped in bunches at short distances from each other so each of the missile sites was covered by several others at the same time. Previously, when the sites were spread out lengthwise, only the site that was attacked by the planes could fire to protect itself; in general, the sites attacked would fire one or two missiles until silenced. Now the system operated differently: a number of the sites in bunched formation fired at the same time.

Fifth, there was greater Soviet participation in operating the antiaircraft network. There was a Russian crew at every missile site; its members acted not only as advisers, but also as the crew that insured the proper operation of the site. The SA-2 sites were operated by Egyptians under close supervision by Russian experts. The SA-3 sites were operated by Russian crews only.

The operation of installing this antiaircraft network was set for the end of June 1970.[67] The first missiles were brought in during the night of June 29 to 30. With Russian assistance, the Egyptians succeeded in bringing in twelve SA-2 missile launchers and two or three SA-3 missile launchers, as well as a large number of antiaircraft guns, to a sector at a depth of about thirty kilometers from the canal in the sector between Ismailia and Suez, halfway between Cairo and the canal.[68] The operation of bringing in the missiles clearly signaled a momentous turning point in the Soviet policy of intervention in the War of Attrition. Until then, Soviet intervention in the war had been limited to defending the Egyptian rear. Now the Russians transferred their activity to the canal front as well. A clash between the IAF and the Soviet missile crews was now unavoidable. The confrontation between Israeli planes and Soviet missiles began the very next day, Tuesday, June 30. The War of Attrition entered its electronic era. From June 30 until the end of the war on August 8, the War of Attrition was marked by the contest between planes and missiles, between the Soviet-Egyptian efforts to install the antiaircraft network solidly near the canal and the Israeli efforts to block them.

In the first clash between Israeli planes and Soviet missiles, Israel lost two Phantoms while the IAF succeeded in wiping out two SA-2 sites.[69] Up to July 7, 1970, five SA-2 sites were wiped out and another two partly damaged. Israel lost three Phantoms, all of them apparently hit by SA-2 missiles of a more advanced type than the previous ones, according to the new method of massive missile fire directed at the attacking planes from all sides.[70]

The Egyptian Perception of Soviet Military Intervention

According to the Egyptian view, the Soviet military intervention in the War of Attrition was directed to securing a number of goals on both the military and political planes. On the military plane, the Soviet military intervention was seen as aimed at liberating Egypt from the strategic constraints imposed on her by the Israeli in-depth raids and at counterbalancing Israeli air superiority in the proximity of the canal by installing an improved air defense network which would enable the Egyptians to utilize their strategic advantages in conducting a war of attrition on land, to cross the canal, and perhaps even to conquer the Sinai. On the political plane, the Soviet military intervention was seen as meant to counterbalance Israeli air strategy and/or threaten globalization of the war, thereby improving the Soviet bargaining posture in contacts with the United States—contacts aimed at bringing the war to an end and reaching a political solution to the conflict.

It was not until after the Israeli government's announcement at the beginning of May that Soviet pilots were participating operationally in the defense of Egypt that Nasser made a public statement to the same effect, declaring that the USSR was helping Egypt defend her skies and air space in order to prevent Israel from bombing deep inside Egyptian territory.[71] In an interview in the newspaper *Die Welt* (of May 20), Nasser disclosed that Soviet pilots were defending Egypt's air space and that the possibility of a clash between Russian and Israeli pilots could not be excluded.[72] In three additional statements during May, Nasser stressed the defensive side of the Soviet intervention in the fighting, i.e., the defense of Egyptian air space and territory against Israeli in-depth raids, since Egypt was not capable of meeting the Israeli challenge on her own. In June and July, Nasser and other Egyptian spokesmen tended to stress the offensive implications of Soviet military intervention which made it possible to neutralize Israeli strategic superiority on the canal front, to wage an effective war of attrition on land, and even to cross the canal and conquer the Sinai. Speaking at Benghazi on June 25,

Nasser openly referred to these hopes and intentions.[73] The stress he laid on the connection between balance in the air and capability to cross the canal probably reflected Egyptian wishes rather than Soviet aims. Nasser's declaration that "no power in the world" could prevent Egypt from crossing the canal testified that Soviet and Egyptian positions were not identical regarding the future development of the war. It is doubtful whether the USSR intended its efforts to secure strategic balance on the canal front to enable the Egyptians to cross the canal, given the escalatory significance of such a development.[74]

Nasser also had to consider the very troublesome question of the "price" Egypt would have to pay in return for Soviet intervention. In speeches at this time, Nasser expressed apprehension lest the threat of globalization of the war because of Soviet intervention be exploited by the Russians themselves to get political concessions from Egypt on her stand regarding the political settlement of the conflict.[75] Egypt herself, when deciding on her strategy of attrition at the start, had hoped to exploit the threat of globalization of the conflict in order to secure political gains. This hope now gave way to fears that this threat might produce an agreement between the two superpowers that would not necessarily be in line with Egypt's wishes.[76] It is against this background of anxiety that Nasser reached his decision to agree to renew direct talks with the United States. The U.S. initiative was taken in the form of a visit of Sisco to Cairo on April 10 to 14. Sisco wanted to persuade Nasser to let the United States propose a new political plan for ending the war and settling the Arab-Israeli conflict. Sisco offered the decision to suspend plane deliveries to Israel as proof of America's desire to earn the trust of the Egyptians as an honest broker.[77]

Nasser had grounds for doubting U.S. sincerity, but he nevertheless saw its efforts as offering a threefold opportunity: to end the War of Attrition that had intensified since the beginning of 1970 and was proving more wearing on Egypt than had been foreseen, to reduce his dependence on the USSR, and to make his acceptance of the renewed U.S. initiative conditional on a change in U.S. policy regarding the Arab-Israeli conflict.[78] In the May 1 speech when he first publicly thanked the USSR for its intervention in the fighting, Nasser also stated his agreement to a renewed U.S. political initiative:

> Despite all that has happened, we have not closed the door finally with the United States. I informed President Nixon that we have reached a decisive moment in Arab-American relations: either we will be estranged forever or there will be a new, serious, and definite start. The future developments will not affect Arab-American relations alone, but will have wider and more serious effects.[79]

In turning to the United States, Nasser was also prepared to bring the war to an end. Once a strategic balance between Israel and Egypt had been secured by means of Soviet intervention, Egypt agreed to negotiate. Insuring the continued existence of this strategic balance was the precondition for ending the war and accepting a political solution of the conflict. Responsibility for ending the war was thus placed on the United States as the supplier of arms to Israel. An undertaking not to supply additional planes to Israel could help bring the war to an end. Sisco's visit to Egypt and Nasser's speech constituted an important turning point on the road to ending the war, once the Soviet intervention in the fighting had become clear to all.[80]

The Israeli Perception of Soviet-Egyptian Efforts to Achieve a Strategic Balance

The Soviet-Egyptian efforts to neutralize Israel's strategic superiority on the Suez Canal front were perceived by the framers of Israeli policy as introducing a new phase of the war from both strategic and political points of view.

From the strategic point of view, the framers of Israeli policy clearly perceived the Soviet-Egyptian efforts to install an antiaircraft system in proximity to the canal as intended to neutralize Israeli Air Force superiority—not only in order to enable Egypt in the first phase to wage an effective war of attrition on land but even perhaps to cross the canal during the next phase.[81] From May 1970 on, Israeli policy makers saw clear indications that the nature of the new Soviet-Egyptian strategy was to increase Egyptian military activity and to neutralize Israel's air superiority in the canal zone in order to be able to cross the canal. The Israelis judged that from the strategic point of view, Egypt and the USSR had initiated something like a division of labor in order to promote the strategic balance they sought. The Russians had taken the air defense of Egypt upon themselves and thereby left Egypt free to take the offensive in the War of Attrition.[82] From the political point of view, the framers of Israeli policy judged that the USSR and Egypt were interested in imposing a political solution on Israel that would include Israeli withdrawal from all the territories and a solution of the Palestinian problem. The Soviet-Egyptian efforts were seen as intended to present the United States with a very grave choice between a worsening of the war situation in the region, including the canal zone, with all that this implied for inter-bloc relations; and acquiescence in a political initiative that would impose Israeli withdrawal from all the territories and the desired solution of the Palestinian problem.[83]

Their evaluation of these politico-strategic changes strengthened the determination of Israeli policy makers to defend the Israeli Defense Forces' superiority on the canal front. The "battle on the canal line" was now defined as "the battle to insure the very existence of the state of Israel." In the face of the Soviet efforts to neutralize Israeli superiority and Egyptian efforts to itensify the War of Attrition, preserving superiority on the canal would insure not only maintenance of the territorial, political, and military status quo, but the very existence of the State at the same time. The connection between this status quo and the survival of the State was thus perceived as a very close one. Israeli Foreign Minister Abba Eban spoke in this context in his address to the Knesset on July 13:

> Nasser affirmed in his Benghazi speech that Egypt's aim is to secure air superiority in the canal zone in order to make it possible to cross over when the time comes, and as if he expected with the help of the USSR to secure this goal and bring about an Israeli withdrawal—something that won't and can't happen. Who would be fool enough to believe that Nasser would stop halfway and not overrun all of Israel in one violent sweep! Hence the battle on the canal line is the battle to preserve the very existence of the state of Israel.[84]

Israel's declared policy that the IDF would fight the Russians in order to insure strategic superiority on the canal was now put to the practical test. The government was facing one of its most difficult moments. On the one hand, there was the question of the credibility of its declared policy of the two previous months that it would defend strategic superiority on the canal front even at the price of a military clash with the Russians, and on the other hand general apprehension over this prospect rose sharply when the clash with the Russians became an immediate reality.[85]

Against this background of apprehension over a clash with the Russians, uncertainty with regard to the real intentions of the USSR, and the growing threat to Israeli strategic superiority on the canal, the framers of Israeli policy reached the view that only a real, concrete threat of globalization of the war would deter the USSR. In spite of U.S. apprehensions about globalization of the war and superpower confrontation, they judged that the United States would then have to take some action to deter the USSR. Israel was indeed not interested in having a superpower confrontation, but the United States would be bound to act to deter the USSR even under the looming threat of confrontation. It was thought that the more the United States did to deter the USSR, the less danger there would be of a superpower confrontation.[86] Furthermore, since Israel was determined to face a clash with the Russians at some stage, this would mean that the United States would eventually be led to act decisively in more difficult circumstances. The Israeli policy makers repeatedly stressed that a clash between Israeli and Russian pilots was becoming more and more likely.[87] The clash was in fact even nearer than they thought. On July 25, Israeli Skyhawks on their way to bomb SA-3 missile bases were attacked by two MIG-21's flown by Russian pilots. One of the Skyhawks was hit, but the pilot succeeded in taking evasive action. The Russian pilots pursued the Skyhawks and even penetrated some distance into the Sinai.[88]

This encounter with Soviet pilots in the band of territory that Israel had defined as over the red line for Soviet air activity meant a real test of the credibility of Israel's declared policy. The choice now lay between direct combat in the air between Israeli and Soviet pilots or else retreating from declared intentions to insure Israeli strategic superiority on the canal front. The decision was taken to make these declarations good by initiating an air clash with the Soviet pilots.[89] On July 30, 1970, Israeli pilots laid an ambush for Soviet pilots in the air space over the Suez Gulf, and in the fighting that ensued the Russians lost five planes.[90] The Egyptians and the Russians did not make any announcement on the incident. Israel also preferred not to make the matter public in order not to give the Russians an excuse for widening the war.[91] Starting a fight with the Russians only a day before the Israeli government accepted the cease-fire agreement would seem superfluous. It was perhaps less a matter of making good the declarations of policy than of punishing the Russians for stepping up their provocation in the air beyond what Israel had defined as the red line for Soviet air activity.[92]

The Effect of Soviet Military Intervention on the Dynamics of the War

The direct Soviet military intervention in the War of Attrition was intended to restore the War of Attrition in its last phase to its level before the strategic process that began with the Israeli destruction of the Egyptian antiaircraft system and the in-depth raids. To a very considerable extent, the intervention succeeded in achieving its aims. From a posture of strategic offensive (the in-depth raids), Israel passed to one of strategic defensive (preserving her strategic superiority on the canal front only). Egypt on the other hand once more expanded her belligerent activity to what it had been before the entry of the Israeli Air Force into the fighting on July 20, 1969. From the moment that the Israeli offensive was blocked, Egypt began working toward strategic balance and a renewed offensive in the War of Attrition. In the last months of the war, from the start of Soviet intervention in the fighting, the belligerent activity on both sides was concentrated on the canal front. While Egypt stepped up the War of Attrition on land to a very considerable extent, Israel was working to put a brake on the effectiveness of the land war of attrition by means of attrition in the air. Escalation in the war on the canal occurred from the beginning of March 1970 to the end of July 1970. In the course of these five months, according to the statements of the Israeli Defense Forces, the Egyptians initiated 3,858 firing incidents, compared with 2,427 in the months between October 1969 and February 1970 (the months preceding the direct Soviet intervention in the fighting), i.e., a rise of 59 percent in the scale of Egyptian belligerent action. An examination of the types of incidents initiated by Egypt indicates intensification of belligerency as well as numerical increase: 85 percent of all the firing incidents from March to July 1970 were artillery and mortar fire as compared with 50 percent in the period preceding the Soviet intervention (see table 6.2).

The intensified belligerency caused a considerable rise in casualties on both sides. From March to July 1970 there were 92 Israelis killed and 249 wounded as compared with 59 killed and 159 wounded from October to February—a rise of 56 percent killed and 57 percent wounded (see table 6.3).

In the last months of the war, Egypt paid a very heavy price in casualties. Over 1,500 Egyptian soldiers were killed in the last three months before the cease fire.[93] There were days when the number of Egyptian casualties reached 300 a day.[94] Thus, toward the close of the war, both sides were on the threshold of mutual attrition. Readiness to end the war was greater than it had been at any point until then.

Table 6.2 Numbers of Incidents Initiated by the United Arab Republic on the Israeli-Egyptian Front, October 1969–July 1970

Months	Light Arms		Mortar Shelling		Artillery		Others		Total	
	No.	%	No.	%	No.	%	No.	%		
October 1969– February 1970	1,124	46.3	577	23.8	641	26.4	95	3.5	2,427	100%
March– July 1970	495	12.8	2,109	54.7	1,172	30.4	82	2.1	3,858	100%

SOURCE: The IDF spokesman, MER (1969–70), p. 167.

Table 6.3 IDF Casualties on the Egyptian Front, October 1969–July 1970

Month	Casualties	Killed	Wounded
October 1969	58	11	47
November 1969	41	12	29
December 1969	32	13	19
January 1970	30	4	26
February 1970	57	19	38
Total	218	59	159
March 1970	41	7	34
April 1970	89	27	62
May 1970	99	36	63
June 1970	60	16	44
July 1970	52	6	46
Total	341	92	249

SOURCE: IDF spokesman, *MER* (1969–70), p. 172.

The U.S. Attitude About Increased Soviet Intervention

The changeover in Soviet aims in the war from blocking the Israeli in-depth raids to restoring strategic balance on the canal front produced a change in the American attitude about direct Soviet intervention in the fighting. As long as Soviet military activity was limited to curbing the Israeli in-depth raids, the United States viewed the Soviet intervention as a development that could be tolerated in view of Egypt's inability to block the in-depth raids by itself. The United States laid the blame for this limited intervention on Israel and denied it the Phantom planes in order to prevent an Israeli-Soviet clash.[95] But once the USSR began to work for a strategic balance on the canal front, the Americans grew increasingly apprehensive over the growing danger of Israeli-USSR confrontation, which would be liable to drag the United States into risking superpower confrontation. At the beginning of 1970 the Americans were already deterred by apprehension lest a local war develop into a global one on the initiative of the clients of both superpowers.[96] In May and June, the United States wished to fix limiting thresholds for Soviet

military intervention on the one hand and on the other to bring
the war to an end by the sole initiative of the United States. The
U.S. attitude was changing as a result of the reappraisal of the
Middle East situation carried out on instructions from President
Nixon, as stated in his announcement of April 29. On the basis of
this reappraisal, stress was laid on the need to reduce the risk of
a superpower confrontation over the Middle East war.[97] The
Americans hoped to do this and more than this—even to get the
Russians out of Egypt or at least restrict their presence there—by
presenting a plan to end the war and to create conditions for a
political settlement of the Arab-Israeli conflict.[98] They founded
their hopes on Nasser's readiness to agree to stop the war and
reduce his dependence on the USSR and on the Israeli Prime
Minister's statement of May 26 that Israel continued to adhere to
United Nations Resolution 242 as the basis for negotiation.[99]

On June 19, the United States presented Israel, Egypt, Jordan, and the three other powers with its proposals regarding a
cease-fire and a renewal of talks between the parties concerned
under the auspices of the United Nations emissary Jarring. Contrary to its efforts in the past, the United States made no attempt
to insure Soviet-American agreement on the plan beforehand,
though the Soviet Union was given information regarding American intentions. At a press conference on June 25, Secretary of
State Rogers announced details of the American plan to end the
war.[100]

From Escalation to De-Escalation

The Soviet success in blocking the IDF in-depth raids and in
achieving a strategic balance on the canal front in fact created
the conditions for ending the war. In spite of the escalatory implications of the Soviet intervention—implications for the local
war and for superpower relations as well—the final result was
de-escalation. The Soviet intervention was mainly what brought
about an end to the war. Once the escalatory dimensions of the
Soviet intervention became clear, Israel, Egypt, and the United
States all wanted the war to end. Israel realized that continuing

the war meant increased danger of military clashes with the USSR; Egypt saw that the price she would have to pay for this intervention was liable to go above and beyond anything it had foreseen. The United States, like the USSR, feared globalization of the war and took action to bring it to a speedy end. The Soviet intervention achieved its goals since the way was opened for ending the war and for renewed attempts to secure a political solution of the conflict. The USSR thereby enabled the United States to play the central role in the moves for ending the war. U.S. diplomacy succeeded in proving to Egypt that while some of Egypt's military ambitions could be achieved with Soviet intervention, its political ambitions could be achieved solely with the help of the United States.

7 Action to End the War

THE DIRECT SOVIET MILITARY intervention in the war with its implicit threat of globalization of the conflict led to significant changes in the nature of the diplomatic initiatives of the powers in the Middle East. The first and most striking of these changes was in the central point on which diplomatic efforts now focused. In 1969 the two-power and four-power talks had directed diplomatic efforts toward finding a political solution to the Arab-Israeli conflict. Now, after the Soviet military intervention, those countries concentrated on working toward a speedy end to the war. With strategic stability on the superpower plane increasingly endangered, a cease-fire was seen as the best way to forestall a superpower confrontation. The second outstanding change was that the Americans made the diplomatic moves to end the war on their own. The Americans and the Russians had been partners at the end of 1969 in attempts to carry out the Rogers Plan, but the USSR was not a full partner in the new U.S. initiative to end the war, although they were kept informed of the details.

The U.S. initiative to end the war marked the breakdown of efforts to secure preliminary superpower agreement, as a result of the lessons learned from the failure of the Rogers Plan at the end of 1969. U.S. policy makers judged that a mistake had been made in trying to deal with the USSR separately from Egypt in diplomatic moves in 1969. The U.S. view that agreement in principle between the two superpowers would be enough to create symmetry of readiness to persuade the respective clients in the region to accept a settlement had proved erroneous. While the United States was ready to bring pressure to bear on Israel to get her to accept the principles of the agreement, the USSR was not prepared to do likewise regarding Egypt. Furthermore, even if there had been symmetry of readiness on the part of the two superpowers to bring pressure to bear, this would not necessarily have insured a positive response from Israel and Egypt.[1]

Since it turned out to be impossible to detach the USSR from Egypt, the Americans thought it worth trying to detach Egypt from the USSR by turning to Nasser. At the same time they felt that the United States should act less pretentiously than it had done in presenting the Rogers Plan and that they should concentrate on a limited proposal for a cease-fire. They should start a process and not try to produce an overall solution.[2] The way to success for the U.S. initiative was opened by the Soviet military intervention in the war and by the U.S. role as the main arms supplier to Israel. The USSR became less acceptable to Israel as a peacemaker by virtue of Russian intervention, and the United States became more acceptable to Egypt by virtue of its capacity to utilize the supply of planes to Israel as an inducement to Egypt to renew talks with the United States. By not supplying the planes, the United States insured renewed talks with Egypt and helped to get the USSR excluded from the negotiating process. Against the background of increased Soviet involvement in Egypt, the Americans, however, holding up the supply of planes made it harder for Israel to agree to U.S. policy.

To promote their initiative, the Americans employed contradictory signaling. They told Nasser that they would hold up the supply of planes to Israel, but when the Israeli Foreign Minister visited the United States on May 21, 1970, President Nixon promised to renew the supply of planes in return for an Israeli declaration of willingness to show political flexibility. The Americans proceeded to elaborate their initiative on the basis of Nasser's May 1 speech, his note to President Nixon of May 2, and Golda Meir's statement in the Knesset on May 26 declaring Israel's willingness to treat United Nations Resolution 242 as a basis for political negotiations and acceptance of Rhodes-type talks.[3]

The new Rogers initiative was communicated to Israel, Jordan, and Egypt on June 19. All three states were requested to sign an identical text in which they notified the Secretary of State that they agreed to Dr. Jarring's being informed that he was empowered to transmit the following in their name to UN Secretary-General U Thant:

(1) That having accepted and indicated their willingness to carry out Resolution 242 in all its parts, they will designate representatives to discussions to be held under my auspices, according to such procedure and at such places and times as I may recommend, taking into account as appropriate each side's preference as to method of procedure and previous experience between the parties;

(2) That the purpose of the aforementioned discussions is to reach agreement on the establishment of a just and lasting peace between them based on (1) mutual acknowledgement by the UAR (United Arab Republic), Jordan, and Israel of each others' sovereignty, territorial integrity, and political independence, and (2) Israeli withdrawal from territories occupied in the 1967 conflict, both in accordance with Resolution 242;

(3) That to facilitate my task of promoting agreements as set forth in Resolution 242, the parties will strictly observe, effective July 1 until (at least) October 1, the cease-fire resolutions of the Security Council.[4]

Israel Refuses

The U.S. initiative, communicated to Israel by the U.S. Ambassador on June 19, was rejected outright by Premier Golda Meir. Mrs. Meir brought the matter before the government two days later, and the decision to reject the proposals was unanimous.[5] The question of the cease-fire was discussed separately from the other provisions of the U.S. proposal, i.e., renewal of the Jarring talks and reiteration of Israeli acceptance of withdrawal, but even then the Israeli government held the view that the American plan meant a measure of acceptance of the Soviet-Arab view that there could be no cease-fire as long as Israel was not ready to return all the territories. Premier Golda Meir was of the opinion that Israel could not accept the idea of a limited cease-fire. Even though Israel was vitally interested in a cease-fire because of the rising casualty rate on the Suez Canal, it was feared that this would enable Egypt to step up preparations for the war of liberation proclaimed by Nasser.[6]

Generally speaking, however, the Israeli rejection of the U.S. initiative was not carefully weighed; the decision was spontaneous and hasty. Even from the tactical point of view, this haste was an error. The U.S. Ambassador had asked the Israeli government to refrain from answering immediately in order to let Egypt be the first to reject the U.S. initiative and thus in fact forestall an American-Israeli clash.[7] Though the government certainly hoped that Egypt would reject this initiative as it had rejected the Rogers Plan, it still failed to accede to the ambassador's request.[8] The immediate rejection of the proposal was conveyed to President Nixon in a personal note from Mrs. Meir, in the hope that since the initiative had originated in the State Department and not in the White House, it would now undergo modification in the White House, as occurred after the presentation of the original Rogers Plan.[9]

Israel's Ambassador to the United States Rabin held up the message of rejection, since he considered it a mistake, and he warned that a rejection of the United States administration's efforts to initiate new consultations in the Middle East would do serious harm to Israel in American public opinion. The American public was apprehensive of a Soviet-American confrontation in the Middle East, and this outright rejection of peace moves could lead to a serious crisis in relations between Israel and the United States. The Israeli government accepted Rabin's view of the situation and agreed to alter the tone of the message but not its content—Israel's declared opposition to the U.S. initiative.[10] In her policy speech to the Knesset on June 29, 1970, Premier Golda Meir refrained from responding to the American initiative and evaded explaining Israel's not accepting a temporary cease-fire. The absence of any mention in the speech of Israel's willingness to accept the United Nations Security Council decision was interpreted as a signal to the Americans that Israel was not prepared to accept the U.S. initiative.[11] This, in effect, ended Israel's part in the first round of reactions to the American proposals. It was now Egypt's and the Soviet Union's turn.

Egypt Agrees

According to Heikal, Nasser welcomed the American initiative while he was still in Libya, even before he went to Moscow on June 29, and his decision came as a surprise to the Soviet leadership.[12] The purpose of the visit to Moscow was to report the Egyptian decision to the Soviet leaders and to shape a common strategy with them vis-à-vis the U.S. call for a cease-fire and a renewal of diplomatic moves in search of a political settlement. This common strategy was intended to increase direct military pressure on Israel in order to make her agree to political concessions, to press the Americans to fix negotiating conditions for a political settlement acceptable to the Arabs, given the changed balance of forces between Israel and Egypt.[13]

Heikal claims that Nasser's response to the U.S. initiative was immediate and positive because he saw it as fitting in with the Egyptian strategy that was emerging in the War of Attrition. Egypt was prepared to agree to an initiative for a cease-fire and a negotiating process now that it felt it was doing so from strength, i.e., once Egypt had secured its rear against in-depth air raids and was on the eve of completing the missile network near the canal.[14] Egypt's consent was not made public until July 22, apparently in order to increase the pressures on Israel and on the United States. The Egyptians wanted to improve their bargaining position in their contacts with the Americans by exploiting Israel's tactical error in rejecting the American initiative so precipitately and by completing their missile network near the Suez Canal at the same time.

Statements by the Egyptians, more particularly after their formal acceptance of the U.S. initiative, emphasized the connection between their consent and Egypt's strategic situation. This was done to make it clear that Egypt's military success in the War of Attrition was in fact what had led the United States to present its initiative and what enabled Egypt to negotiate from the starting point of military strength. In his speech in Cairo on July 23 announcing his acceptance of the U.S. initiative, Nasser affirmed that it was the improvement in Egypt's military position that made it possible for Egypt to accept the initiative, while it had been her military weakness at the end of 1969 that had deterred her from accepting the Rogers Plan:

> We now feel our position is stronger. We are not acting from a weak position, but from a strong one. There have been two main factors in this position. The first has been the increasing ability of our armed forces to strike back; the second has been the increased Soviet political and military backing we have had.[15]

Nasser was also compelled to accept the U.S. initiative for lack of an alternative and for the following reasons:

(1) The Soviet leaders refused to increase their intervention in the war and argued that Nasser would accept the Rogers Plan.[16]

(2) Egypt could not go on with the War of Attrition in face of the high rate of losses and the wear on the army and the population. The army needed time to recover its strength.[17]

(3) Egypt did not have the capability to liberate the territories by force. Securing a better strategic balance could improve Egypt's bargaining position in diplomatic negotiations aimed at an Israeli withdrawal, but to liberate the territories would necessitate strategic superiority and this could only be won by mobilizing the military, political, and economic resources of the whole Arab world and by opening new military fronts against the enemy. (This contention was also meant to counter criticism in the Arab world of the decision to accept the American initiative.)[18]

(4) Accepting the American initiative was thus the only alternative in the existing situation that offered some hope

of a return of the territories since the cease-fire was bound up with Israeli consent to withdrawal. An Egyptian rejection of the American initiative would not only have meant further legitimization of continued Israeli rule of the territories, but would also have insured the continuance of massive U.S. aid, including fighter planes, to Israel. Accepting the initiative made it possible to drive a wedge between Israel and the United States.[19]

(5) The United States was not prepared to offer better terms from the Egyptian point of view for a cease-fire and for starting the diplomatic negotiating process. Egypt's gains in the War of Attrition had not created sufficient pressure on the United States and Israel to realize all of Egypt's wishes.[20]

(6) Israel was not prepared to accept any initiative, such as the joint Soviet-American program, other than that proposed by the Americans.[21]

U.S. Political and Military Pressures

Israel's immediate rejection of the American initiative resulted in the Americans' concentrating their efforts on Israel. Even though the Egyptians did not formally reply until July 22, the Americans had strong grounds for believing that the response would be affirmative. The clearest indication came while Nasser was on his visit to Moscow. The Soviet paper *Novoe Vremya* published an article on July 10 stating formal Soviet agreement and the American initiative.[22] This was interpreted by the Americans in the light of past contacts with the USSR as marking Egyptian agreement as well, since the Russians had refrained from supporting the Rogers Plan in 1969 when it was rejected by Egypt. The U.S. administration headed by President Nixon now took over the campaign to bring Israel around.[23] The main argument was stress on the U.S. commitment to the survival and security of Israel. Once again arms supplies became the key issue in this commitment. In the course of these efforts to persuade Israel, the first step was a personal message from President Nixon to Premier Golda Meir on July 20, 1970, with a commitment to renew the supply of arms to Israel.[24] Signaling of commitment to Israel continued. On July 26, Henry Kissinger, the President's adviser on national security affairs, stated that the United States would work to get the Russians out of Egypt, though he did not go into detail on how this was to be done.[25] On a July 1 television broadcast, President Nixon promised to take action to maintain the balance of power between Israel and the Arab States in view of the aggressive line taken by Israel's neighbors:

> Once the balance of power shifts, where Israel is weaker than its neighbors there will be a war. Therefore it is in the United States' interest to maintain the balance of power, and we will maintain the balance of power. That is why as the Soviet Union moves in to support the UAR, it makes it necessary for the United States to evaluate what the Soviet Union does, and once the balance of power is upset, we will do what is necessary to maintain Israel's strength vis-à-vis its neighbors, not because we want Israel to be in a position to wage war—that's not it—but because that is what will deter its neighbors from attacking it. We look at Israel—a strong, free nation in the Middle East, and we look at its neighbors, its aggressive neighbors, the UAR and Syria. . . . We recognize that Israel is not desirous of driving any of the other countries into the sea. The other countries do want to drive Israel into the sea.[26]

On July 4 the President authorized the shipment of electronic counter-measure (ECM) equipment to be used against the SAM's in the canal zone.[27] The American administration did not agree, however, to make changes in its initiative, which was made public by Secretary of State Rogers at a press conference on June 25.[28] These U.S. signals were welcomed in Israel but they were not enough to produce a substantial change in the Israeli stand.[29] The important turning point in Israeli policy came with the military escalation on the canal and Egypt's agreement to the U.S. initiative on July 22. Israel was now obliged to agree to the initiative or to accept a very serious political confrontation with the United States at the moment when the military situation on the canal was going against her.[30]

The Soviet and Egyptian success in moving up the missile network to the proximity of the canal in the nights of June 29 to

30 constituted at one and the same time a military and a political turning point. The establishment of the missile network was intended as a signal to Israel to respond to the United States initiative, since her strategic superiority on the canal was now in question. The best concrete proof of the new military reality was the downing of five Israeli Phantoms by the missiles.[31] Israel did not possess a military counter to the missiles, and the Israelis were shaken by the evaluation that their planes would be downed in every fight between plane and missile.[32] As Ezer Weizmann ruefully put it, "The missiles wing our wings."[33] Israel's strategic superiority was threatened for the first time since the IAF was sent into the fighting in July 1969, and apprehensions rose accordingly. This state of feeling characterized both the policy makers and the public. Ezer Weizmann wrote at this time:

All the same, I don't get much satisfaction from the government. There too the "Queen in the Bathtub"[34] has spread its infection, I'm sorry to see. Instead of influencing public morale, restoring the people's confidence and stiffening their resolution, the government is itself influenced by the fatigue and weakened morale now characterizing the public. . . . There was no longer complete faith in the right of our cause but merely lip service. Words were all that remained of the massive confidence that we would beat the Arabs even if we didn't have this or that weapon at a given moment, ground or sea or air missiles. . . . The real content of the words had vanished. Naturally, deep depression prevailed in the government because of the loss of planes and the wear on the Air Force. One day Motti Hod (the Air Force Commander), with whom I was having far from easy discussions at the time, came to report to the government. I trod on his foot under the table, "Motti, cheer them up—it reeks of May to June 1967 here."[35]

The question, "What's going to happen? If we don't get the Shrike from the United States, what will happen? What's really going to happen?"[36] summed up the heavy strain on the government, since Israel could not afford the high cost of losing her pilots and planes by attacking more missile sites.[37]

The political turning point in the development of the Israeli response to the U.S. initiative was President Nixon's note to Golda Meir of July 24. Along with his call to accept the U.S. initiative, President Nixon promised not only to guarantee the peace and security of Israel by means of increased military and economic aid, but also to take action to prevent an imposed settlement; the United States would consent to "no return to the 1967 frontiers" and to an Israeli military presence on the cease-fire lines until the signing of a peace treaty.[38] These promises of the U.S. President faced Israel with a very difficult choice— either retreat from its previous policy with the possible breakup of the government, or serious political confrontation with the United States. The Israeli government decided to accept the U.S. initiative even if it meant breaking up the government. It took from July 25 to 31 to reach this decision. When the Labor Front cabinet ministers expressed their general agreement with Israel's accepting the program on July 25, the very day after the receipt of President Nixon's note, it was clear that the main problem then was how to prevent the breakup of the government and a severe internal crisis after a long period of national unity.[39] In the internal debate the fundamental problem was not in fact the cease-fire. Even though most members of the government were of the opinion that the Egyptians needed a temporary cease-fire more than Israel, all of them were ready to accept the proposal for a cease-fire. The problem was mainly the political aspect of the U.S. initiative, the demand that Israel declare her readiness to withdraw on all fronts including Judea and Samaria.[40] This demand was firmly opposed by the Gahal party leader, Menahem Begin. Not everyone in Gahal was fully in accord with all of Begin's views, but they supported him in his stand against accepting the U.S. initiative because of its political aspect. On July 31, against the opposition of Gahal ministers, the government accepted the Rogers initiative.[41]

The Prime Minister announced the government's decision in the Knesset on August 4. Mrs. Meir stressed American pressure as the prime factor in reaching the decision.

In view of the appeals made by the President of the United States and considering his continuing the U.S. commitment on basic lines of policy and his authoritative declarations, the government has decided to give a favorable answer to the U.S. government's latest peace initiative. In spite of the importance of mutual understanding between the USA and Israel on fundamental security and political matters, we cannot ignore the differences of outlook between us on certain subjects. And *in spite of these differences, we cannot ignore the fact that we are discussing the issues with a friendly power* that has proved in the past and continues to prove in the present that it sincerely wants to see Israel living in peace and security.[42]

Particular stress in the remarks of the Minister of Defense was laid on the role of U.S. pressure in reaching the decision. Unlike his colleagues in the Cabinet, he admitted that Israel had now formally agreed to things she had previously rejected by the very fact of using the term "withdrawal" and by accepting negotiating procedures to be laid down by Ambassador Jarring.[43] Consequent to Israel's agreement, the cease-fire between Israel and Egypt became effective on August 8. It included agreement between the parties to freeze positions on both sides of the canal. Thus ended the War of Attrition.

8 Results, Evaluations, Conclusions

THE WAR OF ATTRITION initiated by Egypt was mainly intended to change the "rules of the game" that had come into being as the result of the Six-Day War. The outcome of the Six-Day War had for the first time created a certain potential for changing the nature of the Arab-Israeli conflict from a "zero sum" to a "mixed motive" game. For the first time since 1948 there was the possibility of real bargaining over the issues. Israel could offer to return territories she had conquered in exchange for a political settlement of the Arab-Israeli conflict. However, the enormous disproportion in the relation of forces between the two sides to the conflict as indicated by the results of the Six-Day War would not allow changing the "rules of the game" and even hardened the ideological concepts of the parties to the conflict. Israel hoped that its strategic superiority and its hold on territories would enable it for the first time to secure real peace and security. The Arabs, on the other hand, regarded the disproportion in the relation of forces as the root of an imposed political settlement that would necessarily represent Israel's wishes.

Arab opposition to negotiating from a starting point of strategic inferiority took shape in the Khartoum Conference resolutions shortly after the Six-Day War. When Israel had to face that the Arabs were not prepared to accept the idea of territories as a bargaining tool in a political settlement of the Arab-Israeli conflict, Israel decided to buttress its hold on the territories and insure its strategic superiority. Israel's determination to negotiate from a position of strength in light of the Arabs' refusal to negotiate from a position of strategic inferiority made a mockery of the hopes for starting an era of dialogue in the Arab-Israeli conflict. Israel now saw continuation of the territorial, political, and military status quo as the condition for securing the wished-for peace and security, while the Arabs saw it simply as the perpetuation of the Israeli conquest.

The two superpowers with their opposite commitments to the conflicting parties could not or would not consult each other even given the possibility of providing an option for a dialogue between their respective clients; thus the conditions for a deadlock were created. The central condition for a dialogue was some measure of change in the strategic balance. Faced with the imbalance of forces between the parties, Egypt adopted the means for initiating controlled response to bring about a change in the strategic balance. The Egyptian concept was that such a change would break the deadlock and increase the degree of involvement of the superpowers in securing a political settlement acceptable to Egypt, i.e., Egypt would get back the territories without agreeing to the political settlement of the conflict sought by Israel. Israel saw the War of Attrition as Egypt's attempt to change the territorial status quo by changing the strategic balance; preserving Israel's strategic superiority was the condition for insuring the territorial and political status quo.

When Egypt's military challenges became effective, Israel decided to demonstrate its strategic superiority. Sending the Israeli Air Force into the fighting in July 1969 was meant to counter Egypt's military gains of the War of Attrition and to prevent the superpowers' initiating plans to impose a political settlement that would go against the stand taken by Israel. The more military gains made by Egypt, the readier the United States became to initiate plans for a political settlement running counter to Israel's views. The Israeli in-depth raids were meant to make it clear that not only was there no change in the strategic balance but that Israel's strategic superiority was more decisive than ever—the proof being that the whole Egyptian rear was at Israel's mercy. This strategy turned out to be counterproductive. The effort to demonstrate Israel's strategic superiority produced a countereffort to reduce that superiority. Egypt's success in involving the Soviet Union in the war forced Israel to take action in order to insure her strategic position in the proximity of the canal. Once Israel's strategic superiority was threatened and there was growing apprehension of a clash with the USSR, the country's political position was considerably weakened as well. Israel's attempt to perpetuate the territorial status quo by making use of strategic superiority could not be tolerated by the USSR. As long as Israel succeeded in preventing a change in the territorial status quo without exercising strategic superiority the USSR was faced with U.S. constraints making it difficult to take action to change the strategic balance and force Israel to give way on a political stand. As soon as Israel affirmed its strategic superiority by means of the in-depth raids, it thereby considerably reduced the constraints on Soviet intervention. The United States in fact agreed to Soviet military intervention as the only way to insure the survival of the Nasser regime, once the United States had failed to curb Israel. The USSR and Egypt now aimed to achieve strategic balance as the necessary condition for breaking the deadlock and producing diplomatic moves to change the territorial status quo established after the Six-Day War.

Soviet military intervention in the War of Attrition achieved its purpose. The United States was forced to reappraise its policy in the region. The new U.S. policy was intended, first, to reduce the risk of confrontation between the two powers and limit the presence of the USSR in the Middle East; and second, to extend U.S. influence to the Arab countries and secure acceptance as a factor capable of promoting a political settlement in the region. As Israel's main supplier of arms, and hence guarantor of its strategic superiority, the United States succeeded in maneuvering both Egypt and Israel into agreeing to end the war and beginning a dialogue.

Unlike the wars that preceded it, the War of Attrition ended without a clear-cut military decision. It ended in a strategic draw and the wearing down of both contestants.

In the whole history of violent confrontation in the Arab-Israeli conflict, this was the first war where it was not possible to foresee the victor from the purely military point of view. For all that, there is no doubt that the strategic balance between Egypt and Israel was clearly changed as compared with the situation at the end of the Six-Day War. Egypt had very considerably improved its strategic position by means of the direct Soviet military intervention in the war, which enabled Egypt to find a military and political answer to Israel's decisive strategic superiority as affirmed by the in-depth air raids. Israel's strategic standing, however, had declined in striking fashion from the decisive superiority affirmed in the brilliant victory of the Six-Day War. When Israel tried to translate its strategic superiority into operative political and military terms, it was soon obliged to fight to maintain strategic equilibrium. Maintenance of its strategic superiority depended on refraining from any operative translation of that superiority, on attaining a fine balance between limited operative exploitation of its superiority when and as called for in a given military situation, and the imperative need to refrain from raising military and political constraints on the part of the superpowers to the level where that superiority was completely neutralized. With the in-depth raids, Israel missed this balance. The raids were intended to secure real military and political gains, but the possibility that they would raise the military and political constraints of the superpowers to the level of Soviet military intervention in the war was ignored. This intervention neutralized Israel's strategic superiority and the War of Attrition ended without Israel's finding an answer to the missiles.

The altered strategic balance altered the political balance, even though the territorial status quo was not changed. Completely altered was the connection between the strategic and the political balance that had existed since the Six-Day War. The military and political consequences of the War of Attrition—chiefly the Soviet military presence in Egypt—reduced Israel's political ability to hold out against the superpowers' diplomatic moves directed to settling the conflict. The proof that Israel had lost a measure of its self-confidence and ability to withstand political pressures opposed to its accepted policy was in fact the acceptance of the American peace initiative, acceptance of withdrawal as part of the conditions for a cease-fire and an end to the war, and agreement to return to the Jarring talks after the missile crisis—in spite of the unwillingness of the USSR and Egypt to restore the military position that existed before the missiles were moved. The changed strategic balance resulting from the absence of military and political capacity to measure up to the missile network backed by the Russians led to changed relations between Israel and the United States. As long as Israel was able to insure the territorial, political, and military status quo alone, it could block diplomatic moves counter to its political positions. But when it became apparent that Israel was unable to measure up to the military and political challenges of the War of Attrition alone, and when desperate efforts to do so aroused the United States to the danger of a confrontation with the USSR, the United States took action to bring the war to an end and to reopen a dialogue between the superpowers for this purpose, even if it meant going counter to Israel's positions. Thus the in-depth raids, which were meant to block the implementation of the Rogers Plan, finally led to adoption of the American peace plan for ending the war. Israel's acceptance was bound up with its need to insure the continuance of U.S. political and military support, which was now made conditional on Israeli political concessions. Israel's political and military dependence on the U.S. increased and Israel lost a measure of political and military autonomy because it had to have superpower assistance when it stood on the brink of confrontation with another superpower.[1] Israel's main success in the War of Attrition was preventing Egypt from securing any territorial gains whatsoever. What had guided Israel throughout the war was the fear that any change in the territorial status quo, however limited, might lead in the future to military and political pressures on the part of the superpowers to secure a substantial Israeli withdrawal.

Egypt's gains in the War of Attrition were in direct contrast to her military achievements or lack of them. Its strategy of attrition failed from the purely military point of view but succeeded politically. It was precisely military failure in the war that it turned into a source of strength. By managing to get direct Soviet military intervention in the war when militarily driven to the wall, Egypt succeeded in improving its strategic balance vis-à-vis Israel, and this improved its political stance. By manipulating the superpower political and strategic reality that had now come into being in the region, Egypt managed to produce an American initiative and even to impose it on Israel by merely accepting it. In spite of his military failure, Nasser succeeded in making Israel give way on demands for direct negotiations and an unlimited cease-fire and, for the first time since the Six-Day War, to state its readiness to withdraw. The irony is that it was precisely Israel's governmental efforts to bring about Nasser's downfall that finally led to Israel's own discomfiture. Egypt's political and military dependence on the USSR increased considerably in the course of the war, but by agreeing to the American peace initiative and to a dialogue with the United States, Nasser opened the way for future limitation of Egyptian dependence on the USSR. His heir, Anwar Sadat, later utilized this possibility.

Perceptions of the Results

The results of the war were perceived differently by the two sides. Each judged that the war had ended in victory for itself and that this victory finally set in motion the political processes that ended the war. Both sides were mainly interested in evaluating the relationship between the results of the war and their aims and expectations before and during the war, but this evaluation was not always carried out with entire objectivity but rather according to the hopes and desires of each side.

The two sides' perceptions of the results of the war—and their misinterpretations in their perceptions—had an important effect on their political and military conduct in the period from the end of the War of Attrition to the October 1973 War. The lessons of the war as perceived by the parties were applied in one way or another during the October War.

Israel's Perception
In Israel's perception of the results of the war there were two main sets of evaluations. One was by the government—the version that Israel had won the war both militarily and politically. The other was that of people outside the government, outstand-

ing among them being Ezer Weizmann and Major General (of the reserves) Matti Peled, who thought that Israel had lost the war both militarily and politically because those in charge had not conducted the war properly or had failed to understand its various phases.

The version of Israel's policy framers, politicians and military, was that Israel had won the War of Attrition both militarily and politically since she had succeeded in preventing any erosion of her basic political and military aims as they emerged after the Six-Day War. In the absence of concrete goals in the War of Attrition other than maintaining the territorial, political, and military status quo, Israel's policy framers saw as their main successes their having prevented any Egyptian gains on the ground and having reimposed a cease-fire.[2]

Israel had succeeded in preventing any change in the territorial status quo. Israel's having accepted the U.S. initiative was not interpreted as marking failure; on the contrary, the initiative itself signaled Israel's success and expressed her wishes. "The American initiative fitted in with our main aim—to secure a cease-fire. There was in fact no reason not to accept it."[3] Israel's successes in the War of Attrition even led the United States to abandon the Rogers Plan, or at least to pigeonhole it in the period between the end of that war and the October War, and even, according to the Chief of Staff in the War of Attrition, helped to get the USSR out of Egypt.

I have no doubt that the main factor—not the only factor perhaps, but certainly the main one—in getting the Russians out of Egypt was the fact that Russia learned in the War of Attrition that limited involvement cannot tip the scales. If Israel had displayed weakness in the War of Attrition—or if the USSR had judged that she could turn the scales with limited forces—she would not have got out of Egypt.[4]

Israel's successes were thought to have been the result of finding the right military answers to the Egyptian War of Attrition: standing firm on the lines, sending the Israeli Air Force deep into Egypt, and holding out against the limited Soviet military intervention. The in-depth raids were perceived (in spite of their results) as the main factor that forced Egypt to agree to the cease-fire. The capacity of Israel to maintain her strategic superiority obliged Israel and the Russians to accept the cease-fire.[5]

In contrast to the efforts to present the outcome of the War of Attrition as success for Israel, Ezer Weizmann—during the war the second-highest ranking military officer and Minister in the National Unity Government—described the war as a military and political defeat for Israel. In the War of Attrition Israel failed, according to him, for several reasons: first, the failure to frame a serious, long-term military policy with clear strategic aims; second, the Israeli leadership's "fundamental failure to comprehend the art of combining our massive military power with political moves"; and thirdly, an overestimation of the external political pressures that prevented proper use of Israel's strategic superiority. "Deep in our hearts we were too afraid—of the Russian bear, the American eagle, and even the Arab serpent, and we did not let loose the Israeli lion." Israel refrained from forcing a military decision and weakened its strategic and political stance. The military policy adopted by Israel was partial—mainly a response to the Egyptian military initiatives. "The battles of 1969 to 1970 were characterized by partial military thinking, the main principle being to avoid confrontation and make no effort to defeat the main Egyptian forces. Instead of seeking to defeat the Egyptian army in those years when it was still possible, we were busy delivering stabs on the flanks and attempting to wear the Egyptians down by air power alone."

Weizmann put the blame for the partial security thinking on the Minister of Defense Moshe Dayan, with his exaggerated fears of the USSR:

The Defense Minister of a nation at war has to weigh hesitations and fears in closed conclave in the process of reaching fateful decisions— and to display absolute courage, confidence, and decisiveness in public. Instead he displayed fear, hesitation, and insecurity, not only inside the government, but in public as well. His attitude undoubtedly influenced the conduct of the war in 1969 and 1970. He did nothing to prevent the wrong military moves that were made, and more than that he held back from decreeing a policy of fighting to win. The failure to exploit the in-depth raids effectively—though these were supposed to force a decision against Egypt—because of fear of Russia damaged the entire Israeli military effort. This hesitancy was what encouraged the USSR in the end to intervene. . . . The Soviets exploited this hesitancy and there is no question that it encouraged them to appear in force and quickly. [Instead of persisting with the in-depth raids, the Defense Minister pulled back the Israeli Air Force in view of the Russian moves and once more limited its actions to the canal front only.] Thus the Air Force finally was sent to fight one of its hardest battles—attacking the missiles in Egypt. . . . These acts of commission and omission knocked away the support props of the military leadership, and without question contributed greatly to the troubled atmosphere in mid-1970, when we had the phenomena of "Goldmann-ism," the letter of the final year graduating students, and the "Queen in the Bathtub." [6]

The absence of clear strategic and political aims, the partial military policy, the unsuccessful conduct of the war, and the overestimation of political pressures led to the war's ending without a decisive victory. The military gains that had been achieved were thrown away—the heavy losses inflicted on the Egyptians, the destruction of the missile networks, and the silencing of the Egyptian artillery.

The enormous losses we inflicted on the enemy brought us no benefit politically. This is not surprising, for wars' results are not measured by losses. The serious thing was that after a year and a half of bitter warfare we had not made the enemy feel that we were fighting according to a firm, clear military policy of a kind to lead us to the political goal we had set ourselves: real peace by direct negotiations. When the Defense Minister contends that we broke the Egyptians and the Russians and forced them to agree to a cease-fire, he is flaunting false feathers. [7]

Israel's acceptance of the American initiative did not follow any Israeli successes in the War of Attrition, but on the contrary resulted from the lack of success and the failure to gain a decisive victory in the fighting. The government accepted the U.S. initiative as a godsend: "It is simple stupidity to contend that we succeeded in the war. It was the Egyptians who succeeded in spite of their heavy sacrifices. The War of Attrition must be recorded as the first war in which Israel was defeated." [8] "When we surrendered to the supposition that we could not beat the Egyptian missile system without a technological solution which the Americans had and we did not have, from that moment on in principle we stopped being an independent state carving out our own destiny according to our own judgment and we settled it that we had become a client country."[9]

Like Ezer Weizmann, Matti Peled was of the opinion that Israel failed in the War of Attrition: first, Israel failed to overthrow the Egyptian regime by means of the in-depth raids; second, Israel forfeited her strategic superiority; and third, Israel failed in the attempt to fix "thresholds of limitation" for Soviet military action because the Russians penetrated the entire zone that Israel wanted to protect; and fourth, Israel was so apprehensive of Russian intervention that it agreed to a cease-fire without even insuring a control mechanism that would prevent the Russians from exploiting the cease-fire to their own advantage. "The War of Attrition was the first since the establishment of the state where the IDF was defeated in the field." Unlike Weizmann, Matti Peled put the blame for the defeat on Israel's failure to give sufficient weight to the political constraints because the country wanted to affirm its strategic superiority and because it failed to understand that Egypt could not acquiesce in the territorial status quo resulting from the Six-Day War.[10]

A closer look at the different Israeli perceptions and evaluations of the results of the War of Attrition produces a sense of surprise. The evaluations on the government level are particularly surprising. They were reached without any objective examination of successes and failures. Weizmann judged that the government refrained from any such accounting due to narrow prestige considerations. It brainwashed the public through all the media at its disposal with "explanations," "commentaries," and "doctrines" in order to explain away its failures and in the end, Weizmann said, the government itself believed it all.[11] It looks as if the government really did believe that it had succeeded. Thus, for example, the government said that accepting the U.S. initiative for a cease-fire was fully consistent with its main aims in the war—at the very moment when this same government was struggling to block the U.S. initiative and saw it as very damaging to Israeli interests. Given the political and strategic pressures, acceptance of the initiative was in fact much more a matter of "no choice" than the result of any military success. The government pointed to the in-depth raids as a central element in promoting the cease-fire, but deliberately ignored the causal connection between those raids and the Soviet military intervention in the war with all the consequent damage to Israel's strategic and political stance. The government pointed to its success in preventing Egypt from making any territorial gains and to its having broken the Arabs' iron principle of no direct negotiations as its main achievements, but it ignored the fact that the Israeli Defense Force had failed to find an adequate answer to the Egyptian missiles.

Weizmann was right in declaring that Israel had failed on both the military and the political planes, but it is difficult to accept his explanations for the failure. He was right in pointing to "the failure to frame a serious, long-term military policy with clear strategic aims," but it is difficult to agree with his contention that Israel did not exploit its strategic superiority. It was precisely when Israel attempted to display this superiority in the in-depth raids, ignoring superpower political pressures, that the breakdown of its strategic and political position began. If the government had fully exploited its military power after the Russians intervened in the war, would not this have sharpened the confrontation with the USSR? If Israel had carried out a large-scale land operation on the west bank of the canal or had wiped out the Egyptian missile network after it was moved in August, would not Israel have fallen into an even worse trap than that of the in-depth raids? The war ended without a decisive answer to the missile problem.

Perhaps the most striking failure of the Israeli government was its conviction that maintenance of strategic superiority was enough to block all diplomatic moves counter to Israeli views. Clinging to this conviction, the government gave no thought to initiating diplomatic moves on its own account in order to end the war. In February and March 1970 the government blocked proposals for concluding a temporary cease-fire as an Israeli gesture to Egypt and starting some sort of dialogue with Egypt.[12] In February 1970, the government turned down the proposal of Foreign Minister Abba Eban to launch a peace offensive. His idea was that Israel should not only declare and justify her policies, but also give dramatic expression to her readiness for a temporary cease-fire on the Suez Canal as the first step toward lessening military tension and preventing additional escalation. The government also ignored Interior Minister Moshe Shapiro's suggestion that in order to halt the worsening of the military situation on the canal, Israel should declare an unconditional, unilateral cease-fire, a halt to her air raids for forty-eight or seventy-two hours, as the United States had done in Vietnam as a step toward stopping the war. Still more serious was the government's opposition to the proposal made in March 1970 by Dr. Nahum Goldmann, President of the World Jewish Congress, to go to Egypt and find an opening for Israeli-Egyptian talks, even though he did not intend, according to him, to represent Israel in his talks with Egypt. Mrs. Meir's government turned down the cease-fire suggestions of Eban and Shapiro on the grounds that Nasser must not be allowed to evade his responsibility for the breach of the cease-fire in March 1969 and must declare his readiness to go back to observing it because he had been defeated in the War of Attrition. The view prevailing in the government was that a public declaration by Nasser on ending the War of Attrition was the minimum political price that Israel must demand in return for restoring the fixed cease-fire.[13] Thus Israel failed to seize opportunities to end the war on her own initiative at the strategically best moment and was forced to do so precisely under conditions of strategic inferiority.

Distorted evaluation of the results of the war by Israel's policy makers produced mistaken applications of the lessons of the war, and the results were only too clear in the Yom Kippur War. The illusion that a victory had been won in the War of Attrition and confidence in the correctness of the path taken meant no change among the political and military echelon regarding basic conceptions: first, continued reliance on the territorial and military status quo and distrust of any political initiatives that might be liable to change it; second, overestimation of Israel's military strength and underestimation of the opponent, to a point where the contemptuous conviction took the shape of the absence of a military option for the enemy;[14] and third, continued reliance on a defensive military doctrine in disregard of the failure of the static defense system.[15]

This last point is of particular interest in examining what the lessons of the war were thought to be for Israel's security doctrine. Israel continued to cling to its defensive military doctrine and its corollary, the static defense system, even though the War of Attrition had shown it to be ineffective. This doctrine persistently negated an Israeli preventive war and continued to preach taking the first Arab blow. In June 1973 Dayan said:

> If a new war erupts, the question is whether it will be an Israeli preventive war. The answer is no. We have no intention of starting a preventive war and we are not operating on such assumptions. We do not intend to declare a widening of the war nor will we be responsible for its escalation. . . . We shall do our best to deter the enemy and prevent him from organizing a new war. . . . We are not planning to implement a policy of preventive war.[16]

The belief that a security doctrine based on a static defense system such as the Bar-Lev Line had proved itself in the War of Attrition prevented any thorough examination of what had in fact resulted from basing security on static defense lines. The debate was reopened in the IDF between adherents of mobile defense (Sharon and Tal) and adherents of static defense (Bar-Lev), but no substantial changes were made in the static defense concept. In January 1972 Bar-Lev was succeeded by David Elazar, Tal was appointed Deputy Chief of Staff and Head of the General Staff, while Sharon was put at the head of the Southern Command. It was expected that now that Sharon and Tal had taken over key posts they would succeed in introducing a mobile defense system, but they made no substantial changes. The reasons were the enormous investments that had gone into rebuilding the Bar-Lev Line, the powerful inertia of routine and inadequate will to change things.[17]

In continuing to rely on the static defense system, Israeli framers of security policy ignored some basic facts bound up with the results of the War of Attrition: first, the tactical proximity of the Bar-Lev Line to the Egyptian lines had made it possible for Egypt to force Israel to fight the War of Attrition;[18] and second, the advance of the missiles to the proximity of the canal necessarily meant a measure of neutralization of Israel's air superiority in the canal sector and hence created real difficulties for effective defense on the Bar-Lev Line in a future war, which became clear in the Yom Kippur War.[19] Even after the missiles were moved up to the canal, Dayan and the IDF commanders continued to be of the opinion that no substantial change had taken place in the military status quo. Even though the IDF had not found a military answer to the missiles in the War of Attrition, people in Israel continued to be of the opinion that the Egyptian missile system did not represent a problem for the IDF and that the air force was capable of wiping out the missile network.[20] Immediately after the missiles were moved, the Egyptians began organizing themselves for another war and a canal crossing, while the political and military leaders of Israel considered these contingencies operatively impossible. Israel's political and military blunders in the Yom Kippur War were rooted in mistaken evaluation of the results of the War of Attrition.

Egypt's Perception

Egypt evaluated the results of the War of Attrition as an Egyptian victory from both the military and political viewpoints. From the military viewpoint, they saw the most striking achievement in the war as the changed strategic balance between Egypt and Israel. The change in the strategic balance also led to important political gains: the initiation of the American plan for a cease-fire and Israel's consenting to withdraw from territories it had occupied by virtue of accepting the plan. All the same, the feeling existed that these gains were not enough to enable Egypt to achieve its basic aims.

According to Nasser, the change in the strategic balance was made possible by two things: "The first was the increased ability of our armed forces to strike back; the second was the increased Soviet political and military backing given us."[21] His presenting these two factors indicates the ambivalent Egyptian perception of the results of the war. The increase in Egypt's military capacity was not a result of military achievement in the war. The War of Attrition that Egypt initiated as a strategy for changing the territorial, political, and military status quo failed from the purely military viewpoint since the Egyptians did not succeed in forcing Israel to withdraw from the Sinai or from the Suez Canal by means of raising the "price threshold" of their staying put on the water line; nor did they succeed in imposing on Israel the limitations of conducting a limited war on the ground. The failure of attrition as a military strategy was what made possible its success as a political strategy. Egypt's success in getting the USSR involved in real military intervention was what prevented Israel from affirming its strategic superiority. The changed strategic balance was the result of the changed balance of superpower pressures as viewed by Israel, rather than the changed balance of strength between Israel and Egypt. The changed balance of superpower pressures indeed prevented Egypt's defeat, but it was not sufficient to bring about Israeli withdrawal from the territories. The Egyptians saw that to accept the Rogers initiative was not enough to produce changes in the territorial status quo. During his visit to Moscow, Nasser told Brezhnev, "I don't think the initiative stands any chance of success. I wouldn't rate its chances at more than .5 percent." [22]

To get a change in the territorial status quo it was not enough to have a changed strategic balance based on a changed balance of superpower pressures; it was necessary to change the balance of forces in Egypt's favor. "Our force must be above his [the enemy's] force. We must try by every means to be superior to Israel, particularly in the air. To achieve superiority over Israel we must pool all resources for the battle. We must mobilize our military and economic resources. We must pool the Arab nations' resources." [23] Egypt's acceptance of the cease-fire was mainly intended to permit working toward a change in the balance of forces between Israel on the one hand, and Egypt and the Arab world as a whole on the other, given the judgment that the results of the war were not sufficient to enable Egypt to realize the aims it had set herself since the Six-Day War. The first step toward changing the balance of forces was to step up efforts to neutralize Israel's air superiority, not only on the canal front but also in the Sinai, by moving up the missile network to the proximity of the canal. The cease-fire was meant to prevent Israel from wrecking Egyptian efforts to set up the missile network in the proximity of the canal. Evidence of this is to be found in Heikal: "The most important thing in Nasser's view was to finish building the missile wall. When completed this would not only protect our armed forces on the west bank of the Suez Canal, but would give protection over a strip fifteen to twenty kilometers wide on the east bank, and so give cover for our troops crossing the canal when the time came." [24]

The roots of the Yom Kippur War are thus discerned in the lessons learned in the War of Attrition. Even though toward the end of the War of Attrition Egypt felt that it had succeeded in securing certain military and political gains, Nasser judged that these were insufficient to bring about an Israeli withdrawal. To reach more substantial military and political results, it was necessary to change the balance of forces between Israel and the Arabs, and to change Egypt's military strategy from protracted attrition to a swift offensive. The Egyptian forces crossing the canal under the protection of a missile umbrella—the strategy that would be put into practice in the Yom Kippur War—was based on the plan framed by Nasser at the end of the War of Attrition, as Heikal testifies: "Nasser gave General Fawzī orders to prepare for 'Operation Granite,' which was to provide for crossing the canal and pushing as far as the Sinai passes." [25]

Was the War of Attrition a Limited War?

The War of Attrition between Israel and Egypt is defined as basically a limited war, but it was characterized by striking transgressions of the limitations that characterize such a war. These transgressions arose from two main sources: first, Egypt's basic lack of understanding of how to conduct a limited war of attrition; and second, the temptation offered both sides to widen the war in the belief that it would thereby be possible to realize significant political and strategic gains.

The Egyptians' planning of the War of Attrition was flawed on the tactical and strategic levels by lack of understanding of the limitations of a war of attrition as a limited strategy. The choice of attrition as a strategy was based mainly on an evaluation of Egypt's limited capability to embark on a total war or on other limited strategies, but without any overall concept of a war of attrition as limited. Most of the mistakes the Egyptians made arose out of a faulty understanding of limited war. The Egyptian leadership tried to make the advantages of a limited war suit Egypt's needs, without having a clear idea of the limitations implicit in this strategy. The Egyptian leadership thought that the military and political constraints characteristic of a limited war would prevent Israel from developing her full military ascendancy, but would enable Egypt to realize all its politico-strategic aims. Thus, for example, Heikal presented Egyptian strategy in the War of Attrition as intended to realize all the aims that could be realized in a total war, without asking whether it was in fact possible by means of a limited war to achieve the aims of a total war, or whether trying to achieve Egyptian aims in this fashion challenged the basic concept of a limited war.[26] The assumption that Egypt was capable of inflicting 10,000 Israeli casualties in a limited, static war was not compatible with the concept of limited war. How could results like these possibly be reached in a war conceived as fundamentally limited, static, and lasting from six to eight weeks? And if Egypt had succeeded in achieving results like these, would the war have continued to be limited? The view that Egypt must choose a strategy linked to its politico-strategic advantages was correct, but it did not logically follow that Egypt's politico-strategic advantages would necessarily be Israel's disadvantages. The premise that a prolonged war suited Egyptian conditions did not necessarily negate the premise that this strategy may in a given situation have suited Israel as well, notwithstanding that the Israeli security doctrine proscribed prolonged war. Another flaw in the Egyptian strategy was its overestimation of Egypt's staying power in a static war of attrition and its underestimation of Israel's staying power and potential success in such a war. Heikal judged that Israel's staying power in a lengthy war would be limited because of limited human and material resources. In the first stage of the war, in the phase when it was conducted the way Egypt wanted and without significant Israeli escalation, Israel displayed staying power well beyond the period of six to eight weeks that Heikal had thought was its limit.[27] In spite of the war's being prolonged, Israel did not need to mobilize any very large part of its economic and military resources, while Egypt was obliged to do just that.

Furthermore, the Egyptian view that crossing the Suez Canal

would be feasible without altering the limited nature of the war was not well founded. It is highly probable that if Egypt had effected a canal crossing, the war would have developed very considerably beyond the bounds of its supposed limitations, given the great importance attached by Israel to the preservation of the status quo. The view that Egypt had an advantage in the war because it had more vital interests at stake then Israel was also unsound. Egypt's determination to change the status quo was no greater than Israel's determination to maintain it. Israel's readiness to take the risks involved in widening the war in order to preserve the status quo was also underestimated.

The fundamental flaw in the Egyptian planning of the War of Attrition was that all Egypt's moves in the war were based on manipulating Israel's limitations, without consideration of the conditions under which Israel would be liable to transgress the limitations of a static war while still keeping within the accepted framework of limitations characterizing a limited war. The Egyptian attempt to distinguish between a static war of attrition and a limited war did not take into account that a war of attrition is only one specific type of limited war, and that a limited war can develop different variations outside the bounds of a lengthy, static war of attrition.

The Egyptians failed to realize the possibility—or failed to correctly gauge—that a static war of attrition would be liable to change in character even while remaining within the bounds of a limited war. Egypt failed to give sufficient weight to possible escalation in this type of war. When Israel escalated the air war, the Egyptians had no suitable alternative plan. This was perhaps the clearest sign of the failure of Egyptian strategy. The belief that a limited war was based on the common interest of the parties in staying within certain bounds was perceived to hold for Israel's behavior alone. On this perception Egypt founded its presumed capacity to dictate the bounds of the war, its character, its desired duration, and its results. The biggest blunder of Egyptian strategy was thus a mistaken concept of Egypt's capacity to dictate a certain kind of war. The use of the Soviet threat against Israel as a deterrent worked only as part of a development toward total war, or at least a striking breakdown of the limited war framework. Once Israel evaluated the dangers from an Egyptian canal crossing as worse than the risks involved in escalating the war, the whole Egyptian strategic concept of the war collapsed.

Up to the destruction of the Egyptian antiaircraft network at the end of 1969, Israel was careful to restrict itself to controlled military responses that did not go beyond the framework of a limited war. Israel's adding the air force to the war after July 1969, though a military escalation, was aimed at deescalatory goals—to prevent an Egyptian canal crossing. By wrecking the Egyptian preparations for a crossing and forcing Egypt to give up the idea for the time being, Israel prevented a widening of the war. However, the Israeli Air Force's destruction of the Egyptian antiaircraft network during the in-depth raids after January 1970 led to serious escalation of the war. The war continued to be basically limited, but it now went well beyond its previous bounds. With the in-depth raids, many of the limitations that had characterized the war from March to December 1969 now disappeared. From January to April 1970 the war was in many respects a new type of war, for the in-depth raids introduced substantial changes in the nature of the war on both the political and the military planes.

First, a significant escalation took place in the political aims of both sides in the war. From a situation of limited and defensive political and military aims, Israel moved toward formulating general, offensive, political aims which differed markedly from the political aims characteristic of a limited war. To aim at breaking Egypt's political determination and its will to fight was certainly more characteristic of a general than of a limited war. Even if the military means for attaining this goal were relatively limited (raids on strategic military targets), they were not limited enough to prevent it looking as if Israel had set general political aims. Even if Israel's leaders repeatedly affirmed that they were not interested in bringing about Egypt's total defeat or overthrowing the regime, once Israel's war aims appeared to her opponents—both Egypt and the USSR—as total ones, the war was necessarily perceived by them as general and not limited. Second, the in-depth raids led to real changes from the purely military viewpoint as well. The war stopped being local—limited to the canal front—and it widened to such an extent that a large part of Egypt's territory became part of the front. The targets selected also changed. They were still basically military targets, but they now included targets not on the front line.

The Egyptian decision to call in Soviet military intervention was also without question political and military escalation. Though the primary aim behind the efforts to get the USSR to intervene militarily was to deter Israel from proceeding with the in-depth raids, it turned out that by actually bringing about this intervention Egypt hoped to be able at a later stage to opt for a more general war in order to achieve the liberation of the Sinai.

Although the Soviet military intervention led to the breakdown of various limitations, increasing the number and type of participants in the war (a direct role played by a superpower) and the military means employed (introducing SA-3 missiles, a new kind of missiles in the region), its character was nevertheless mainly limiting. The political constraints bound up with the Soviet military intervention brought the in-depth raids to a stop, changed the strategic balance, and ended the war.

Theoretical Implications

We turn, finally, to an examination of the relationship between the empirical results of the case study and the framework for the study of limited local war outlined in chapter 1. The theoretical framework was highly relevant and useful for analyzing and explaining the interactions that took place during the War of Attrition and its outcome. The general theoretical framework identified the relevant variables and helped to assess their reciprocal relationships. Identifying the factors relevant for limiting and expanding a war between local actors and consideration of the kinds of relationship that may exist between "constraints" and "limitations" made it possible to better distinguish the various factors behind the dynamics of limited local war. The findings of this study strongly support the conclusion that constraints rather than limitations were the major factors limiting and finally terminating the war.

Despite several important escalations in objectives, in level and scope of military means employed, and in participants, the war remained limited. But the limitations were not consensual limitations. Egypt and Israel did not succeed in achieving consensual limitations because they did not share the same understanding of limitations. At the outset Egypt believed that war limitations were based on capacity to control the bounds of the war, its character, and its results. The Egyptian concept that a favorable set of limitations in the war would result from ability to manipulate Israel's political and strategic position was contrary to the concept of consensual limitations. Consensual limitations were also difficult to achieve because there was no parity of power between Egypt and Israel and because it was difficult to conceive of an equalization of advantages within consensual limitations. The only attempt to achieve consensual limitations was made by Israel in the last stage of the war. Israeli leaders attempted to convince the Soviet Union to accept two consensual limitations—both geographic. These limitations were based on the assumption that failure to accept them by tacit or formal bargaining would bring both sides to a military confrontation, but they failed because the USSR refused to accept consensual limitations that stood in the way of Soviet aims. Soviet acceptance of consensual limitations with Israel might have reduced the prestige and the credibility of the Soviet Union as a superpower. This experience suggests that a small state attempting to agree on consensual limitations with a superpower encounters special difficulties.

External political constraints on Israel and military capability constraints on Egypt, rather than consensual or self-interest limitations for either, appear to have been the most effective sources for limiting the war. External political constraints proved to be particularly important—indeed necessary—for several reasons: there was no parity in power between the local actors, there was no equalization of advantages from the limitations, and there were special patron-client relationships between Egypt and the Soviet Union and between Israel and the United States. The element of uncertainty regarding the superpowers' reactions or direct superpower pressures or threats—including actual direct military intervention—forced limitations on Israel and Egypt. The pattern of limitations changed according to the degree of this uncertainty. When the expectation of Soviet intervention was low, the Israeli readiness to expand the war was high (Israeli in-depth air raids); when concern over Soviet reaction mounted, Israel's readiness to expand the war was low (nonutilization or restrictions on the air force).

The War of Attrition suggests that in situations in which local actors fail to maintain limitations, the superpowers' roles in management of limitations is likely to become more prominent and decisive. Moreover, when the local actors fail to terminate a war by bilateral agreement, as in this case (in fact, they did not even enter into serious bargaining efforts to reach a cease-fire), the superpowers tend to assume the responsibility for terminating the war. In the War of Attrition, termination was imposed in effect by outside powers.

Additional case studies of limited local war are needed, of course, in order to broaden understanding of the range and variety of interrelationships between sources of constraints and limitations in local war, their interactions, and their roles in determining the outcome of such conflicts.

Notes

Preface

1. The literature available in English includes: Ahmed S. Khalidi, "The War of Attrition," *Journal of Palestine Studies* (1973), 3(1):60–87; Edgar O'Ballance, *The Electronic War in the Middle East 1968–70* (London: Archon, 1974); Avi Shlaim and Raymond Tanter, "Decisions Process, Choice, and Consequences: Israel's Deep-Penetration Bombing in Egypt, 1970," *World Politics* (1978), 30(4):483–516; Lawrence L. Whetten, *The Canal War: Four Power Conflict in the Middle East* (Cambridge: MIT Press, 1974).

Introduction

1. This point is brought out by Dan Horowitz in "Towards a New Conception of Security," in *Alternative Solutions to the Israeli-Arab Conflict* (Hebrew), p. 27, a discussion held in June 1974 in the aftermath of the October 1973 War, in continuation of the international symposium held in May 1973 at the Van Leer Institute in Jerusalem.

1. Framework for the Study of Limited Local War

1. On the development of the strategic theory of limited war see, e.g., Bernard Brodie, "Unlimited Weapons and Limited War," *The Reporter* (November 18, 1954), pp. 16–21; Brodie, "More About Limited War," *World Politics* (October 1957), 10:117–22; Brodie, *Strategy in the Missile Age* (Princeton, N.J.: Princeton University Press, 1959); Alexander L. George, *The Quid Pro Quo Approach to the Study of Limitations in Local War* (Rand D–5690, October 20, 1958); George, *Framework for the Study of the Tac-Air Sanctuary* (Rand D–6360, January 14, 1959); Morton Halperin, *Limited War: An Essay on the Development of the Theory and Annotated Bibliography* (Cambridge, Mass.: Harvard University, Center for International Affairs, Occasional Paper no. 3, May 1962); Halperin, *Limited War in the Nuclear Age* (New York: Wiley, 1963); William W. Kaufmann, "Limited Warfare," in William W. Kaufmann, ed., *Military Policy and National Security*, pp. 102–36 (Princeton, N.J.: Princeton University Press, 1956); Henry A. Kissinger, *Nuclear Weapons and Foreign Policy* (New York: Harper, 1957); Rob-

ert E. Osgood, Limited War: The Challenge to American Strategy (Chicago: University of Chicago Press, 1957); Thomas C. Schelling, The Strategy of Conflict (Cambridge, Mass.: Harvard University Press, 1960); Schelling, Arms and Influence (New Haven, Conn.: Yale University Press, 1966).

2. Robert E. Osgood, "The Reappraisal of Limited War," Adelphi Papers no. 54 (London: Institute for Strategic Studies, 1969), p. 42.

3. Yehoshaphat Harkabi, Nuclear War and Nuclear Peace (Jerusalem: translated from Hebrew, Israel Program for Scientific Translations, 1966), p. 88.

4. Brodie, Strategy in the Missile Age, pp. 309–10.

5. George, Quid Pro Quo Approach, p. 20.

6. Osgood, "Reappraisal of Limited War," p. 61.

7. On the distinction between constraints and limitations, see George, Quid Pro Quo Approach, pp. 21–2.

8. Charles H. Fairbanks, "War Limiting," in Klaus Knorr, ed., Historical Dimensions of National Security Problems, p. 166. (Lawrence, Kansas: Allen Press, 1976).

9. George, Framework, pp. 8–9. See also, Klaus Knorr, On the Uses of Military Power in the Nuclear Age (Princeton, N.J.: Princeton University Press, 1966), pp. 68–71.

10. Halperin, Limited War, pp. 24–5, 36, 45–7.

11. George, Framework, p. 5; Halperin, Limited War, pp. 6, 31; Schelling, Arms, p. 173.

12. George, Quid Pro Quo Approach, pp. 24–5; Framework, p. 5.

13. Schelling, Strategy of Conflict, pp. 53–80; Arms, pp. 131–41, 199–203, 215–20.

14. Schelling, Strategy of Conflict, p. 77; see also Alexander L. George, David K. Hall, and William R. Simons, The Limits of Coercive Diplomacy: Laos, Cuba, Vietnam (Boston: Little, Brown, 1971), ch. 1.

15. Halperin, Limited War, p. 30.

16. George, Quid Pro Quo Approach, p. 25.

17. George, Framework, pp. 22–3. On the problem of maintaining limitations by "tacit bargaining," see George's excellent discussion, Quid Pro Quo Approach, pp. 26–54.

18. Kissinger, Nuclear Weapons, p. 139; Maxwell D. Taylor, The Uncertain Trumpet (New York: Harper, 1959), p. 62.

19. Kissinger, Nuclear Weapons, pp. 123–24; see also Fulvia Attina, "Limited War," Peace Research Reviews, 1974, pp. 59–97.

20. Osgood, Limited War, pp. 22–3. On the principle of primacy of political aims over military means, see Karl von Clausewitz, in Anatol Rapoport, ed., On War (London: Penguin, 1968), pp. 397–410; B. H. Liddell Hart, Strategy (New York: Praeger, 1974), pp. 319–33; Brodie, Strategy in the Missile Age, pp. 312–13.

21. Attina, "Limited War," p. 69; Osgood, Limited War, pp. 248–49; Halperin, Limited War, p. 35.

22. Kissinger, Nuclear Weapons, pp. 152–53.

23. Kissinger is of the opinion that both sides in a limited war should refrain from carrying out in-depth air raids and from striking at economic or civilian targets since the side suffering damage is liable to feel that the war is not limited where he is concerned but total. The more the whole country becomes a war zone, the more certain the limitations to break down. Kissinger, Nuclear Weapons, pp. 152–53. See also Halperin, Limited War, p. 35; George, Framework, pp. 30–35.

24. Attina, "Limited War," p. 68; Halperin, Limited War, pp. 34–35.

25. Attina, "Limited War," pp. 68–69; Kissinger, Nuclear Weapons, pp. 152–53, 170; Edward L. Warner III, "Escalation and Limitation in Warfare" in Richard G. Head and Ervin J. Rokke, eds., American Defense Policy (Baltimore: Johns Hopkins University Press, 1973), p. 183.

26. Osgood, Limited War, p. 245.

27. Attina, "Limited War," p. 50; Halperin, Limited War, p. 28.

28. Kaufmann, "Limited Warfare," p. 109.

29. Schelling, Arms and Influence, p. 164.

30. George, Framework, p. 20.

31. Ibid.

32. Ibid.

33. On the definition of bargaining power and its implications see Glenn H. Snyder and Paul Diesing, Conflict Among Nations (Princeton, N.J.: Princeton University Press, 1977), pp. 190–91.

34. Schelling, Arms and Influence, pp. 216–20.

35. Yair Evron, The Middle East: Nations, Superpowers, and the Wars (London: Elek, 1973), pp. 173–91. See also Robert L. Rothstein, Alliances and Small Powers (New York: Columbia University Press, 1968), pp. 261–64; Robert O. Keohane, "The Big Influence of Small Allies," Foreign Policy (1971), no. 2, pp. 161–82; Ernst B. Haas, "Multilateral Incentives for Limiting International Violence" in Richard Rosecrance, ed., The Future of the International Strategic System (San Francisco: Chandler, 1971), pp. 151–74.

36. Richard Smoke, War: Controlling Escalation (Cambridge: Harvard University Press, 1977), p. 17.

37. John Garnett, "Limited War" in John Baylis, Ken Booth, John Garnett, and Phil Williams, eds., Contemporary Strategy (New York: Holmes and Meier, 1975), p. 126; Warner, "Escalation and Limitation," p. 182.

38. Warner, "Escalation and Limitation," p. 185; George et al., The Limits of Coercive Diplomacy, p. 16.

39. Halperin, Limited War, p. 29.

40. Ibid.

41. Schelling, Strategy of Conflict, p. 104; Schelling, Arms and Influence, pp. 155, 164.

42. Schelling, Arms and Influence, pp. 164–65.

43. Smoke, War: Controlling Escalation, p. 242.

44. Ibid., pp. 250–51.

45. Halperin, Limited War, p. 29; Smoke, War: Controlling Escalation, p. 25.

46. Kissinger, Nuclear Weapons, p. 189.

47. Osgood, "Reappraisal of Limited War," p. 166; Kissinger, Nuclear Weapons, p. 141.

48. Osgood, "Reappraisal of Limited War," p. 166; Liddell Hart, Strategy, p. 334.

49. Halperin, Limited War, pp. 24–25, 45–47; Zeev Schiff, Phantom Over the Nile: The Story of Israel's Air Corps (Haifa: Shikmona, 1970) (Hebrew), p. 44.

50. Osgood, "Reappraisal of Limited War," p. 166; Kissinger, Nuclear Weapons, pp. 139–41; Garnett, "Limited War," p. 126; Kaufmann, "Limited Warfare," p. 112; Smoke, War: Controlling Escalation, p. 24; Brodie, 1963, p. 314.

51. Halperin, Limited War, p. 9.

52. Smoke, War: Controlling Escalation, p. 25.

53. Warner, "Escalation and Limitation," pp. 184–85; Halperin, *Limited War*, p. 3.

54. Warner, "Escalation and Limitation," pp. 185–87; Halperin, *Limited War*, pp. 29–38.

55. Snyder and Diesing, *Conflict*, pp. 207–8.

56. George et al., *Limits of Coercive Diplomacy*, pp. 8–11.

57. Halperin, *Limited War*, p. 9.

58. Kissinger, *Nuclear Weapons*, p. 140.

59. Schelling, *Arms and Influence*, p. 21.

2. The Theory and Definition of "War of Attrition"

1. A short treatment of the theory of "strategy of attrition" is to be found in Alexander L. George, David K. Hall, and William E. Simons, eds., *The Limits of Coercive Diplomacy: Laos, Cuba, Vietnam* (Boston: Little, Brown, 1971), pp. 19–20. Also see Russell F. Weigley, *The American Way of War; A History of United States Military Strategy and Policy* (New York: Macmillan, 1973), pp. 3–17.

2. The term *attrition* is defined by John Quick in *Dictionary of Weapon and Military Terms* (New York: McGraw-Hill, 1973) as "the reduction of the effectiveness of a force caused by loss of personnel and material."

3. Quincy Wright, *A Study of War* (Chicago: University of Chicago Press, 1942), pp. 314–15.

4. On the development of the war on the western front in World War I and on the eastern front in World War II into wars of attrition, see B. H. Liddell Hart, *The Decisive Wars of History: A Study in Strategy* (London: G. Bell, 1929), pp. 161–71; Liddell Hart, *Strategy* (New York: Praeger, 1965), pp. 167–79; Liddell Hart, *The War in Outline* (London: Faber and Faber, 1936), pp. 65–77, 113–27; Basil Collier, *The Lion and the Eagle: British and American Strategy, 1900–1950* (London: Macdonald, 1972), pp. 97–124; Hoffman Nickerson, *The Armed Horde, 1793–1939* (New York: Putnam, 1940), pp. 261–81; Theodore Ropp, *War in the Modern World* (Durham, N.C.: Duke University Press, 1959), pp. 201–5, 228–29, 321–25.

5. See e.g., Alexander George, et al., *Limits of Coercive Diplomacy*, pp. 195, 198–99.

6. This kind of strategy has been dubbed "compellence" by Schelling to indicate an attempt or intention to force the adversary to consent to a given change in the political and/or military situation, in contrast to "deterrence," the attempt to prevent the collapse of a given political and/or military situation. Thomas C. Schelling, *Arms and Influence* (New Haven, Conn.: Yale University Press, 1966), pp. 69–91.

Attrition strategy is also characteristic of guerrilla warfare, which is generally waged by the weaker side in a war. Situations can, however, occur when it is precisely the more powerful side that chooses a war of attrition as the strategy preferred, because of political pressures. Nigeria in the war against Biafra, the United States in Vietnam, and Israel in the War of Attrition (when it activated its Air Force) all utilized the strategy of attrition in order to bring about a decision in the war, believing this to be less escalatory than any other strategy. See e.g., George et al., *Limits of Coercive Diplomacy*, pp. 19–20, 195, 198–99.

Trotsky saw a defensive war of attrition as the only type of war suited to the geographical conditions and the economic backwardness of Soviet Russia after the Revolution and the only type that could reap any military success for the country until it developed its economic and industrial resources. See Edward Mead Earle, "Lenin, Trotsky, Stalin: Soviet Concepts of War," in Edward Mead Earle, ed., *Makers of Modern Strategy* (Princeton, N.J.: Princeton University Press, 1971), p. 344.

7. Liddell Hart gives a similar explanation concerning the adoption of limited aims in war: "The more usual reason for adopting a strategy of limited aim is that of awaiting a change in the balance of force—a change often sought and achieved by draining the enemy's force, weakening him by pricks instead of risking blows. Usually, a war policy of limited aim imposes strategy of limited aim." (*Strategy*, p. 335)

8. This concept was introduced by Prof. Yehoshaphat Harkabi in his book *On Guerrilla* (Tel Aviv: Ministry of Defense, 1971), pp. 29–30.

9. On the question of the relevance of the duration of the war and the tempo of erosion for the strategy of attrition, see also: George, et al., p. 19; Wright, *Study of War*, pp. 793–95.

10. On the manipulation of risk, see Schelling, *Arms and Influence*, pp. 92–125.

11. On the characteristic features of "strategy of threatened defeat," see, e.g., Yair Evron, *The Middle East: Nations, Superpowers, and the Wars* (London: Elek, 1973), pp. 186–89.

3. Egypt Imposes Its Strategy

1. This evaluation appeared in Abdel Nasser's speech of November 6, 1968, quoted by Cairo Radio in *Daily Report* (*DR*), November 8, 1968, and in Muḥammad Heikal's article in *Al-Ahrām*, September 13, 1968.

2. United States support for Israel was seen by the Egyptians as the central factor in the perpetuation of the territorial, military, and political status quo and in preventing the settlement of the conflict by means of a political solution that would be acceptable from the Egyptian point of view. Militarily, American support was seen as helping Israel maintain strategic superiority over Egypt and thereby deterring Egypt from initiating a new war aimed at changing the status quo. Politically, American support was seen as helping to block any international decision that would compel Israel to withdraw from the territories conquered before it secured a satisfactory peace settlement (necessarily contrary to that desired by Egypt). This evaluation of American policy appeared in Abdel Nasser's statements and expressions of opinion and in Heikal's weekly articles in *Al-Ahrām*. See, e.g., the speech by Nasser of July 23, 1968 (quoted by Cairo Radio the same day); *DR*, July 24, 1968; and Heikal's articles in *Al-Ahrām*, February 23, July 25, and October 4, 1968.

3. In his speech of November 6, 1968, Abdel Nasser said: "Why should our enemy in this struggle—any enemy in any struggle—give up the advantages he has secured unless he is forced to do so, when a will stronger than his own compels him to do so?" *DR*, November 8, 1968. See also Heikal in *Al-Ahrām*, July 25, 1968.

4. This concept was voiced by Nasser as early as November 1967, when he coined the expression, "What was taken by force will be retaken by force, and

only by force" (quoted by Cairo Radio on November 23, 1967; *British Broadcast Corporation Summary of World Broadcast* (BBC), part IV, November 25, 1967. For additional pronouncements by Nasser in the same vein, see his speeches of March 12 and 30 and July 23, 1968, on Cairo Radio, March 12 and 30 and July 23, 1968; *DR*, March 14, and July 25, 1968; BBC, April 2, 1968). For Nasser's doubts regarding the possibility of securing an acceptable political solution, see Muḥammad Heikal, *The Road to Ramadan* (London: Collins, 1975), pp. 54–55.

5. These sentences were singled out by Chaim Herzog as the expression of Egypt's military policy in *The War of Atonement* (London: Weidenfeld and Nicolson 1975), p. 15; and by Khalidi as indicating Egypt's aims in the War of Attrition. See Ahmed S. Khalidi, "The War of Attrition," *Journal of Palestine Studies*, (August 1973), 3(1):60–87.

6. Karl von Clausewitz, in Anatol Rapoport, ed., *On War* (London: Penguin, 1968), pp. 118–19.

7. An additional indication that the decision to utilize the military option was reached in the autumn of 1968 was the evacuation of the inhabitants of the towns along the Suez Canal. See Daniel Dishon, ed., *Middle East Record (MER)*, 1968 (Jerusalem: Israel Universities Press, 1973), p. 359.

8. For a discussion of the artillery incidents of September–October 1968 and the Naj' Ḥamādī action and its effects, see *MER* (1968), pp. 358–63; Anwar el Sadat, *In Search of Identity* (New York: Harper and Row, 1978), p. 197.

9. Speech by Nasser on September 14, 1968, at the opening of the National Convention of Egypt's ruling political party of Arab Socialist Unity. Cairo Radio, September 14, 1968; *DR*, September 16, 1968.

10. *Jumhūriyya*, September 10, 1969, quoted by *Middle East News Agency* (Mena), September 10, 1969; *DR*, September 10, 1969; *AKHBĀR*, July 4, 1969; Ṣawt al-'Urūba, March 29, 1969. According to *Military Balance, 1969–70* (London: Institute for Strategic Studies 1969), pp. 33–37, Egypt disposed of about 400 fighter planes in 1969, including 100 MIG-21s and 90 Sukhoi-7s. The number of Israeli fighter planes at that time was only 275—48 Skyhawks and 65 Mirages. At a press conference in September 1968, Israeli Air Force Commander Mordekhai Hod stated that the strength of the Egyptian Air Force was back to its pre-Six-Day War strength and that Egypt's obsolete fighter planes had been exchanged for the new model fighter MIG-21s and Sukhoi-7s. See Robert Jackson, *The Israeli Air Force Story: The Struggle for Middle East Aircraft Supremacy Since 1948* (London: Stacey, 1970), p. 223. Various sources reported that in the spring of 1969 two to three hundred Egyptian airmen had completed eighteen months' training in the USSR on the MIG-21, MIG-23 and Sukhoi-7. Ze'ev Schiff, *Phantom Over the Nile: The Story of Israeli Air Corps* (Haifa: Shikmona, 1970), p. 23; Jackson, *Israeli Air Force Story*, p. 218; *Christian Science Monitor*, July 11, 1969, quoted by *Ha'aretz*, July 13, 1969. In June 1969, besides a large number of antiaircraft guns, the Egyptians also disposed of about 300 SA-2 antiaircraft missiles.

11. Cairo Radio commentary, October 17, 1968; *DR*, October 18, 1968.

12. Speech by Nasser, Cairo Radio, December 2, 1968; *DR*, December 3, 1968. In June 1969, the Egyptians had at their disposal about 207,000 soldiers (including reserves) as opposed to 290,000 Israeli soldiers (including reserves). The number of Egyptian tanks at that time was about 915 as opposed to 1,020 Israeli tanks. The number of guns at the disposal of the Egyptians was 750 as against 300 for Israel. *Military Balance, 1969–1970*, pp. 33–37. According to various sources, a very large part of the Egyptian army was concentrated along the canal. William Beecher, writing in the *New York Times* (quoted by *Ha'aretz*

on May 15, 1969), reported that Egypt had assembled some 600–700 tanks, 800 guns and heavy mortars, and 50,000 to 70,000 soldiers on the west bank of the canal. Similar figures were also given by *Al-Ḥayāt*, Lebanon (quoted by *Ha'aretz*, May 29, 1969). A high-ranking officer in the Israeli Defense Forces estimated that two-thirds of the Egyptian Army was stationed along the canal (*Ha'aretz*, March 13, 1969). According to Beecher, Israel concentrated 4,000 to 7,000 soldiers along the canal, and the same number in the mechanized force was held in reserve to block any Egyptian thrust or sortie across the canal. See London *Times*, September 10, 1968; *Daily Telegraph*, September 13, 1968.

13. Speeches by Nasser (Cairo Radio, March 28, 1969; *DR*, March 29 and May 1, 1969; BBC, May 3, 1969). Interview with Nasser on Egyptian TV on April 29, 1969; Heikal in *Al-Ahrām*, March 7 and 21, 1969; Cairo Radio commentary, March 12 and April 3, 1969; *Akhbār al-Yawm*, May 3, 1969; *Al-Ahrām*, April 25, 1969.

14. For different views on the effect of the construction of the Bar-Lev Line on Egypt's decision to start a war see Schiff, *Phantom Over the Nile*, p. 21; Matti Peled, *Reflections on Defense Topics* (in Hebrew), *Ma'ariv*, August 12, 1971; and Chaim Herzog, *War of Atonement*, p. 8.

15. The USSR turned down Egypt's requests for offensive weapons as part of their attempt to persuade Egypt not to launch a new, general war. *New York Times*, June 18 and October 13, 1968; *Ha'aretz*, October 13, 1968; *Newsweek*, July 22, 1968. High-ranking Soviet advisers in Egypt warned Nasser that his army was not yet ready for an offensive war in spite of the equipment that it had received, and that it was fit only for defensive tasks. Schiff, *Phantom Over the Nile*, pp. 21–22; Yair Evron, *The Middle East: Nations, Superpowers, and the Wars* (London: Elek, 1973), pp. 188–89. And see Edgar O'Ballance, *The Electronic War in the Middle East* (London: Faber and Faber, 1974), p. 73. According to Sadat it was not part of the Soviet Union's plan to have Nasser fight another war; it supplied him the weapons as a courtesy gesture but never intended them to be used (pp. 186–88). Sadat mentioned that Nasser started and continued the War of Attrition against the wishes of the Soviet Union (p. 196).

16. Testimony to the attempt of the Soviets to persuade Egypt to persist with diplomatic efforts can be found in Heikal's book, *Road to Ramadan*, pp. 56–57, and in his articles in *Al-Ahrām*, July 12, 1968 and July 25, 1968; *Guardian*, July 5, 1968; *Daily Telegraph*, July 10, 1968; *Ha'aretz*, January 2, 1969; and London *Times*, February 7, 1969.

17. In his articles in *Al-Ahrām*, March 7 and October 3, 1969, Heikal defined Egyptian aims as those of a general war, which it intended to achieve by means of a limited war.

18. Ahmed Khalidi ("War of Attrition," p. 60) in his study on the War of Attrition, and Herzog on p. 7 of his book *The War of Atonement*, were both of the opinion that if Egypt had succeeded in achieving its aims in the War of Attrition, the nature of the war would not have been what it turned out to be, but instead there would have been a general, large-scale outbreak of war in the whole region. In their opinions, the intention and aim of the Egyptians was "to create a situation which would enable them to cross the canal and recover the Sinai Peninsula by force." (Later in his article, on p. 77, Khalidi states that Egypt's aims were limited ones.)

19. This fundamental precondition was repeated over and over again by Nasser in his speeches and by Heikal in his articles in *Al-Ahrām*. See, e.g., Nasser's speech of March 27, 1969; Cairo Radio, March 28, 1969; *DR*, March 29,

1969; Heikal's article, *Al-Ahrām*, April 11, 1969; and his book, *The Road to Ramadan*, p. 65; see too the Beirut newspapers, *Al-Nahār*, March 30, 1969, and *Al-Ḥayāt*, April 6, 1969.

20. Heikal, *Road to Ramadan*, pp. 60–61, and article in *Al-Ahrām*, March 27, 1969.

21. The air defense system was intended to neutralize the Israeli Air Force while the Egyptian army was crossing the canal, and this was in fact the basis of the Egyptian strategy in the Yom Kippur War. Heikal, *Road to Ramadan*, pp. 60–61.

22. The Egyptian Defense Minister, Muḥammad Fawzī, reporting to the national convention of the Socialist Unity Organization in closed session on March 28, 1969, expatiated on the potential of the armed forces and their capability, both defensive and offensive. Regarding defense, the Egyptian forces were stated to be in a position to repel any Israeli attack anywhere on Egyptian territory, while the air defense network at Egypt's disposal was capable of repelling any attack by Israeli aircraft. But as regards the offensive, Fawzī stressed that the armed forces had not yet reached the stage of capability to effect a general attack; though it was in their power to cross the Suez Canal, the prospects of victory in this case were no better than 50 percent. *Ṣawt al-'Urūba*, March 29, 1968.

23. *Al-Ahrām*, March 27, 1969 and April 11, 1969.

24. For this analysis, see Dan Horowitz, "Towards a New Conception of Security" in *Alternative Solutions of the Israeli-Arab Conflict*, a discussion on the October 1973 War, held in June 1974 in continuation of an international symposium (Jerusalem: Van Leer Institute, June 1974), p. 29. A fuller treatment of the idea of "compellence" will be found in Schelling, *Arms and Influence* (New Haven, Conn.: Yale University Press, 1966), pp. 69–91.

25. Liddell Hart terms this Egypt's "grand strategy" in the War of Attrition. "The term 'grand strategy' serves to bring out the sense of 'policy in execution.' The role of grand strategy—higher strategy—is to coordinate and direct all the resources of a nation, or band of nations, towards the attainment of the political object of the war." See B. H. Liddell Hart, *Strategy* (New York: Praeger, 1974), p. 322.

26. See e.g., Nasser's speeches of May 1 and July 23, 1970. Cairo Radio; May 1, July 23; BBC, May 4, July 26.

27. Heikal in *Al-Ahrām*, August 13, 1968, and April 29, 1970.

28. After the direct military intervention of Russia in Egypt in April 1970, Heikal, in *Al-Ahrām*, April 29, 1971, laid special emphasis on this strategy.

29. Heikal, *Road to Ramadan*, pp. 47–48. See also Nadav Safran, *Israel—The Embattled Ally* (Cambridge: Harvard University Press, 1978), p. 261.

30. Heikal, *Road to Ramadan*, pp. 47–48.

31. Heikal, *Al-Ahrām*, March 7, 1969.

32. Speech of Abdel Nasser, Cairo Radio, May 1, 1969; BBC, May 3, 1969; Heikal, *Al-Ahrām*, March 7 and March 27, 1969.

33. Even though these aims were not stated in express terms by Abdel Nasser or his spokesmen, they are indicated in Nasser's speech of July 23, 1969, where he coined the term "war of attrition" for Egypt's strategy. Further supporting evidence can be found in what Nasser said a year later, on July 23, 1970, at the Congress of the Arab Socialist Unity Party. In this speech, he hinted that he had agreed to the cease-fire (Rogers' initiative) only in order to make it possible to push the deployment of the missiles forward to the canal and to establish a bridgehead on the other side of the canal under the protection of this missile

umbrella, which would neutralize the Israeli Air Force. Additional testimony to this effect is provided by Heikal in his book, *The Road to Ramadan*, p. 60. See too interview with Sadat in *Newsweek*, April 9, 1973. This evaluation is supported by Evron, *Middle East*, p. 188; Schiff, *Phantom Over the Nile*, pp. 19–22; Khalidi, "War of Attrition," p. 77; and Herzog, *War of Atonement*, pp. 7–8.

34. Thus, for example, in his article in *Al-Ahrām* of March 7, 1969, Heikal explained why a *blitzkrieg* was not a suitable choice as a strategy for taking the eastern bank of the canal or establishing footholds there. First, a *blitzkrieg* demands prolonged planning and the utilization of decisive technological superiority. Since Egypt was technologically inferior to Israel, it could not secure the capability for such an attempt except after a long period of time. This particular limited military option was therefore out of the question for Egypt. Second, *blitzkrieg* demands air superiority since it calls for a heavy blow to be dealt by the air force in the first phase of the war. Egypt had not yet achieved this capacity. Third, *blitzkrieg* is a type of war characteristic of Israel and therefore cannot be suited to Egypt. According to Heikal's evaluation, one of the basic tenets of military strategy is that one has to annul the enemy's superiority by exploiting his shortcomings and not by adopting the military strategy in which the enemy enjoys superiority.

35. Heikal, *Al-Ahrām*, February 2 and September 20, 1968; March 7 and October 3, 1969; *Al-Muṣawwar*, August 1, 1969.

36. Heikal, *Al-Ahrām*, February 16, 1968.

37. Heikal, *Al-Ahrām*, March 7, 1969; Nasser's speech of March 27, 1969 (Cairo Radio, March 27, 1969; Itim Mizrah News Agency: Monitoring Service of Middle East Broadcasts) [IMB]; Nasser interview in *Toronto Daily Star* (quoted by *Ha'aretz*, August 15, 1969), *Al-Muṣawwar*, August 1, 1969.

38. Heikal, *Al-Ahrām*, March 7, 1969. Heikal's figures certainly exceed the bounds of limited war. For criticism of this line of Heikal's, see chapter 8.

39. Heikal, *Al-Ahrām*, March 7, 1969; *Al-Muṣawwar*, August 1, 1969; *Akhbār al-Yawm*, November 1, 1969.

40. For Egypt the War of Attrition, in spite of being defined as a strategy, was not the final battle. Attrition was not in itself the phase of liberation but a preparation for the phase of liberation. (See Nasser's speeches of July 23 and 25, 1969, Cairo Radio, *DR*, July 24, and 28, 1969.)

41. Heikal, *Al-Ahrām*, March 7, 1969.

42. In his speeches of July 23 and 25, 1969, Nasser put the duration of the war at between three and four years (Cairo Radio, *DR*, July 24 and 28, 1969). In the interview with the *Toronto Daily Star* (*Ha'aretz*, August 15, 1969), he put the length of the War of Attrition at five years.

43. Heikal, *Al-Ahrām*, April 25, 1969.

44. On the relation of forces between Israel and Egypt in general and along the canal in particular, see pp. 44–46 in this chapter.

45. Heikal, *Al-Ahrām*, March 7 and October 3, 1969; *Al-Ḥayāt*, May 13, 1969.

46. Examples are February 2 and 16, August 23, September 13 and 20, 1968. Nasser's Chief of Staff, General 'Abd al-Mun' im ar-Riyaḍ convinced Nasser that operations in restricted areas best suited to Egypt might succeed. See Joseph Churba, *The Politics of Defeat* (New York: Cyrco Press, 1977), p. 49.

47. Speech by Nasser on March 27, 1969 (Cairo Radio, March 27, 1969; IMB, March 28, 1969. See too Schiff, *Phantom Over the Nile*, p. 24).

48. In his speeches of March 27 and May 1, 1969, Nasser disclosed that

Egypt took into account the possible damage to economic and civilian installations along the canal and the possibility of evacuating the civilian population from the canal towns. This evacuation began even before the incidents of September and October 1968. See *MER*, 1968, p. 359.

49. In his speech of May 1, 1969, Nasser claimed that Egyptian artillery fire had succeeded in knocking out 60 percent of the Bar-Lev Line and that in the Egyptian army's view it would soon be possible to destroy the other 40 percent.

50. In his articles of 1968 regarding the kind of war Egypt wanted, Heikal expressed doubts about the possibility of imposing a prolonged war on Israel (see also *Al-Ahrām* on February 2 and April 26, 1968); in his articles in 1969, and particularly in that of March 7, 1969, he expressed no such doubts.

51. Heikal, *Al-Ahrām*, March 7, 1969.

52. According to Schiff, *Phantom Over the Nile*, pp. 23–25, the entire Egyptian plan was supposed to be executed in the summer of 1969. It was limited to the capture of certain positions or footholds on the eastern bank of the canal. The Egyptian army was supposed to seize a strip on the eastern bank some 30 kilometers long, or an even smaller sector according to operational developments. The idea was that the crossing would be affected at two points, with the main thrust directed at the northern sector, which was chosen because it was an area of swamps where Israeli armored forces would have difficulty launching an attack. The planners of the operation (after consulting Soviet experts in Egypt) considered the key to the whole operation to be the air force. The Egyptian view was that given the minimal objectives of the operation, the Egyptian Air Force could secure local air superiority along the canal, which would insure the passage of the forces doing the crossing and would also make it possible to block the Israeli armor and air force and thus prevent their wrecking the operation. This Egyptian view was founded on two main considerations: the proximity to the front of the Egyptian airfields, and the Egyptian air defense system along the canal; these two combined would help cover the crossing and hold off Israeli Air Force attacks. Another important consideration for the success of the operation, besides air superiority along the canal, was speed in execution. The Egyptian evaluation was that the first twenty-four hours of the operation would be decisive. If the Egyptian army succeeded in winning real successes in that space of time, it would be possible to secure a cease-fire with the help of the Soviets, and this would open the way for further diplomatic initiatives. In the event of the operation's getting bogged down, the Egyptians thought that the USSR would provide an air umbrella to protect vital targets in Egypt. (See too Khalidi, "War of Attrition," pp. 62–63; Herzog, *War of Atonement*, p. 8; *New York Times*, December 25, 1968.) There are no descriptions in Egyptian sources of these plans for the operation of crossing the canal, but there is a vague reference to them by Heikal, *Road to Ramadan*, p. 60.

53. Moshe Dayan, *Ha'aretz*, April 30, 1969; Golda Meir, *Ha'aretz*, July 1, 1969; *Divrei Ha'knesset* (Knesset Records) (Hebrew), July 8, 1969, vol. 55:3465.

54. Haim Bar-Lev, in *Album of 1,000 Days* (Hebrew), Yitzhak Arad, ed. (Tel Aviv: Defense Ministry, no date), p. 1.

55. Dayan, *Ha'aretz*, March 23, 1969; Dayan, *A New Map—New Attitudes* (Hebrew) (Tel Aviv: Shikmona, 1969), p. 82; *Ha'aretz*, July 2, 1969; Foreign Ministry spokesman, *Ha'aretz*, July 8, 1969; Bar-Lev, *Zahal Monthly Review* (Hebrew), April 18, 1969; Dan Horowitz, *The Israeli Concept of National Security: Fixed Factors and Variables in Israeli Strategic Thinking* (Hebrew) (Jerusalem: Hebrew University, 1973), pp. 35–36.

56. Dayan, Ha'aretz, March 23, 1969; Bar-Lev, Zahal Monthly Review, April 18, 1969; Dayan, Ha'aretz, April 30 and May 29, 1969; Dayan, New Map, p. 94; Foreign Ministry spokesman, Ha'aretz, July 8, 1969.

57. Dayan, Ha'aretz, April 30 and May 29, 1969.

58. Dayan, Ha'aretz, October 20 and November 26, 1968.

59. Dayan, New Map, December 26, 1968, p. 53; Dayan, Ha'aretz, May 29, 1969.

60. Bar-Lev, Lamerhav and Ha'aretz, January 1, 1968; Dayan, New Map, February 6, 1968, p. 63.

61. Dayan, New Map, December 26, 1968, p. 53; Abba Eban, Ma'ariv, February 7, 1969.

62. Dayan, Ha'aretz, January 19, 1968.

63. Dayan, Ha'aretz, January 7, February 14 and May 26, 1968; Dayan, New Map, p. 86. In 1968 and 1969 when Dayan used the term "war," it denoted in most instances general war.

64. Dayan, Ha'aretz, October 29, 1968; Dayan, New Map, p. 88.

65. Herzog, War of Atonement, p. 14; Ze'ev Schiff, October Earthquake (Tel Aviv: University Publishing Projects, 1974), p. 136.

66. Dayan, New Map, February 6, 1968, pp. 63, 66; Jerusalem Post, January 7, 1968.

67. Bar-Lev, Ha'aretz, and Lamerhav, January 1, 1968.

68. Golda Meir, Knesset Records, May 26, 1970, 57:1857. See also Bar-Lev, Album of 1,000 Days, pp. 1–2.

69. Schiff, October Earthquake, p. 136. Chaim Herzog, War of Atonement, p. 5. Hanoch Bartov, Daddo—48 Years and 20 More Days (Tel Aviv: Ma'ariv, 1978), pp. 174–76, Avraham Adan (Bren), On Both Banks of the Suez (Jerusalem: Edanim, 1979), p. 44.

70. Schiff, October Earthquake, p. 137; Herzog, War of Atonement, p. 5.

71. Schiff, p. 137; according to Adan, On Both Banks of the Suez, p. 4, all in the Israeli military high command accepted the idea of the Bar-Lev Line.

72. Schiff, p. 138; Bar-Lev, Album, p. 21; Herzog, War of Atonement, p. 6.

73. Herzog, War of Atonement, p. 6.

74. Schiff, October Earthquake, pp. 138, 140, 141; Herzog, War of Atonement, pp. 5, 11–12. The arguments of Tal and Sharon were fully vindicated in the October War.

75. For the changes in the Israeli security concept, see Dan Horowitz, Israeli Concept, p. 36; Yigal Allon, Screen of Sand (Tel Aviv: Ha'Kibbutz Ha'meuhad, 1968), p. 442.

76. This was pointed out by Dayan at the very beginning of the War of Attrition: "The distance of only 200 meters separating the Egyptian soldiers from ours and our unwillingness to move back even a single meter, not even for the operative need of increasing the range in our own interest, these things of course have their consequences. And the consequences are these flare-ups and the whole price we have to pay." New Map, March 19, 1969, p. 86 (Stress added.) Major General Matti Peled summed the issue up as follows: "Basing the defense on the very bank of the canal was the result of political considerations. Instead of the political calculation's attaching superiority to the entirety of the area held, the forces were ordered to maintain a static defense on the first line of contact with the attackers." Ma'ariv, September 19, 1971. Bar-Lev himself told the newspaper, Davar, only a few days before the outbreak of the October War: "Any deployment that enables them to make a significant gain of terrain in this sensitive area can

turn into a setback for us that it will be very hard to conceal or that will cost us very dear politically. . . . Our will to insure security and our forming up in the form it took was the correct answer." *Davar*, August 3, 1973. See also Adan, *On Both Banks of the Suez*, p. 46.

77. Senior IDF officer, *Ha'aretz*, March 13, 1969; Dayan, *Ha'aretz*, March 9, March 27, and April 7, 1969; *New Map*, April 17, 1969, p. 77. *Ha'aretz* leading article, March 10, 1969.

78. Dayan, *Ha'aretz*, May 19, 1969.

79. Ze'ev Schiff, in *Phantom Over the Nile: The Story of the Israeli Air Corps* (Hebrew) (Haifa: Shikmona, 1970), pp. 19 and 26, expresses the opinion that in the first months of the war no final evaluation was reached in Israel regarding the Egyptian plan of operations, that is, a canal crossing and capture of footholds on the eastern bank. Herzog, on the other hand, thinks that as early as 1968 the Israeli command believed in the possibility of an extensive Egyptian attack involving a canal crossing, such as the offensive launched by Sadat in the Yom Kippur War (*War of Atonement*, p. 5). Herzog does not show, however whether or to what extent this evaluation was operative at the beginning of the War of Attrition.

80. Senior IDF officer, *Ha'aretz*, March 13, 1969; Dayan, *Ha'aretz*, March 9, 1969.

81. The "powder keg" phrase was used by President Nixon in his first press conference on January 27, 1969, *New York Times*, January 28, 1969. The significance of what he had to say on that occasion on the interaction between military and diplomatic activity is discussed later.

82. Announcement by Foreign Ministry spokesman, *Ha'aretz*, March 9, 1969; senior IDF officer, *Ha'aretz*, March 13, 1969; Golda Meir, *Ha'aretz*, May 9, 1969; Dayan, *Ha'aretz*, May 29 and June 27, 1969; *Ha'aretz* leading articles, March 10 and April 22, 1969; Schiff, *Phantom Over the Nile*, pp. 26–77.

83. Schiff, *Phantom Over the Nile*, p. 26.

84. Dayan, *Ha'aretz*, May 29, 1969; Schiff, *Phantom Over the Nile*, p. 27.

85. Senior IDF officer, *Ha'aretz*, March 13, 1969; Dayan, *Ha'aretz*, April 11 and 24, 1969; *New Map*, May 12, 1969, p. 94; Israel Galili, *Ha'aretz*, April 27, 1969; *Ha'aretz* leading articles, April 22 and 24, 1969.

86. Schiff, *Phantom Over the Nile*, p. 27.

87. Dayan, *New Map*, April 17, 1969, p. 77; Dayan, *Ha'aretz*, May 29, 1969 and June 27, 1969; Galili, *Ha'aretz*, April 25, 1969 and June 18, 1969.

88. Dayan, *New Map*, May 12, 1969, p. 93; *Ha'aretz*, May 29 and June 18, 1969; Golda Meir; *Ha'aretz*, July 1, 1969.

89. Dayan, *New Map*, May 12, 1969, p. 93; Dayan, *Ha'aretz*, April 30, 1969.

90. Dayan, *New Map*, May 12, 1969, p. 93; Dayan, *Ha'aretz*, April 30, 1969; the senior IDF officer estimated that about two-thirds of the Egyptian army was stationed along the canal, *Ha'aretz*, March 13, 1969.

91. Dayan, *New Map*, March 19, 1969, p. 168; Bar-Lev, *Album*, pp. 1–2.

92. Dayan, *Ha'aretz*, March 9 and 11, and April 7, 1969; Galili, *Ha'aretz*, April 7, 1969.

93. Dayan, *Ha'aretz*, March 23 and April 30, 1969; Dayan, *New Map*, April 6, 1969, pp. 78–79.

94. Dayan, *Ha'aretz*, March 9, 1969; Allon, *Ha'aretz*, March 19, 1969; senior IDF officer, *Ha'aretz*, March 13, 1969; *Ha'aretz* leading article, March 10, 1969.

95. Dayan, *New Map*, March 9, 1969, p. 86; Allon, *Ha'aretz*, March 12, 1969.

96. Doubts were also expressed in the Israeli press and news media with

regard to the speed and accuracy of the reports on the numbers of losses published by army spokesmen. The appearance of photographs of the fallen in the press also added to the feeling of anxiety and alarm over Israel's finding itself in a state of protracted war from which it was difficult to extricate itself. At a meeting with students in Haifa on March 19, 1969, Dayan spoke of the price paid: "We are paying the highest price in loss of life—are we doing everything in our power to secure something in return for the price we are paying for our presence on the Suez line of fire? . . . Or are we only paying a price and not trying to secure the basic changes that we want to see and that we need to have and for the sake of which—in order to bring them about—we have waged and are waging war?" (*New Map*, p. 170.)

97. The speech of Nasser on May 1, 1969, when he announced that his army had succeeded in destroying 60 percent of the Bar-Lev Line, was the main reason for the Israeli view that some military action was needed that would have a greater deterrent effect.

98. Ezer Weizmann, *Thine the Sky, Thine the Land* (Tel Aviv: Ma'ariv, 1975), pp. 309–10.

99. Weizmann, pp. 309–10.

100. Weizmann stresses his efforts to persuade the military and political leadership to abandon defensive policy. *Ha'aretz* leading articles, May 2, and July 3 and 11, 1969. Ze'ev Schiff, "We must extricate ourselves from our routine defensive," *Ha'aretz*, May 9, 1969. Nathan Yellin-Mor, "War or a political solution?" *Ha'aretz*, May 16, 1969.

101. Dayan, *New Map*, May 12, 1969, p. 94.

102. Dayan, *Ha'aretz*, May 19, 1969.

103. Dayan, *New Map*, May 12, 1969, p. 94; *Ha'aretz* leading article, May 12, 1969.

104. This is the type of escalation called "expansion": a gradual rise in military activity without significant alteration in the character of the war.

105. Allon, *Ha'aretz*, March 12, 1969; *Ha'aretz* leading article, March 10, 1969; Schiff, *Phantom Over the Nile*, p. 26.

106. Schiff, p. 26.

107. In his speech of March 27, 1969, Abdel Nasser admitted that 350,000 inhabitants of the towns along the canal had been evacuated (Cairo Radio, March 27, and 29, 1969; *DR*, April 1, 1969; see too *Al-Nahār*, March 30, 1969).

108. In the speech by Abdel Nasser on March 27 and again on May 1, 1969. Cairo Radio, March 27 and May 1, 1969; *DR*, April 1, 1969; BBC, May 3, 1969.

109. In speeches on March 27, May 1, and July 23, 1969, Abdel Nasser pointed out that reprisals against Israel were almost impossible, given the price to be paid in Israel: counterreprisals (Cairo Radio; *DR*, April 1, 1969; BBC, May 3, 1969; *DR*, July 24, 1969).

110. Abdel Nasser, Cairo Radio, July 23, 1969; *DR*, July 24, 1969.

111. Schiff, *Phantom Over the Nile*, pp. 27–28. There were, however, air fights in the March–July period in the course of which thirteen Egyptian planes and one Israeli Piper plane were downed.

112. See William B. Quandt, *Decade of Decisions: American Policy Toward the Arab-Israeli Conflict, 1967–76* (Berkeley: University of California Press, 1977), pp. 72–104.

113. *Le Monde*, April 4, 1969; *New York Times*, April 4, 1969; London *Times*, April 5, 1969; *International Herald Tribune*, April 2, 1969.

114. Lawrence L. Whetten, *The Canal War: Four Powers Conflict in Middle East* (Cambridge, Mass.: MIT Press, 1974), p. 79.

115. *Christian Science Monitor*, May 21, 1969; *Washington Post*, May 8 and June 7, 1969; *New York Times*, April 9, 1969; *Observer*, May 3 and 25, 1969.

116. Quandt, *Decade of Decisions*, pp. 86, 87; *International Herald Tribune*, April 25, 1969; *New York Times*, April 3, 1969.

117. *International Herald Tribune*, June 28, 1969. Quandt, *Decade of Decisions*, p. 86; Safran, *Israel—Embattled Ally*, p. 433. The proposals were not disclosed by American sources but were first published in *Al-Ahrām* on June 27, 1969. According to *Al-Ahrām*, the plan included the following points: an end to the state of war, demilitarization of the Egyptian territories evacuated by Israel, Israeli withdrawal to the June 4, 1967 frontiers, cessation of Egyptian aid to the terrorists, opening of the Straits of Tiran and the Suez Canal to free transit, solution of the refugee question, direct negotiations between Israel and the Arabs at a certain stage of the talks in order to sign an agreement, and stationing of United Nations forces (to be withdrawn only with the consent of the Security Council). The question of the Gaza Strip would remain open for further discussion.

118. *New York Times*, June 15, 1969; Quandt, *Decade of Decisions*, p. 86.

119. Whetten, *Canal War*, pp. 73–74; Quandt, *Decade of Decisions*, p. 87.

120. *Akhbār al-Yawm*, March 15, 1969; *Al-Nahār*, March 30, 1969. Jean Lacouture states in his book about pressures exerted by the Egyptian army and particularly by the War Minister, General Fawzī, on Abdel Nasser to reject the proposed plan, that Fawzī even told Nasser: "If you sign this agreement, I shall no longer be responsible for the Army." See *Nasser and His Heirs* (Hebrew) (Tel Aviv: Am Oved, 1972), p. 216. Safran, *Israel: Embattled Ally*, p. 433.

121. *Al-Ahrām*, June 19, 1969.

122. *Middle East News Agency*, June 13, 1969; IMB, June 14, 1969; Daniel Dishon, ed., *Middle East Record 1969–1970* (Jerusalem: Israel Universities Press, 1977), p. 13.

123. *Economist*, June 14, 1969; *New York Times*, June 11, 15, and 18, 1969; *International Herald Tribune*, June 14, 1969; *London Times*, June 20, 1969; *Washington Post*, June 29 and July 1, 1969. According to Quandt, some within the American administration doubted that the Soviets would be prepared to sacrifice regional interests for the sake of improved American-Soviet relations. They argued that the Soviet Union had worked hard to build a position of influence in the Middle East; to maintain that position, it depended chiefly on providing arms to key clients and if peace were established, these arms would no longer be needed in large quantities. The Soviets therefore had an interest in preventing a real peace agreement (*Decade of Decisions*, pp. 86–87).

124. *International Herald Tribune*, July 2, 1969; *New York Times*, June 26, 1969. The hardening Soviet attitude was marked by reversion to the line that a timetable must be set for Israeli withdrawal from all the territories and by abandonment of the idea of direct negotiations at a given stage in talks between the sides. The formal rejection of the American plan came on June 17.

125. *New York Times*, June 26, 1969; *International Herald Tribune*, July 2, 1969.

126. Rogers Press Conference on July 2, 1969, *Department of State Bulletin*, July 21, 1969.

127. Abba Eban, *Ha'aretz*, October 3, 1968; *Ma'ariv*, December 11 and 13, 1968; Israel Galili, *Lamerhav*, October 10, 1968.

128. Statement by Foreign Ministry spokesman, *Ha'aretz*, March 9, 1969; Dayan, *Ha'aretz*, April 7, 11, and 17, 1969; Dayan, *New Map*, p. 77.

129. Dayan, *New Map*, April 17, 1969; p. 77.

130. Golda Meir, *Ha'aretz*, July 1, 1969.

4. Egyptian Strategy Breaks Down

1. In the month of June 1969 there were 404 shooting "incidents," 331 of them (77 percent) artillery fire. In July there were 355 incidents, 207 (58 percent) artillery fire. (This decrease would seem to be the effect of the Israeli Air Force sorties that began on July 20.) After April 19, 1969, ten Egyptian raids took place including attacks on Israeli posts and clashes with Israeli patrols. The Egyptian commando raid of July 10 on the Israeli tank depot at Port Tawfīk produced the conviction that the large measure of Egyptian success in this raid would give an impetus to increased military activity, including canal crossings. In his book *Phantom Over the Nile: The Story of Israeli Air Corps* (Haifa: Shikmona, 1970) (Hebrew), journalist Ze'ev Schiff stresses the decisive influence of this Egyptian raid in producing the Israeli decision to send in the air force. "When future military historians come to sum up what happened between Egypt and Israel," he writes, "they will doubtless be surprised at the extent to which this raid on the quayside at Port Tawfīk was decisive in bringing about one of the gravest escalations in the war" (p. 46). In the air actions in June and July up to the massive entry of the Israeli Air Force, nine Egyptian planes were downed in fights in the air. Schiff, *Phantom Over the Nile*, p. 27.

2. Dayan, *Ha'aretz*, June 27 and July 1, 1969; Schiff, *Phantom Over the Nile*, p. 27. Changes of appreciation of this type are seen by Osgood and Kissinger as factors liable to produce an extension of limited war. Robert E. Osgood, "The Reappraisal of Limited War," *Adelphi Papers* no. 54 (London: Institute for Strategic Studies, 1969), p. 155; Henry A. Kissinger, *Nuclear Weapons and Foreign Policy* (New York: Harper, 1957), p. 141.

3. In a BBC interview, May 9, 1970, Bar-Lev said that in the summer of 1969 Israel had definite information that the Egyptians were preparing to cross the canal. See also Bar-Lev, *Ha'aretz*, July 27 and September 8, 1969; Dayan, *Ha'aretz*, August 5 and 19, 1969; *Ma'ariv*, April 10, 1970.

4. *Ha'aretz*, September 12, 1969; Schiff, *Phantom Over the Nile*, p. 27 et seq.

5. Presumably the repeated reports in the media of belligerent activity along the canal and Israeli losses made people very conscious of the reality of the fighting on the front, which for the first time in modern Israel's history was a very long way from the civilian rear. Despite the great distance from the front, there was an atmosphere of disenchantment in the country at the time—"slackening of spirit, loss of direction, lack of trust, doubts as to the worthwhileness of all the bloodshed and as to the prospects of ever living in this country without black-framed notices in the papers." (Ezer Weizmann, *Thine the Sky, Thine the Land* [Hebrew] (Tel Aviv: Ma'ariv, 1975), p. 310.

6. Weizmann recounts that the straw that broke the camel's back for him personally was his being caught in a massive Egyptian artillery bombardment on a visit to the canal in mid-July 1969, when he experienced the "hellish fire" of the Egyptians for the first time, something he had not previously realized. *Thine the Sky, Thine the Land*, p. 311. On the influence of internal stresses in the

Korean War, see Morton Halperin, *Limited War in the Nuclear Age* (New York: Wiley, 1963), pp. 45–47.

7. Bar-Lev, *Ha'aretz*, July 27 and September 8, 1969; Dayan, *Ha'aretz*, August 5 and 19, 1969; *Ma'ariv*, April 10, 1970; *Ha'aretz* leading articles, July 21 and 28, 1969.

8. Galili, *Ha'aretz*, July 27, 1969; Golda Meir, *Ha'aretz*, July 28 and August 3, 1969; Bar-Lev, *Ha'aretz*, September 8, 1969; Dayan, *Ha'aretz*, November 13, 1969.

9. Dayan, *New Map*, May 12, 1969, p. 94; Dayan, *Ha'aretz*, August 5, November 13, and December 15, 1969; Bar-Lev, *Ha'aretz*, July 27 and September 8, 1969; Foreign Ministry spokesman, *Ha'aretz*, July 27, 1969; Schiff, *Phantom Over the Nile*, pp. 43–7; Ahmed S. Khalidi, "The War of Attrition," *Journal of Palestine Studies* (August 1973), 3:64–65.

10. Dayan, *Ha'aretz*, August 15 and 19, 1969.

11. Dayan, *Ha'aretz*, August 5, 1969.

12. Weizmann, *Thine the Sky, Thine the Land*, pp. 309–10. Weizmann even recommended front-line military action on land, to include capturing footholds on the western shore of the canal.

13. *Ibid.*

14. *Ibid.*

15. Dayan, *Ha'aretz*, August 4, 5, and 15, October 24, and November 14, 1969; Schiff, *Phantom Over the Nile*, p. 28; Weizmann, *Thine the Sky, Thine the Land*, p. 314; Weizmann in preface to Schiff, *Phantom Over the Nile*, p. 14; Bar-Lev, in *Album of 1000 Days*, Yitzhak Arad, ed. (Tel Aviv: Defense Ministry, no date), pp. 1–2.

16. Schiff, *Phantom Over the Nile*, p. 45. Similar views are hinted at in statements by Dayan, Bar-Lev, and Golda Meir in 1970; Dayan, *Ma'ariv*, April 10, 1970; Golda Meir, *Knesset Records* (May 26, 1970), 57:1857.

17. Ezer Weizmann, *Thine the Sky, Thine the Land*, p. 312; Schiff, *Phantom Over the Nile*, p. 47. The air force command opposed also the possibility of operation of the air force without a plan which combined ground and armored forces.

18. Weizmann, *Thine the Sky, Thine the Land*, pp. 313–4; Schiff, *Phantom Over the Nile*, p. 47.

19. Schiff, *Phantom Over the Nile*, p. 27.

20. Bar-Lev, *Ha'aretz*, September 8, 1969.

21. Foreign Ministry spokesman, *Ha'aretz*, July 27, 1969; Bar-Lev, *Ha'aretz*, July 27 and September 8, 1969; Galili, *Ha'aretz*, July 27, 1969; Golda Meir, *Ha'aretz*, August 1, 1969; Dayan, *Ha'aretz*, August 1, 5, and 19, 1969.

22. Dayan, *Ha'aretz*, August 5 and November 13, 1969.

23. Dayan, *Ha'aretz*, August 1 and 15 and November 13, 1969; Bar-Lev, *Ha'aretz*, September 8, 1969; Golda Meir, *Knesset Records* (December 15, 1969), 56:193.

24. Schiff, "The IDF aims at quieting down Suez" (Hebrew), *Ha'aretz*, October 9, 1969; Khalidi, "War of Attrition," p. 65.

25. Khalidi, "War of Attrition," p. 65; Schiff, "The IDF aims at quieting down Suez," *Ha'aretz*, October 9, 1969; *Ha'aretz* leading article, December 28, 1969.

26. Khalidi, "War of Attrition," p. 65; Schiff, "Controlled Escalation at Suez," *Ha'aretz*, August 1, 1969.

27. Dayan, *Ha'aretz*, August 5, October 24, and November 13, 1969.
28. Weizmann, *Thine the Sky, Thine the Land*, p. 312; Schiff, *Phantom Over the Nile*, p. 47.
29. Dayan, *Ma'ariv*, April 10, 1970; Schiff, *Phantom Over the Nile*, p. 53; Weizmann, *Thine the Sky, Thine the Land*, pp. 312–13.
30. Weizmann, *Thine the Sky, Thine the Land*, p. 313.
31. Schiff, *Phantom Over the Nile*, p. 53.
32. Dayan, *Ha'aretz*, August 5, October 24, and November 13, 1969.
33. Weizmann, *Thine the Sky, Thine the Land*, p. 313; Schiff, *Phantom Over the Nile*, p. 53.
34. The bombings focused on a strip to a depth of 30 km. from the canal: Robert Jackson, *The Israeli Air Force Story: The Struggle for Middle East Aircraft Supremacy Since 1948* (London: Stacey, 1970), p. 230. Schiff puts the width of the strip at 20 km. (*Phantom Over the Nile*, p. 66).
35. After October 15 the air force bombings were more intensive and longer (one to four hours). There were bombings on October 15, 16, 23; November 4, 5, 6, 7, 9, 10, 11, 13, 18, 19, 23, 27, 28, and 30; and December 1–11, 14–18, and 25.
36. As a result of an Egyptian attempt to set up fresh missile sites along the canal at the end of December, the IAF carried out its biggest operation since the Six-Day War. For more than eight hours on December 25, scores of planes rained down hundreds of tons of bombs on the missile sites. At the end of the day, the Egyptian front was again clear of missile sites. Schiff, *Phantom Over the Nile*, p. 65; Jackson, *The Israeli Air Force Story*, p. 230; Khalidi, "War of Attrition," p. 66. Presumably at this point the Israeli General Staff believed that after it had been proved that the Egyptian Air Force was incapable of confronting the Israeli Air Force, any Egyptian plan for crossing the canal would have to be based on an Egyptian missile system's providing an "umbrella" against the IAF.
37. Bar-Lev, *Ha'aretz*, September 8, 1969; Eban, *Ha'aretz*, August 17, 1969; Dayan, *Ha'aretz*, August 19, 1969 and October 24, 1969; Golda Meir, *Knesset Records* (December 15, 1969), 56:193; Dayan, *Ma'ariv*, April 10, 1970.
38. Bar-Lev, *Ha'aretz*, September 8, 1969.
39. Schiff, *Phantom Over the Nile*, p. 65.
40. It would have been preferable to end the first period on July 19, but the data were compiled by months, so the whole of July was put into the first period. The data are those of the IDF and they refer only to belligerent activity initiated by Egypt. The IDF published no data on the number of incidents or belligerent actions initiated by the IDF.
41. This figure does not include air actions initiated by Israel, i.e., it does not give the number of air sorties flown by the air force between July and December. Chief of Staff Bar-Lev reported over 1,000 sorties flown by the air force between July 20 and the beginning of September (*Ha'aretz*, September 18, 1969). Dayan reported sixty-five aircraft attacks (*Ha'aretz*, November 13, 1969).
42. Weizmann, *Ha'aretz*, May 3, 1970.
43. Weizmann, *Thine the Sky, Thine the Land*, p. 313; the air activity was not affecting the Egyptian commando raids.
44. Schiff, *Phantom Over the Nile*, p. 65.
45. Weizmann in his preface to Schiff's book, *Phantom Over the Nile* (p. 144): "By sending the Air Force into action on the canal on July 20, we saved hundreds of lives—prevented much blood from being shed."
46. High-ranking IDF officer, *New York Times*, November 11, 1969;

Ha'aretz, December 26, 1969; Weizmann, *Thine the Sky, Thine the Land*, p. 313; Schiff, *Phantom Over the Nile*, pp. 63, 69; Khalidi, "War of Attrition," pp. 65–66; Jackson, *The Israeli Air Force Story*, p. 230.

47. IDF officer, *New York Times*, November 11, 1969; *Ha'aretz*, December 26, 1969; Jackson, *The Israeli Air Force Story*, p. 230, gives the figure of twenty radar stations.

48. Schiff, *Phantom Over the Nile*, p. 65.

49. Dayan, *Ha'aretz*, November 13, 1969; *Ma'ariv*, January 7, 1970, Schiff, *Phantom Over the Nile*, p. 65.

50. These included twenty-one MIG-21's and ten Sukhoi-7's.

51. Dayan, *Ha'aretz*, August 19, 1969: "We cannot get the lines completely quiet." Bar-Lev, *Ha'aretz*, September 8, 1969: "I for my part am not certain that the Egyptians or Nasser are really capable of remaining indifferent to what will or will not happen to them. In reality Egypt will at present, in my opinion, do everything to keep up its current activity along the canal. We are capable of bringing about a moderation of this activity of theirs, but I do not think that it is at present within our power to force them to observe a total cease-fire." Dayan, *Ha'aretz*, August 15, 1969: "I agree with Nasser when he believes that he can hold out for a long time in the present situation."

52. Weizmann, *Thine the Sky, Thine the Land*, pp. 313–14.

53. *Ibid.*, p. 314.

54. Given the consistently limited nature of the IAF action and the non-intervention of the USSR, it was thought in Israel that the USSR was not against this limited type of escalation. See Ezer Weizmann's preface to Schiff's book, *Phantom Over the Nile*, p. 14: "The apprehensions we had felt over intervention on the part of the Russians and the Americans were seen to have been exaggerated." Dayan and Allon gave indications to the same effect in what they were saying at this time: *Ha'aretz*, August 16, September 18, and October 24, 1969.

55. See e.g., Kissinger, *Nuclear Weapons*, pp. 152–53.

56. Abdel Nasser in his speech of May 1, 1969 (Cairo Radio, May 1, 1969; BBC, 2 May 1969).

57. Abdel Nasser's speeches of July 25, and November 6, 1969 (Cairo Radio, July 25, and November 6, 1969; *DR*, July 28, 1969; *BBC*, November 6, 1969).

58. Heikal, *Al-Ahrām*, July 25, 1969; January 30, May 14 and 21, 1970.

59. Heikal, *Al-Ahrām*, October 3, 1969 and January 30, and May 14 and 21, 1970.

60. Heikal, *Al-Ahrām*, July 21 and 25, 1970; *Al-Anwār*, July 23, 1969.

61. Heikal, *Al-Ahrām*, January 30, 1970.

62. Heikal, *Al-Ahrām*, July 25, 1969.

63. Heikal, *Al-Ahrām*, July 25, 1969.

64. *Al-Jumhūriyya*, December 4, 1969.

65. Heikal, *Al-Ahrām*, May 21, 1970.

66. Heikal, *Al-Ahrām*, October 3, 1969, and January 30, 1970.

67. Abdel Nasser in his speech of November 6, 1969; Heikal, *Al-Ahrām*, October 3, 1969, and January 30, 1970.

68. Heikal, *Al-Ahrām*, October 3, 1969, and January 10 and 30, 1970.

69. Heikal, *Al-Ahrām*, January 30, 1970.

70. Heikal, *Al-Ahrām*, October 3, 1969, and January 30, 1970; *Al-Akhbār*, October 9, 1969; *Al-Jumhūriyya*, December 4, 1969.

71. Heikal, *Al-Ahrām*, October 3, 1969.

72. Khalidi, "War of Attrition," p. 66.

73. The destruction of the Egyptian air defense deployment deprived the Egyptian canal crossing plan of its basis.

74. An explanation of this kind had already been made by Heikal in an article in *Al-Ahrām* as early as March 7, 1969, but the War of Attrition had not been given formal mention in Nasser's speeches up to July 23.

75. The Soviet advisers in Egypt helped Abdel Nasser reach this decision. They pressed him to postpone the crossing for the time being and to concentrate on sustained attrition of Israel and continued training of the Egyptian army. In addition to that persuasion, the Soviets put a partial embargo on spare parts of aircraft to force the Egyptians to give up the plan for the crossing. (Schiff, *Phantom Over the Nile*, p. 53.)

76. See for example Abdel Nasser's speeches of July 23 and 25, and November 6, 1969; Heikal, *Al-Ahrām*, October 13, 1969; *Al-Muṣawwar*, August 1, 1969; *Akhbār al-Yawm*, November 1 and 13, 1969.

77. Abdel Nasser in his speeches of July 23 and 25, 1969, defined the war as very protracted, a matter of years. In an interview he gave to the *Toronto Daily Star* (cited in *Ha'aretz*, August 15, 1969), Nasser estimated the length of the war at three to four years. Talking to representatives of the PLO in Cairo, Abdel Nasser put the War of Attrition at five years (*Aṣ-Ṣayyād*, November 13, 1969).

78. See e.g., Abdel Nasser's speeches of July 23 and 25, 1969.

79. Abdel Nasser in his speeches of July 23 and 25, 1969.

80. *Akhbār al-Yawm*, November 1, 1969. Since the war had failed to secure any concrete gains in its first phase, stress was now laid on the political aims.

81. The other Arab countries not in immediate confrontation with Israel such as Saudi Arabia and Kuwait should assist with massive financial support. Abdel Nasser himself announced that Egypt had mobilized more than half a million soldiers and had earmarked more than 500 million Egyptian pounds in the 1969 budget for the needs of the War of Attrition. Cairo Radio, July 23, 1969; *Aṣ-Ṣayyād*, November 13, 1969.

82. Abdel Nasser in an interview in the *Toronto Daily Star* (*Ha'aretz*, August 15, 1969); *Akhbār al-Yawm*, November 1, 1969.

83. *Akhbār al-Yawm*, November 1, 1969; October 2, 1969.

84. Abdel Nasser's speech of July 23, 1969; Heikal, *Al-Ahrām*, October 3, 1969; *Akhbār al-Yawm*, November 1, 1969.

85. Heikal, *Al-Ahrām*, October 3, 1969; *Akhbār al-Yawm*, November 1, 1969.

86. Abdel Nasser in his speech of July 23, 1969, and in his interview in the *Toronto Daily Star* (*Ha'aretz*, August 15, 1969).

87. Lawrence L. Whetten, *The Canal War: Four Powers Conflict in Middle East* (Cambridge: M.I.T. Press, 1974), p. 70.

88. Whetten, *Canal War*, p. 75; *International Herald Tribune*, October 1–5, 1969; January 13, 1970; Nadav Safran, *Israel—The Embattled Ally* (Cambridge: Harvard University Press, 1978), p. 434.

89. London *Times*, *Daily Telegraph*, *Guardian*, *Morning Star*, September 22, 1969.

90. Whetten, *The Canal War*, p. 75; William B. Quandt, *Decade of Decisions: American Policy Toward the Arab-Israeli Conflict, 1967–76* (Berkeley: University of California Press, 1977), pp. 88–89.

91. The plan was made public on instructions from President Nixon, who was disappointed by the Soviet rejection of the plan. Marvin Kalb and Bernard Kalb, *Kissinger* (Boston: Little, Brown, 1974), p. 189.

92. *New York Times*, December 10, 1969.

93. Michael Brecher, *Decisions in Israel's Foreign Policy* (London: Oxford University Press, 1974), p. 479. The Israeli policy makers did not expect the Rogers Plan to be made public as the official policy of the American government, at least not in the near future. The United States and the USSR presented the plan to Egypt on October 10. See William B. Quandt, *Decade of Decisions: American Policy Toward the Arab-Israeli Conflict, 1967–76* (Berkeley: University of California Press, 1978), p. 90.

94. These aims were: stable and permanent peace; direct negotiations; free navigation; agreed, recognized and secure boundaries; and solution of the refugee problem within the Arab States in the region after the signature of a peace treaty. (Eshkol's speech of December 1, 1967.) See Brecher, *Decisions*, pp. 480–2. The Rogers Plan was also an indication that the United States would be ready to impose a settlement on Israel that went counter to the latter's views (Kalb and Kalb, *Kissinger*, p. 180); Yitzhak Rabin, *Pinkas Sheirut* (Hebrew) (Tel Aviv: Ma'ariv, 1979), pp. 264–72.

95. Brecher, *Decisions*, p. 481.

96. *Ibid.*

97. *Jerusalem Post*, December 12, 1969, quoted by Brecher, *Decisions*, p. 483.

98. Brecher, *Decisions*, pp. 484–85.

99. *Ha'aretz*, December 23, 1969; the Yost Document, like the Rogers Plan, dealt with the territorial arrangements to be reached between Israel and Jordan, in essence involving almost complete Israeli withdrawal to the June 4, 1967 boundaries.

100. *Knesset Records*, 56:344–45; Brecher, *Decisions*, p. 486.

101. Cairo Radio, November 6, 1969.

102. Whetten, *The Canal War*, p. 78; Safran, *Israel*, p. 435.

103. *Al-Ahrām*, November 12 and 26, 1969.

104. *Le Monde*, December 14, 1969; London *Times*, December 19, 1969; *Washington Post* and *New York Times*, November 10, 1969. This in spite of Kosygin's promise in his speech at the luncheon in honor of the mission that the USSR would reinforce Egypt's defense potential. *Pravda*, December 10, 1969.

105. Sadat interview in *Al-Akhbār*, December 17, 1969.

106. *New York Times*, December 24, 1969.

107. Whetten, *The Canal War*, p. 79.

108. *Ibid.*, p. 82.

109. *Ibid.*, p. 84.

110. Abdel Nasser's speech of July 23, 1970.

111. Whetten, *The Canal War*, pp. 84–5.

112. *New York Times*, January 1, 1970.

113. In the course of 1969, beginning from April 3, there were twenty-one meetings between representatives of the four countries.

114. *New York Times*, November 19, 1969.

115. *Le Monde* and *International Herald Tribune*, December 4, 1969.

5. Israel Imposes Its Strategy

1. The Israeli Embassy in the United States believed that the only way to prevent a solution's being imposed on Israel by the superpowers was by means of

an Israeli military solution to the Egyptian War of Attrition. The United States had proposed the Rogers Plan when it was seen that Israel was not succeeding in winning the war. Yitzhak Rabin, *Pinkas Sheirut* (Hebrew) (Tel Aviv: Ma'ariv, 1979), pp. 248, 261–64.

2. Information from former high-ranking IDF commanding officers.

3. Weizmann, *Thine the Sky, Thine the Land* (Tel Aviv: Ma'ariv, 1975), p. 312–3. Conversation with a former high-ranking IDF commanding officer.

4. Conversation with a former high-ranking IDF commanding officer. Yitzhak Rabin proposed that the government definitely decide about in-depth bombing in Egypt. Rabin, *Pinkas Sheirut*, pp. 253–54, 261.

5. Dan Margalit, *Message from the White House* (Hebrew) (Tel Aviv: Ot-Paz, 1971), p. 30; *Ha'aretz*, June 23, 1970.

6. Ze'ev Schiff, *Phantom Over the Nile: The Story of Israeli Air Corps* (Hebrew) (Haifa: Shikmona, 1970), p. 190. (See also the statistical analysis of Egyptian belligerent activity in the previous chapter.) Yitzhak Rabin, *Pinkas Sheirut*, p. 248.

7. Conversations with former high-ranking commanding officers and a former senior official. Some "hawks" in the Israeli top echelon were critical of the fact that Israel was not exerting its full military strength and in fact was not making itself felt in the Middle East. But it was not only the "hawks" that advanced this contention. (Schiff, *Phantom Over the Nile*, pp. 191–92.)

8. The plan for a large-scale land operation was worked out by Major General Ariel Sharon (Ezer Weizmann, *Thine the Sky, Thine the Land*, p. 313).

9. Schiff, *Phantom Over the Nile*, pp. 190–91.

10. The Intelligence appraisals were that the raids would offer a good prospect of overthrowing Nasser. (Conversation with former high-ranking commanding officer.) In her memoirs published in 1975 Golda Meir throws light on the government's aims: "The only way we could possibly prevent the total war which Nasser himself proclaimed day and night to be the ultimate goal of his War of Attrition was by striking back, and striking hard, at the Egyptian military installations; by bombing Egyptian military targets, not only at the cease-fire line but inside Egypt itself; and, if and when necessary, even bringing our message to the very doorstep of the Egyptians by raiding deep into Egyptian territory. . . . So we reluctantly began our in-depth retaliatory bombardments, using our planes as flying artillery and trusting that the Egyptian people, hearing those planes over the military airfield near Cairo, would understand that they couldn't have it both ways: war for us and peace for themselves." *My Life* (London: Weidenfeld and Nicholson, 1975), pp. 319–20. See also Dayan interviews, Israel Broadcasting Authority (IBA), January 13 and 28; *DR*, January 14 and 29, 1970.

11. Schiff, *Phantom Over the Nile*, p. 190. (My stress.)

12. The Israeli attempt to draw a distinction between the Nasser regime and the Egyptians as a whole was also intended to make clear the limited character of Israel's escalatory activity.

13. In private conversation, a former high-ranking Israeli commanding officer contended that the political constraints were in fact scrupulously examined in the plan for the raids submitted by the IDF, but given the prevailing feeling that if the raids were carried out they would succeed operationally, these constraints were pushed aside.

14. Dan Horowitz, *The Israel Concept of National Security: Fixed Factors and Variables in Israeli Strategic Thinking* (Hebrew), (Jerusalem: Hebrew University, 1973), p. 5.

15. Yigal Allon, *A Curtain of Sand* (Hebrew), (Tel Aviv: Ha'kibbutz Ha'mouchad, 1968), pp. 417–18. These views were also held by the Minister for Transport, Ezer Weizmann. See, e.g., pronouncements of his reported in the *Jerusalem Post*, July 12, 1970, and *Ha'aretz*, May 3, 1970.

16. Allon, *A Curtain of Sand*, p. 418. See similar views expressed by Ezer Weizmann, *Thine the Sky, Thine the Land*, pp. 321–22.

17. Margalit, *Message*, p. 53.

18. Moshe Dayan, *Milestones* (Hebrew), (Tel Aviv: Dvir, 1976), pp. 475, 485.

19. Moshe Dayan, *New Map: Different Attitudes*, February 6, 1968 (Haifa: Shikmona, 1969), p. 64.

20. Dayan, *New Map*, December 4, 1967, p. 68.

21. Margalit, *Message*, p. 54.

22. *Ibid.*, p. 55.

23. *Ibid.*, pp. 42–3.

24. Conversation with former high-ranking Israeli commanding officer. See too Margalit, *Message*, p. 43.

25. *Ha'aretz*, July 24, 1970.

26. Conversation with Israeli former senior official.

27. "It wasn't an easy decision to make, particularly since we knew that the Soviets might extend their involvement in Egypt even further. . . . But one can't always choose one's opponents." Meir, *My Life*, pp. 319–20. Golda Meir saw the raids as vitally necessary: "What enraged us, though, was that we were also being questioned whether our bombing in depth was 'really' necessary and a matter of self-defense, as though one must wait until a murderer actually reaches one's home before it is morally possible to stop him from trying to kill one, particularly when—as in Nasser's case—we were being left in no doubt whatsoever as to his intentions." *My Life*, p. 322.

28. Rabin, *Pinkas Sheirut*, pp. 253–54, 274.

29. Rabin, pp. 248, 252–54, 261–64. See also Margalit, *Message*, pp. 37–38; Schiff, *Phantom Over the Nile*, p. 191.

30. Rabin, *Pinkas Sheirut*, pp. 252–54, 261–64.

31. Ibid. Various sources state that Rabin was given clear hints to this effect from a very senior personality in the American administration (Margalit, *Message*, p. 37), one of the heads of the State Department (Schiff, *Phantom Over the Nile*, p. 191). Rabin was told that the United States had never attempted to restrict Israel in taking measures against Egypt. If Israel extended her air raids deep into Egypt, the United States would not support the raids but would not oppose them. A somewhat different version is to be found in the interview with the Foreign Minister, Abba Eban, in *Ha'aretz* of January 2, 1970: "If fate wills it that Nasser should fall, in the way that regimes do fall, I assume that there will be no mourning in the United States. But one should not conclude from this that the United States encourages actions taken deliberately in order to overthrow him. . . . There is understanding in the United States of our defense needs, but there is no sign of a desire for an energetic increase of activity beyond the cease-fire lines if Egypt does not force us into this." According to Margalit, a different version of what the high-ranking American personality said to Rabin was heard later, to the effect that the person in question had not confined himself to a "laconic remark," but had explained why he was in favor of in-depth raids into Egypt. "Heavy bombing of the Egyptian rear might well force Cairo and Moscow to repent their refusal to accept the 'Rogers Plan' of October 1969 and to agree to a political settlement in the spirit of Washington's views." He was quoted as

saying that in the end Israeli air raids on the suburbs of Cairo might well improve the chances of the political program that had been rejected outright by Cairo, Moscow, and Jerusalem (Margalit, *Message,* p. 38). Sisco warned Rabin about American isolation in the Arab world. Rabin, *Pinkas Sheirut,* p. 249.

32. E. Weizmann, *Thine the Sky, Thine the Land,* p. 321; Schiff, *Phantom Over the Nile,* p. 192; Margalit, *Message,* pp. 35–38.

33. Speaking to a group of commanding officers in December 1967, Dayan put the question in all its seriousness: "If the USSR intervenes or threatens to intervene, will the United States stop them? Will the United States be prepared for confrontation with the Russians and say to them, 'If you send in your forces, we shall send in ours against them,' and this would mean, if not a world war, certainly a war between the two great powers. . . . I should feel relieved if I could say with any certainty that if the USSR wanted to intervene with its forces in the Middle East conflict, the United States would stop them or present them with a real threat. But that is a question that so far I have no answer to." (*New Map,* p. 68.)

34. Interview in *Al-Anwār,* April 17, 1970. See too Heikal, *The Road to Ramadan,* p. 84.

35. Heikal, *Al-Ahrām,* February 12, 1970.

36. Heikal, *The Road to Ramadan,* p. 82.

37. Heikal, *Al-Ahrām,* January 30 and May 21, 1970. In his article of May 21, 1970, Heikal gave the number of sorties effected by the Israeli Air Force from January to April at 3,300 and the weight of explosives dropped at 7 to 8,000 tons.

38. Heikal, *Al-Ahrām,* January 23, 1970.

39. Muḥammad Fawzī, War Minister, *Al-Ahrām,* March 6, 1970; Heikal, *Al-Ahrām,* January 23, 1970; *Al-Jumhūriyya,* February 23, 1970.

40. Heikal, *Al-Ahrām,* January 16, February 12 and March 5, 1970; Heikal, *Road to Ramadan,* p. 82. It is worth noting that these views on American policy were the same as Rabin's when he decided that the Americans were not opposed to the in-depth raids.

41. In an interview with an Indian journalist, quoted in *Al-Ahrām* of April 17, 1970, Nasser said that the Americans were threatening the Egyptians with more raids as long as they refused to honor the cease-fire agreement. He voiced similar views in his speeches on May 1, and July 23, 1970.

42. In an article in *Al-Ahrām* of February 12, 1970, Heikal wrote: "Some of our friends asked the Americans if they were of the same opinion as Israel that the pressure of the air raids deep into Egypt would lead to a weakening of the position of Abdel Nasser. Their answer was: 'It is possible that this may weaken Nasser's position, but it is more likely that it will influence Nasser himself. We know that he is a sentimentalist who loves his people and hates to cause them harm or heavy losses. If the loss of life increases as a result of the raids and their extension, sentimental Nasser is liable to act—either to agree to terms imposed on him or else to decide on his own account to leave the arena, and he himself will choose a leader who can reach an understanding.' "

43. *Al-Ahrām,* February 12, 1970.

44. Heikal, *Al-Ahrām,* February 12, 1970. Nasser said much the same things in his speech on May 1, 1970.

45. Heikal, *Al-Ahrām,* March 5, 1970.

46. Heikal, *Al-Ahrām,* March 11, 1970.

47. Lawrence L. Whetten, *The Canal War* (Cambridge, Mass.: M.I.T. Press, 1974), p. 78; Edgar O'Ballance, *The Electronic War in The Middle East* (London:

Faber, 1974), p. 98. The later version of Israeli policy makers was that the Soviets promised the delegation to supply Egypt with SA-3 missiles. (See chapter 6.)

48. Heikal, *Road to Ramadan*, p. 83.

49. In spite of the great secrecy surrounding this visit, the *New York Times* knew on January 30, that it had taken place. It was confirmed by Nasser himself in his speech of July 23, 1970.

50. Heikal, *Road to Ramadan*, p. 84; *New York Times*, January 30, 1970; *Al-Ahrām*, July 27, 1970. See also Muḥammad Heikal, *Sphinx and Commissar: The Rise and Fall of Soviet Influence in the Arab World* (London: Collins, 1978), p. 179.

51. According to Heikal, Nasser contended that the SA-2s were completely ineffective against planes flying below 500 meters and not very effective between 500–1000 meters. To support this contention, Nasser asked for an opinion from Soviet experts in Egypt. Heikal, *Road to Ramadan*, p. 84.

52. It is difficult to accept Heikal's version that Nasser did not know that the Egyptian SA-2 teams were not capable of operating the SA-3 missiles and that it would need six months to train them, when Heikal himself recounts that Nasser asked the Soviet experts in Egypt for an opinion on the matter.

53. Heikal, *Road to Ramadan*, p. 86.

54. *Ibid.*, p. 87.

55. In exchange for their support the Soviets demanded from Nasser that once Egypt's bargaining position was sufficiently restored, he would make an earnest effort to seek a political solution on terms akin to those of the Rogers Plan. Nasser agreed to these demands. Nadav Safran, *Israel—The Embattled Ally* (Cambridge: Harvard University Press, 1978), p. 437.

56. *Al-Ahrām*, January 22, 1970. London *Times*, February 10, 1970.

57. Liddell Hart points out that air raids on industrial targets have no very great prospect of exercising an immediate and decisive influence. Perhaps the prospects are greater of causing an additional prolonged war of attrition of a new kind—air attrition. (This would apply to raids on army camps like those carried out by the Israeli Air Force in the Egyptian-Israeli War of Attrition.) *Strategy*, pp. 348–50. See also George Quester, "Bargaining and Bombing during World War II in Europe," *World Politics* (April 1963), 15(3):417–37; Ernest R. May, *"Lessons" of the Past* (New York: Oxford University Press, 1973), pp. 125–42.

58. Weizmann, *Thine the Sky, Thine the Land*, p. 313. (My stress.)

59. In the opinion of the Israeli former high-ranking commanding officer, the limited effectiveness of the in-depth raids was also connected with limited supplies of ammunition, problems of precision, and the attacking airmen's incomplete information on the objectives they were to attack.

6. Soviet Military Intervention

1. The Kremlin apparently gave Nasser this understanding during his visit to Moscow in July 1968. See e.g., Yaakov Ro'i, *From Encroachment to Involvement: A Documentary Study of Soviet Policy in the Middle East* (Jerusalem: Israel Universities Press, 1974), p. 514; Interview with Anwar Sadat, Arnaud de Borchgrave, *Newsweek*, December 13, 1971. See also John D. Glassman, *Arms for the Arabs: The Soviet Union and War in the Middle East* (Baltimore: Johns Hopkins University Press, 1975), p. 216; Anwar Sadat, *In Search of Identity* (New York: Harper and Row, 1978), p. 187.

2. Close Soviet control more than once led to clashes between Soviet experts in Egypt and Egyptian military, and also between the experts and Nasser himself. For details, see Edgar O'Ballance, *The Electronic War in the Middle East* (London: Faber, 1974), pp. 64, 73, 91, 93.

3. Ro'i, *From Encroachment to Involvement*, p. 514; Ze'ev Schiff, *Phantom Over the Nile: The Story of Israeli Air Corps* (Haifa: Shikmona, 1970), pp. 208–9; Glassman, *Arms for the Arabs*, p. 73; O'Ballance, *Electronic War*, p. 89, states that the fresh arms deliveries to Egypt included the very latest Soviet tank, the T-62.

4. According to O'Ballance, *Electronic War*, p. 92, the number of Soviet "advisers" in Egypt in September 1969 had reached 10,000—4,000 of them military advisers. (Some 3,000 were employed in completing the Aswan Dam, while the remainder were mainly concerned with economic and technical aid in different fields.) Ezer Weizmann, *Thine the Sky, Thine, the Land* (Tel Aviv: Ma'ariv, 1975), p. 309, states that some 20,000 Russians poured into Egypt from March to June 1969; part of them were posted at command levels as low as the brigade, in armor, artillery, and infantry. See also Glassman, *Arms for the Arabs*, pp. 73–74.

5. Schiff is of the view that the decision in favor of direct Soviet military intervention in the War of Attrition took shape at two meetings of the Warsaw Pact countries, the first in Prague in November 1969 and the second in Moscow five weeks later. At the Prague meeting of the Warsaw Pact Foreign Ministers, it was decided to increase military aid to Egypt. At the Moscow meeting, attended by the Warsaw Pact Heads of State and Defense Ministers, the Soviet Union representatives told those present that there was apparently no prospect of avoiding actual military intervention in defense of Egypt in order to save Nasser's regime and the enormous sums the USSR had invested in Egypt. Schiff nevertheless thinks that though the Israeli destruction of the SA-2 missiles was an important element in reaching this decision, it was not what actually produced the decision. It was the operational failure of Nasser and his whole army at all levels that led to the decision. (*Phantom Over the Nile*, p. 209.)

6. Ro'i, *From Encroachment to Involvement*, pp. 514–15; Glassman, *Arms for the Arabs*, p. 74.

7. This argument was put forward by Dayan (*Ma'ariv*, April 10, 1970) and was endorsed by the rest of Israel's policy makers: Golda Meir, *Knesset Records* (May 26, 1970), 57:1859; Abba Eban, *Ha'aretz*, June 5, 1970; and Bar-Lev, *Davar*, May 13, 1970; *Ma'ariv*, June 5, 1970. See Yigal Allon, "The Soviet Involvement in the Arab-Israeli Conflict," in Michael Confino and Shimon Shamir, eds., *The USSR and the Middle East* (New York: Wiley, 1973), p. 152. The Israeli former high-ranking commanding officer admitted in conversation with the author that the IAF raids were probably decisive in bringing about Soviet intervention. Yitzhak Rabin, *Pinkas Sheirut* (Hebrew) (Tel Aviv: Ma'ariv, 1979), p. 279.

8. Dayan, *Ma'ariv*, April 10, 1970; Glassman, *Arms for the Arabs*, p. 74.

9. Dayan, *ibid.*, Dan Margalit, *Message from the White House* (Tel Aviv: Ot-Paz, 1971), p. 57, states that the Americans did not believe that Soviet intervention would have become a fact had it not been for the in-depth raids.

10. In the *Road to Ramadan* (London: Collins, 1975), pp. 86–87, Muḥammad Heikal states that what made the biggest impression on the Soviet leaders was Nasser's threat to resign and that this was what made them agree to meet his requests.

11. Heikal reports on the Kremlin leaders' evaluation of the escalatory significance of Soviet intervention in the fighting: "Brezhnev said that this would be

a step with serious international implications. It would provide all the makings of a crisis between the Soviet Union and the United States. . . . This will involve a considerable risk, and I don't know whether we are justified in taking it." *Road to Ramadan*, p. 86. See also Muḥammad Heikal, *Sphinx and Commissar: The Rise and Fall of Soviet Influence in the Arab World* (London: Collins, 1978), p. 197. On July 23, 1970, Nasser disclosed that during his visit (January 22 to 25), the USSR had decided to support Egypt "with all its power" and had promised him that "all this support" would be provided within thirty days at the most (Cairo Radio, July 23, 1970; BBC, July 25, 1970).

12. The contents of the note were not published officially, but TASS news agency reported details concerning it. Similar reports appeared in the press in the West. TASS in English, February 12, 1970; *BBC/SU*, February 14, 1970; London *Times* and *New York Times*, February 4, 1970; see also Rabin, *Pinkas Sheirut*, pp. 175–76.

13. Lawrence L. Whetten, *The Canal War: Four Powers Conflict in the Middle East* (Cambridge, Mass.: M.I.T. Press, 1974), p. 91; O'Ballance, *The Electronic War*, p. 107; Glassman, *Arms for the Arabs*, p. 75. It is even contended that the USSR informed the United States that the supply of Soviet arms necessitated dispatch of Soviet personnel and that the sa-3 missiles would only be installed near vital Egyptian centers—Cairo, Alexandria, and the Aswan Dam. J.C. Hurewitz, "Superpower Rivalry and the Arab-Israeli Dispute: Involvement or Commitment?" in Michael Confino and Shimon Shamir, eds., *USSR and the Middle East* (New York: Wiley, 1973), p. 160; and Glassman, *Arms for the Arabs*, p. 75.

14. Radio Moscow in English and Arabic, February 4, 1970; *BBC/SU*, February 6, 1970; *Pravda*, February 1, 1970; *Izvestia*, February 4, 1970.

15. London *Times*, February 6, 1970; Yair Evron, *The Middle East: Nations, Superpowers and the Wars* (London: Elek, 1973), p. 115; Yitzhak Rabin, *Pinkas Sheirut*, pp. 275–76.

16. Richard Nixon, *U.S. Foreign Policy for the 1970's—Building for Peace: A Report to the Congress*, February 25, 1971, pp. 62–63.

17. Whetten, *The Canal War*, p. 83; Evron, *The Middle East*, pp. 113–14.

18. Whetten, *The Canal War*, pp. 93–94, is of the opinion that "the straw that broke the camel's back" for the Kremlin was the February 12 raid on the Egyptian factory at Abū-Za'bel. After this raid, they concluded that it was necessary to block the Israelis immediately. The only question was what form Soviet military intervention should take. The American refusal at the Four-Power meeting on February 19 to condemn the Israelis for the Abū-Za'bel raid strengthened the Soviet belief that the Americans were not prepared to put a stop to the in-depth raids. (See too Glassman, *Arms for the Arabs*, p. 76.) In an interview with the IDF weekly, *Bamahaneh* (May 6, 1970), Prime Minister Golda Meir said that there had been no American pressure on Israel to refrain from utilizing her capacity on the cease-fire line.

19. In this way the Soviet government took care to make it clear that their intervention was strictly defensive, intended to curb the in-depth raids rather than sustain the War of Attrition. (Heikal, *Road to Ramadan*, pp. 82, 84; Schiff, *Phantom Over the Nile*, pp. 210–11; O'Ballance, *Electronic War*, p. 111.) According to Heikal, the missiles were put in near the canal because of the high concentration of Egyptian troops there and also because the Egyptian High Command believed that when the time came, the fate of the Middle East would be decided in this area. (Heikal does not explain exactly what was meant by this expression.)

20. Schiff, *Phantom Over the Nile*, p. 211, points out that at first Israel

thought that the Egyptians were building a second line of fortifications, and this in spite of the fact that the trenches or ditches that they were digging were disposed in unusual fashion, mostly in twos, with considerable distances between each group of two.

21. Israeli planes carried out nineteen attacks on the Egyptian construction sites between March 1 and 25; according to Heikal (*Road to Ramadan*, p. 82), about 4,000 Egyptian workers engaged in digging were killed.

22. The *International Herald Tribune* of March 20 reported that American officials stated that SA-3 missiles and Soviet soldiers as well began to reach Egypt on February 25. Whetten, *The Canal War*, p. 94, gives the dates as March 12–16. The Beirut paper, *Le Jour*, of February 5, put their arrival at the beginning of February.

23. The Russians took not the slightest pains to hide the arrival of the missiles, in spite of the fact that in Moscow they had asked Nasser to keep their dispatch a secret. On the contrary, Heikal says that the Russians wanted the missiles to be transported through the streets of Alexandria in broad daylight, with the Soviet crews waving at the crowds in the streets and shouting *"aṣdiqa"* (friends). Heikal explains this contradiction as follows: "My own theory was that this was how the game was played between the superpowers: it would have been a signal to the Americans that the Russians had arrived in Egypt" (*Road to Ramadan*, p. 90).

24. At the end of January 1970, Dayan declared that for the time being there was no hint or sign of any Soviet intention to intervene actively against Israel. (Israel) Government Press Office, January 28, 1970. On February 2, 1970, the Israel Foreign Ministry spokesman denied that the USSR had transmitted an ultimatum to Israel through western nations to stop the in-depth raids. (Israel) Government Press Office, February 13, 1970. Answering a question in the Knesset on March 16, 1970, Foreign Minister Abba Eban denied that the Foreign Ministry had received a Soviet warning not to attack the Aswan Dam. (*Knesset Records*, Vol. 57, p. 1187.) In an interview on Paris Radio on February 20, 1970 (quoted in the *Jerusalem Post*, February 22, 1970) Bar-Lev discounted the possibility of direct Soviet intervention in the Middle East fighting. Yitzhak Rabin, *Pinkas Sheirut*, p. 277.

25. Margalit, *Message*, p. 57.

26. *Jerusalem Post*, February 23, 1970.

27. *Jerusalem Post*, March 22, 1970.

28. *Ibid.*

29. Margalit, *Message*, p. 53; Horowitz, *The Israel Concept of National Security: Fixed Factor and Variables in Israeli Strategic Thinking* (Hebrew) (Jerusalem: Hebrew University, 1973), p. 36; *Ma'ariv*, May 3, 1970; IBA, May 5, 1970; DR, May 6, 1970.

30. Margalit, *Message*, p. 53. This view was shared in one form or another by other ministers: Ezer Weizmann, Israel Galili, Haim Landau. Margalit, *Message*, p. 77.

31. Schiff, *Phantom Over the Nile*, p. 214.

32. *Ma'ariv*, April 10, 1970. (Stress added.)

33. The decision was made to stop the in-depth raids when news was received on April 13 that Russian crews were manning twenty missile sites. (Whetten, *The Canal War*, p. 95.) Glassman is of the opinion that the U.S. decision of March 23, 1970, to suspend deliveries of Phantoms and Skyhawks to Israel was the central factor in the decision to stop the in-depth raids. (*Arms for the Arabs*,

p. 77.) Israeli former high-ranking commanding officers and a former senior official in conversation with the author rejected Glassman's argument that at the time Israel did not have enough crews at her disposal to operate the Phantoms.

34. Israeli planes flying deep inside Egyptian territory for patrol and reconnaissance purposes were surprised by an interceptor plane of MIG-21 type bearing Egyptian Air Force insignia but flown by Russian pilots. Schiff, *Phantom Over the Nile*, p. 213.

35. Dayan, *Ma'ariv*, May 5, 1970; Bar-Lev, *Davar*, May 13, 1970.

36. Dayan, *Ma'ariv*, April 10 and May 5, 1970; *Jerusalem Post*, May 8, 1970.

37. Dayan, *Ma'ariv*, May 5, 1970; *Jerusalem Post*, May 8, 1970. Bar-Lev even wanted a distinction between Soviet "involvement" west of the canal and "intervention" east of it. Dan Horowitz, *The Israel Concept of National Security*, p. 36.

38. Dayan, *Ma'ariv*, May 5, 1970; *Jerusalem Post*, May 8, 1970.

39. *Ma'ariv*, May 5, 1970.

40. *Ha'aretz*, May 15, 1970.

41. Golda Meir, *Jerusalem Post*, April 30, 1970; Begin, *Ma'ariv*, May 4, 1970; Dayan, *Jerusalem Post*, May 9, 1970.

42. During the first stage of the Soviet involvement, some Israeli Ministers, Allon and Eban among them, held the contrary view that in contacts with the United States, Israel should avoid enlarging on the dangerous implications of Soviet involvement. After the clash with the Soviet pilots, however, there was an increasing consensus on this question in Israel for turning to the Americans. Rabin, *Pinkas Sheirut*, pp. 288–91.

43. Dayan, *Ma'ariv*, April 10, 1970; Golda Meir, *Jerusalem Post*, April 20, 1970; Israel Galili, *Jerusalem Post*, May 28, 1970; Peres, *Ma'ariv*, June 28, 1970.

44. Margalit, *Message*, pp. 57, 104.

45. On March 23, 1970, only four days after the *New York Times* published its disclosures on the delivery of SA-3 missiles to Egypt and the arrival of Soviet teams to operate them, U.S. Secretary of State Rogers announced that the United States had decided to hold up the delivery of Phantoms to Israel. *New York Times*, March 24, 1970.

46. Glassman, *Arms for the Arabs*, p. 77. The *New York Times* of March 24, 1970, stated that American aims were "to regain some favor in the Arab world by a show of American restraint, and to win Soviet support for a limitation of the arms race in the Middle East."

47. Dayan, (Israel) Government Press Office, May 9, 1970; Eban, *Ha'aretz*, June 5, 1970; Bar-Lev, *Davar*, May 13, 1970.

48. Message from the Israeli Prime Minister to President Nixon on April 29, 1970. Margalit, *Message*, p. 108.

49. Immediately after the U.S. statement, Israeli Foreign Minister Abba Eban publicly expressed Israel's disappointment. *Jerusalem Post*, March 24, 1970. Rabin, *Pinkas Sheirut*, p. 289.

50. Elliot Richardson, *Department of State Bulletin*, May 18, 1970; Melvin Laird, *Jerusalem Post*, May 25, 1970; William Rogers, *Jerusalem Post*, May 27, 1970.

51. *New York Times*, May 1, 1970. The reappraisal ended with Secretary of State Rogers' presentation of the American program for ending the War of Attrition on June 25, 1970.

52. Golda Meir, *Jerusalem Post*, April 20, 1970; Rabin, *Davar*, June 5, 1970. Foreign Minister Abba Eban visited Washington on May 20–21, 1970, in a fruitless effort to persuade the American administration to supply the planes to Israel.

Jerusalem Post, May 24, 25, 1970; IBA, May 24, 1970; BBC, May 27, 1970. Rabin, *Pinkas Sheirut*, pp. 290–91.

53. *Ma'ariv*, June 5, 1970.

54. Eban, *Ha'aretz*, June 5, 1970.

55. Rabin, *Ma'ariv*, June 5, 1970.

56. Eban, *Ha'aretz*, June 5, 1970; Margalit, *Message*, p. 116; Rabin, *Pinkas Sheirut*, p. 288.

57. It is not clear whether the expansion of Soviet intervention signified a new decision or whether it was an additional step in implementing the previous decision on involvement in the war as a matter of policy. See Glassman, *Arms for the Arabs*, p. 78.

58. Glassman, pp. 70–78.

59. The Egyptians on the other hand hoped that with Israel's strategic superiority neutralized, they could cross the canal. Nasser said as much in his speech at Benghazi, Libya, on June 25, 1970: "Once the Army acquired a balance in the air, no power in the world could stop it from crossing the canal, for which the UAR Army had completed its training." Libya Radio, June 25, 1970; BBC, June 27, 1970.

60. Glassman, *Arms for the Arabs*, pp. 79–80.

61. Schiff, *Phantom Over the Nile*, p. 219; O'Ballance, *The Electronic War*, p. 90.

62. The raids lasted for consecutively long hours—on May 5, 13, 18 and 19 for about three hours, on May 7 for about four hours; while on May 14 and 16 the raids went on for six hours.

63. Bar-Lev, *Bamahaneh*, July 7, 1970.

64. Schiff, *Phantom Over the Nile*, p. 222.

65. Israeli former senior official, in conversation with the author.

66. Bar-Lev, *Bamahaneh*, July 7, 1970; Mordekhai Hod, *Bamahaneh*, July 14, 1970.

67. Nasser hinted at this operation in his Benghazi speech, June 25, 1970: "Very soon we shall be able to establish complete air defense in the canal zone. We shall very soon be able to make up for the Israeli air superiority by achieving a balance in the air."

68. Whetten, *The Canal War*, p. 109; Schiff, *Phantom Over the Nile*, p. 224.

69. Bar-Lev, *Bamahaneh*, June 30, 1970.

70. Bar-Lev, *Bamahaneh*, July 7, 1970.

71. Cairo Radio, May 1, 1970; BBC, May 4, 1970.

72. *Die Welt*, May 20, 1970.

73. See notes 59 and 67.

74. Glassman, *Arms for the Arabs*, pp. 78–79. According to Nadav Safran, Nasser urged the Soviets to allow their pilots to intervene in the battle zone and strongly enough to permit the Egyptian forces to establish a missile defense system. This would enable him to enter into negotiation from a position of strength and seek a settlement that avoided a contractual agreement. The Soviets, long suspecting that Nasser was bent on embroiling them in the war, argued that further military intervention on their part was dangerous and unnecessary. Safran, *Israel: The Embattled Ally* (Cambridge: Harvard University Press, 1978), pp. 444–45.

75. His apprehensions were not unfounded. "In a secret meeting with Rogers on March 11, Ambassador Dobrynin stated that the Soviet Union had managed to obtain political concessions from Nasser in return for the new arms

shipments that were just beginning to Egypt." William Quandt, *Decade of Decisions: American Policy Toward the Arab-Israeli Conflict: 1967–1976* (Berkeley: University of California Press, 1977), p. 79.

76. When Soviet intervention in the fighting began in March, satisfaction was expressed over the globalization of the war (articles by Heikal, *Al-Ahrām*, March 2 and 27, 1970), but a couple of months later this satisfaction had moderated somewhat (articles by Heikal, *Al-Ahrām*, May 21 and June 11, 1970).

77. Quandt, *Decade of Decisions*, p. 98; Safran, *Israel: The Embattled Ally*, p. 438.

78. According to Sadat, Nasser told him: "Whether we like it or not, all the cards of this game are in America's hands. It's high time we talked and allowed the United States to take part in this. *In Search of Identity*, p. 128.

79. Cairo Radio, May 1, 1970; BBC, May 4, 1970.

80. Whetten, *The Canal War*, pp. 98–9; Quandt, *Decade of Decisions*, p. 98; Margalit, *Message*, p. 98.

81. Dayan, *Jerusalem Post*, May 8, 1970; Eban, *Ha'aretz*, May 3, 1970; Golda Meir, *Knesset Records* (May 26, 1970), 58:1859; *Ma'ariv*, June 30, 1970; Bar-Lev, *Bamahaneh*, July 7, 1970.

82. *Jerusalem Post*, May 8, 1970; Golda Meir, *Knesset Records* (May 26, 1970), 58:1859; *Ma'ariv*, June 30, 1970; Galili, *Ha'aretz*, May 30, 1970.

83. Golda Meir, *Knesset Records* (May 26, 1970), 58:1859; *Ma'ariv*, June 30, 1970; Abba Eban, *Ha'aretz*, May 3, 1970; Galili, *Ha'aretz*, May 3, 1970; Yosef Tekoa, IBA, May 6, 1970; DR, May 6, 1970; Bar-Lev, *Davar*, May 13, 1970; Dayan, *Jerusalem Post*, May 8, 1970.

84. *Knesset Records* (July 13, 1970), 58:2426.

85. In the government, Transport Minister Ezer Weizmann stated his opinion that the Russians had crossed the red line set by Israel, and that therefore Israel could no longer be deterred from clashing with the Russians. "We have to behave towards every military entity in Egypt within the necessary broad band west of the canal as an enemy. . . . We have to act so as to make it perfectly clear to the Russians that in this band, if attacked, we would not tolerate Russian intervention—if it was Russian, we would hit the Russians and planes piloted by Russian pilots." *Ma'ariv*, March 16, 1974. See Weizmann, *Thine the Sky, Thine the Land*, pp. 321–22.

86. Margalit, *Message*, p. 140.

87. *Ma'ariv*, July 8, 1970; Bar-Lev, *Ma'ariv*, June 5, 1970; *Bamahaneh*, July 7, 1970.

88. *Daily Express* and *Jerusalem Post*, July 29, 1970; *Ma'ariv*, July 29, 1970; Schiff, *Phantom Over the Nile*, p. 220; Weizmann, *Thine the Sky, Thine the Land*, p. 322; Glassman, *Arms for the Arabs*, p. 79.

89. Glassman, p. 79; *New York Times*, August 12, 1970.

90. The Israeli evaluation at the time was that only four Soviet planes were brought down (Weizmann, *Thine the Sky, Thine the Land*, p. 322). It was not known until later that according to the Egyptian version, five Soviet planes were brought down in this fight. (Heikal, *Road to Ramadan*, p. 162.)

91. After the war, Golda Meir revealed the story publicly for the first time on October 25, 1970, at a meeting with Jewish students in New York. According to her, Israel refrained from making the story public for the following reasons: "We were not interested in appearing to the world as heroes, and we did not wish to fight the Russians." (IBA, October 26, 1970, DR, October 27, 1970.)

92. Conversation with Israeli former high-ranking commanding officer.

93. *Los Angeles Times*, August 6, 1970.

94. This is the figure given by Egyptian Vice-Premier and Minister of Defense Ṣādiq, on April 4, 1972. (*Jumhūriyya*, April 5, 1972.)

95. Quandt, *Decade of Decisions*, p. 95.

96. Marvin Kalb and Bernard Kalb, *Kissinger* (Boston: Little, Brown, 1974), pp. 189, 190.

97. During the period from April 29 to the beginning of June, the National Security Council with Henry Kissinger at its head was busy reappraising the Middle East situation. At a press conference on June 25, Secretary of State Rogers stated that the reappraisal had been completed. *Department of State Bulletin*, July 13, 1970.

98. Quandt, *Decade of Decisions*, p. 100; Kalb and Kalb, *Kissinger*, pp. 192–93; London *Times*, July 8, 1970. On July 5, Sisco said in an interview that to use the word "expel" with regard to the Russians in Egypt was "too harsh"; the word should not be taken to mean that the United States wanted to get rid of the Russians by using physical force. At the same time he did not deny that the aim of the United States was in fact to get the Russians out of Egypt. (TV interview, Meet the Press, July 12, 1970; *Department of State Bulletin*, August 3, 1970.) On July 12, the *New York Times* reported differences of opinions between Kissinger and Rogers over Soviet military intervention in Egypt. Rogers was reported saying that the United States "never thought of expelling" the Russians from Egypt. While the United States believed it "desirable" for the Soviet presence to disappear from the Middle East, the concept of "expulsion" of the Soviet personnel was meant in the context of a Middle East peace agreement. See Quandt, *Decade of Decisions*, pp. 100–01.

99. Quandt, *Decade of Decisions*, pp. 98–99; Whetten, *The Canal War*, pp. 100–01.

100. Quandt, *Decade of Decisions*, pp. 99–100; Whetten, *The Canal War*, p. 102; *New York Times*, July 26, 1970.

7. Action to End the War

1. William B. Quandt, *Decade of Decisions: American Policy Toward the Arab-Israeli Conflict* (Berkeley: University of California Press, 1977), pp. 92–93; Marvin Kalb and Bernard Kalb, *Kissinger* (Boston: Little, Brown, 1974), pp. 188–89. Kissinger was not enamored of the idea of a settlement to be accomplished by the United States putting pressure on the Israelis and the Russians on the Egyptians, since its outcome would depend mostly on how effective the United States alone managed to be. "Why should we let the Russians have credit for an agreement that is largely due to American pressure on Israel?" See Henry Brandon, *The Retreat of American Power* (New York: Delta, 1972), p. 116.

2. Quandt, *Decade of Decisions*, p. 93.

3. Michael Brecher, *Decisions in Israel's Foreign Policy* (London: Oxford University Press, 1974), p. 489; Quandt, *Decade of Decisions*, p. 99; Lawrence L. Whetten, *The Canal War: Four Powers Conflict in the Middle East* (Cambridge, Mass., MIT Press, 1974), pp. 101–2; Dan Margalit, *Message from the White House* (Tel-Aviv: Ot-Paz, 1971), pp. 128–29; Muḥammad Heikal, *Road to Ramadan* (London: Collins, 1975).

4. *Jerusalem Post*, July 31, 1970, quoted by Brecher, *Decisions*, pp. 490–91.

5. Yitzhak Rabin, *Pinkas Sheirut* (Tel Aviv: Ma'ariv, 1979), p. 194; Margalit, *Message*, p. 130; Brecher, *Decisions*, p. 490.

6. Already at this stage Israel feared that a temporary cease-fire would be utilized by Egypt and the USSR to move the SA-3 missiles up to the canal. *Ha'aretz*, June 26, 1970. See too Margalit, *Message*, pp. 130–32.

7. Rabin, *Pinkas Sheirut*, p. 244; Margalit, *Message*, p. 127; Brecher, *Decisions*, p. 490.

8. Rabin believed that Egypt would refuse the American initiative, and this led the Israeli government to accept his views. See Rabin, IBA, August 8, 1970; DR, August 10, 1970; Rabin, *Pinkas Sheirut*, pp. 292–93; Margalit, *Message*, p. 127.

9. Brecher, *Decisions*, p. 490; Margalit, *Message*, p. 129.

10. Rabin, *Pinkas Sheirut*, pp. 194–95; Margalit, *Message*, pp. 135–37; Brecher, *Decisions*, p. 491.

11. *Ma'ariv*, June 30, 1970; Margalit, *Message*, p. 138.

12. Heikal, *Road to Ramadan*, pp. 93–95. Muḥammad Heikal, *Sphinx and Commissar: The Rise and Fall of Soviet Influence in the Arab World* (London: Collins, 1978), pp. 201–2.

13. *Observer*, July 19, 1970.

14. "But then Nasser himself took a closer look at the plan and decided that it fit in with his overall strategy. By now the army was ready and the Soviet Union was actively engaged in the defense of our civil population against air attacks. *The most important thing in Nasser's view was to finish building the missile wall. When completed this would not only protect our armed forces on the west bank of the Suez Canal but would give protection over a strip fifteen to twenty kilometers wide on the east bank, and so give cover for our troops crossing the canal when the time came.*" Heikal, *Road to Ramadan*, p. 93. Heikal, *Sphinx and Commissar*, pp. 198–201.

15. Cairo Radio, July 23; BBC, July 25, 1970.

16. Anwar Sadat, *In Search of Identity* (New York: Harper and Row, 1978), p. 198; Heikal, *Sphinx and Commissar*, p. 199.

17. Heikal, *Road to Ramadan*, p. 95. Note from Nasser to the President of Iraq, *Al-Ahrām*, August 3, 1970. Heikal, *Sphinx and Commissar*, p. 201.

18. Speech by Nasser, July 23, 1970 (Cairo Radio, July 23; BBC, July 25, 1970). Note from Nasser to President of Iraq, *Al-Ahrām*, August 3, 1970, Heikal, *Sphinx and Commissar*, pp. 199–200.

19. Nasser's speech, July 23, 1970; Heikal, *Al-Ahrām*, July 2 and 30, 1970.

20. Nasser put this argument to the Soviet leaders during his visit to Moscow. See Heikal, *Road to Ramadan*, p. 95, and his articles in *Al-Ahrām*, July 2 and 30, 1970.

21. Heikal, *Road to Ramadan*, p. 95.

22. Formal Soviet agreement to the initiative was transmitted to the United States by Dobrynin the very next day after Egypt's positive reply, i.e., on July 23.

23. On July 17, 1970, the *New York Times* reported that responsibility for United States Middle East policy had passed from the State Department to the White House.

24. Quandt, *Decade of Decisions*, p. 100.

25. Kalb and Kalb, *Kissinger*, p. 193; London *Times*, July 4 and 8, 1970; *New York Times*, July 6, 1970.

26. *Department of State Bulletin*, July 27, 1970.

27. Quandt, *Decade of Decisions*, p. 101.

28. *Department of State Bulletin,* July 13, 1970.

29. Margalit, *Message,* p. 140; Brecher, *Decisions,* p. 491.

30. Rabin, *Pinkas Sheirut,* p. 295. Professor Brecher points out in his research on the Rogers initiative that the operative environment of Israeli decision makers at the time was influenced by two main variables: the structure of Israeli-U.S. relations and Israel's military strength. *Decisions,* pp. 464–78.

31. According to IDF announcements, 2 planes were downed on June 30, one on July 15, one on July 18, and one on August 3. Rabin, *Pinkas Sheirut,* p. 295.

32. The loss of planes and pilots was a very bad blow for the I.A.F., which had only about twenty planes and twenty pilots available for bombing the missiles at the beginning of this period. (Conversation with Israeli former high-ranking commanding officer).

33. This phrase is the title Weizmann gave to the last chapter of his book. The pun in the Hebrew is on similar-sounding words for "bend," "compel compliance," and "wing."

34. *"Queen in the Bathtub"* was a play staged during the War of Attrition satirizing the government and mocking traditional values held sacred by many people.

35. Ezer Weizmann, *Thine the Sky, Thine the Land* (Hebrew) (Tel Aviv: Ma'ariv, 1975), pp. 317–19.

36. *Ibid.,* p. 319.

37. *Jerusalem Post,* July 31, 1970.

38. Rabin, *Pinkas Sheirut,* p. 295; Brecher, *Decisions,* p. 493; Margalit, *Message,* pp. 158–60; Nadav Safran, *Israel: The Embattled Ally* (Cambridge: Harvard University Press, 1978), p. 446.

39. On the debate within the government, see Margalit, *Message,* pp. 157–83.

40. *Ibid.,* pp. 163–4.

41. The text of the decision reached by the government differed from the original text of the American initiative. Minister of Defense Moshe Dayan demanded that Israeli reservations be included in the decision, stating that the government regarded itself as bound only by its own foreign policy principles.

42. *Knesset Records* (August 4, 1970), 58:2757. (Stress added.)

43. (Israel) Government Press Office, August 7, 1970.

8. Results, Evaluations, Conclusions

1. David Vital, in his book *The Survival of Small States* (London: Oxford University Press, 1971), points out that in every instance when a small country needed aid from one superpower against the other, it suffered loss of autonomy. "Conflict with a great power is, ultimately, conflict over autonomy. If it seeks and gains protection from another great power it loses autonomy" (p. 12).

2. Golda Meir, *Bamahaneh,* May 6, 1970; *Knesset Records* (May 26, 1970), 58:1859; *Ha'aretz,* September 1, 1970; Abba Eban, *Knesset Records* (July 13, 1970), 58:2426–27; Moshe Dayan (Israel) Government Press Office, August 7, 1970.

3. Bar-Lev, *Ma'ariv,* October 8, 1970; *Davar,* August 3, 1973.

4. *Davar,* August 3, 1973.

5. Dayan, *Ha'aretz,* October 4, 1970; Bar-Lev, *Ma'ariv,* October 8, 1970; *Davar,* August 3, 1970.

6. *Ma'ariv*, May 14, 1971.

7. *Ma'ariv*, May 14, 1971.

8. Ezer Weizmann, *Thine the Sky, Thine the Land* (Hebrew) (Tel Aviv: Ma'ariv, 1975), pp. 313, 318.

9. *Ibid.*, p. 323.

10. *Ma'ariv*, May 8, 1971.

11. *Ma'ariv*, May 14, 1971. Yitzhak Rabin, *Pinkas Sheirut* (Tel Aviv: Mariv. 1979), p. 295.

12. Dan Margalit, *Message from the White House* (Tel Aviv: Ot-Paz, 1971), pp. 61–65, 87–96.

13. *Ibid.*, p. 63.

14. Weizmann, *Thine The Sky, Thine The Land*, pp. 319–20.

15. Matti Peled, "Thoughts on Defense," *Ma'ariv*, September 19, 1970.

16. *Ma'ariv*, June 5, 1973. See Amos Perlmutter, *Politics and Military in Israel, 1967–1977* (London: Frank Cass, 1978), p. 54.

17. Ze'ev Schiff, *October Earthquake* (Tel Aviv: University Publishing Projects, 1974), pp. 139–40; Avraham Adan (Bren), *On Both Banks of the Suez* (Jerusalem: Edanim, 1977), pp. 49–52.

18. Matti Peled, *Ma'ariv*, September 19, 1970.

19. *Ibid.*, p. 140.

20. Weizmann, *Thine The Sky, Thine The Land*, p. 319.

21. Cairo Radio, July 23, 1970; BBC, July 25, 1970.

22. Muḥammad Heikal, *Road to Ramadan* (London: Collins, 1978), p. 95.

23. Speech by Nasser, Cairo Radio, July 23, 1970; BBC, July 25, 1970.

24. Heikal, *Road to Ramadan*, p. 93.

25. *Ibid.*, p. 97.

26. Heikal, *Al-Ahrām*, October 3, 1969.

27. For a searching criticism of Egyptian strategy in the war see Ahmed S. Khalidi, "The War of Attrition," *Journal of Palestine Studies* (August 1973), 3:77–87.

Index